ADVANCE PRAISE FOR *ANTHROPOLOGY AND LAW*

"An updated introduction and overview of the field of legal anthropology is long overdue and *Anthropology and Law* will be welcome in many quarters. Mark Goodale has done a service to the discipline, and his volume is likely to become a classic text, required reading in a variety of courses, and a touchstone for years to come."
—Rosemary Coombe, Tier One Canada Research Chair in Law,
   Communication and Culture, York University, Toronto, Canada

"In *Anthropology and Law*, Mark Goodale elucidates how anthropology detaches the concept of law from its western moorings and takes a global perspective on the various ways that societies resolve disputes, enforce social norms, regulate power and authority, and articulate ideas of the person. Goodale's sparkling prose and brilliant analysis of the history and most recent developments in legal anthropology will appeal to experts and students alike.
—Richard Ashby Wilson, Professor of Anthropology and Law,
   University of Connecticut

"*Anthropology and Law* presents a much-needed recent history of the field, focusing on its shifting contours and concerns in a post–Cold War era. It shows how tensions and debates amongst scholars have fueled theoretical innovation and moved research forward in productive ways. Rich in illustrative case studies and encompassing in theoretical depth and breadth, the book shows the importance of grounded real-world ethnographic scholarship to better understand the legal complexities of our current age."
—Eve Darian-Smith, author of *Laws and Societies in Global Contexts:
   Contemporary Approaches*

"Mark Goodale uses a global palette to paint a vivid and accessible account of what contemporary anthropologists have to say about law as meaning, regulation, and identity. If, as might be expected, his discussion of human and cultural rights is particularly convincing, the overall thesis of the path to legal cosmopolitanism and beyond is a stimulating contribution in its own right."
—David Nelken, Professor of Comparative and Transnational Law in
   Context, Vice Dean and Head of Research, the Dickson Poon School
   of Law, King's College London

# Anthropology and Law

*A Critical Introduction*

Mark Goodale

*Foreword by Sally Engle Merry*

NEW YORK UNIVERSITY PRESS
New York

NEW YORK UNIVERSITY PRESS
New York
www.nyupress.org

References to Internet websites (URLs) were accurate at the time of writing. Neither the author nor New York University Press is responsible for URLs that may have expired or changed since the manuscript was prepared.

Library of Congress Cataloging-in-Publication Data
Names: Goodale, Mark, author.
Title: Anthropology and law : a critical introduction / Mark Goodale ;
foreword by Sally Engle Merry.
Description: New York : New York University Press, [2017] |
Includes bibliographical references and index.
Identifiers: LCCN 2016041138| ISBN 978-1-4798-3613-0 (cl : alk. paper) |
ISBN 978-1-4798-9551-9 (pb : alk. paper)
Subjects: LCSH: Law and anthropology.
Classification: LCC K487.A57 G66 2017 | DDC 340/.115—dc23
LC record available at https://lccn.loc.gov/2016041138

New York University Press books are printed on acid-free paper, and their binding materials are chosen for strength and durability. We strive to use environmentally responsible suppliers and materials to the greatest extent possible in publishing our books.

Manufactured in the United States of America

10 9 8 7 6 5 4 3 2 1

Also available as an ebook

*For Simon Roberts, who introduced me—and many others—to the anthropology of law at the LSE back in the good old days.*

# CONTENTS

*Foreword*                                                              ix
SALLY ENGLE MERRY

*Preface*                                                               xiii

Introduction: From Status to Contract to Cosmopolitanism                1

PART I. LAW AND THE PRODUCTION OF MEANING

1. Speaking the Law                                                     33
2. History, Heritage, and Legal *Mythoi*                                53

PART II. LAW AND AGENCY, LAW AS REGULATION

3. Justice between the Devil and the Deep Blue Sea                      75
4. Human Rights and the Politics of Aspiration                         96
5. Shaping Inclusion and Exclusion through Law                         117

PART III. LAW AND IDENTITY

6. Law and the Fourth World                                            141
7. Law and the Moral Economy of Gender                                 163
8. Ethnonationalism and Conflict Transformation                        184

Conclusion: Law in a Post-Utopian World                                203

*Notes*                                                                223
*References*                                                           241
*Index*                                                                277
*About the Author*                                                     289

# FOREWORD

SALLY ENGLE MERRY

*Silver Professor of Anthropology, New York University*

Despite past predictions of the demise of the anthropology of law, it is clearly flourishing. As this wonderful book shows, legal anthropologists are now tackling an amazing range of issues, from legal responsibility for genocide to rectifying past injuries to indigenous people. Law is everywhere, and so are legal anthropologists. They are working in many different places—local, national, and transnational—to develop theories that make sense of the creation of social order, however fragile, in a rapidly changing world. This book offers a broad and strikingly comprehensive view of what Mark Goodale sometimes refers to as the "new" legal anthropology, work of the post–Cold War era. This legal anthropology is far broader than the legal anthropology of the past, covering relations between law and language, poetics, indigeneity, and gender, among many other issues. The book concludes by considering the future of the field, discussing new issues such as the role of measurement and law, the juridification of politics, the possibility of a cosmopolitan legality, the potential for universal conceptions of law, and the implications of law for growing national and global inequality, both its complicity and its possibilities for redistribution.

Goodale's synthesis of legal anthropology since the early 1990s shows how the field has moved from past concerns with the nature of legal mechanisms in villages and bands to a vast array of new issues such as human rights, legal sovereignty for indigenous communities, and international criminal tribunals. While the focus on disputing served as a valuable method for legal anthropological research in the past, the contemporary field has moved into a far wider set of theoretical and methodological frameworks from multisited ethnography to Foucauldian analyses of the production of knowledge.

To some extent, this flourishing of anthropological scholarship on law reflects a historical transformation in the role of law in social justice movements. During the late nineteenth and early twentieth centuries, social justice activism often focused on the possibilities of social revolution. Social movements inspired by Marxist theory searched for a more just society by radically restructuring economic relationships. Revolutionary movements sought to destroy the power of the property-owning classes, an approach central to the Russian, Cuban, and Chinese revolutions, for example. At the same time, anticolonial movements also saw violence as a path to the decolonization of their societies and their consciousness, a position vividly articulated by Franz Fanon. Law was not seen as a vehicle for social transformation, but rather as an obstacle, part of the existing structure of power that had to be changed.

With the end of the Cold War, however, there was a new turn to law as a mode of producing a just society. Disillusion with Communism in practice, although not in theory, and distrust of the violence of revolutionary change ushered in a new era of enthusiasm for law as the path to social justice. The expansion of global capitalism required a legally based world order to facilitate production and trade. Past failures in economic development projects inspired a turn to governance, in particular to programs that sought to prevent corruption and enhance accountability and the rule of law. The expansion of human rights, international criminal courts, the global regulation of trade, and UN peacekeeping are all indications of a turn to law as the path to promoting social order. Producing a global legal order clearly benefits states as well as international corporations. It pulls domestic conflicts under the authority of state governance, thus enhancing state control over populations. It also empowers what is called the "international community" as a central source of governance and legal order. But this term conceals the extent to which this community is made up of powerful nation-states which exercise disproportionate power in international institutions and international law.

During this period, critical legal studies critiques of law and its complicity with supporting the dominant segments of society gave way to movements for access to justice, alternative dispute resolution, and enhanced legal protections for vulnerable populations such as victims of domestic violence, sexual assault, and human trafficking. These issues were framed largely as criminal justice problems, demanding greater investments in prosecution and punishment. This requires more state resources but enhances state control over populations. Thus, along with a turn to the law as the way to regulate international affairs, there is a similar increase in the use of law by states to regulate their populations. The mass incarceration in the United States is well known, but work on governmentality shows the extent to which more socially embedded forms of control, acting both on bodies and on subjectivity and person-hood, are also fundamental to contemporary forms of governance.

This florescence of law as the favored mode of building more just societies and at the same time as a way to enhance state surveillance and control provides fertile ground for a post–Cold War anthropol-ogy of law. This is the terrain that this book engages. Its historical ap-proach highlights these dramatic changes in the scope of work on the anthropology of law and provides valuable background to contemporary scholarship. The book presents and analyzes a rich collection of research studies on the intersections between law and social and cultural for-mations. Its organization provides an effective framework for exploring contemporary legal anthropology. The studies it describes are well con-textualized and clearly presented and explained. The historical approach and focus on the post–Cold War period offer a valuable context, while the discussion of contemporary scholarship provides dramatic evidence that the anthropology of law is a vibrant field. As law is increasingly seen as a salvation from endless wars and conflicts and a mode of social order fundamental to economic development, its analysis becomes in-creasingly important. These developments offer new opportunities for anthropologists interested in questions of justice and power.

As this book shows, the object of study has moved out of the court-room into issues as diverse as state failure to provide birth registration or secure land titles to the way new regulations about sexual violence reshape gender identities. In the United States, the conservative fight against transgender identities has taken the form of passing laws requir-ing people to use the bathrooms of their birth gender identity, using the specter of men sexually assaulting women in restrooms to generate political support for this position. Indeed, the law is very often at the center of political struggles over justice and state power, an instrument both of transformation and resistance.

One of the strengths of this text is its engagement with the question of justice. Although legal anthropology has long focused on questions of the nature of law and the sources of order, it has been less engaged with the concept of justice. The term is hard to define. It has both procedural and substantive aspects, for example. Yet it is central to the legitimacy of law. From an anthropological perspective, concepts of justice grow out of particular cultural understandings and practices. What justice means, and for whom, must be answered in terms of contexts and situations. However, some of the recent developments in international law, such as the human rights system and the international criminal courts, claim to define a universal conception of justice and seek to enforce it.

While achieving justice, in any sense, is clearly challenging and usually impossible, it is a critically important aspiration. With the turn to international legal instruments that assert universal authority, the question of whether they are producing justice for everyone takes on new importance and complexity. Is there a universal standard of justice? Are these standards relevant, at least aspirationally, to people living in a wide range of societies? In my own work on human rights and gender violence, I have found that even in relatively remote local communities, many activists and even some victims had an awareness that there was an international system of human rights according to which women could "stand up for themselves." The existence of a transcendent system of human rights, even vaguely defined, gave strength to local demands for justice. That the human rights system is a legal one was clearly important to its legitimacy and power. Local activists whom I have studied in the United States, China, India, and Peru reinterpreted and vernacularized these global standards, making them understandable within local systems of meaning and practice. At the same time, these ideas of justice remain tethered to the conception of a global, universal system of law, although the ties are sometimes long and tenuous.

It is not surprising that there is so much terrific new scholarship in this field. This volume is an excellent way to discover this exciting new work and to appreciate its range and power. Mark Goodale has done a great job of showing us the richness and excitement of this field, presented in a comprehensible and engaging way. The book is a real pleasure to read and an essential guide to understanding how law intersects with social and cultural life in the contemporary period.

# PREFACE

This book is both a critical introduction to the contemporary anthropology of law and an attempt to contextualize the ways and means of law more generally within broader currents of history, conflict, and the ethics of everyday life. It is an intervention whose scope is meant to reveal questions as much as suggest answers. It is, more than anything else, an extended tribute to the rigor and creativity of scholars working at the ethnographic crossroads where some of the most significant forces now meet, spaces of violence and ambiguity, but also of possibility, in which law has come to play a central role.

Because several fine studies of "comparative law and society" now exist, both as single volumes and as edited collections and readers, I have tried to focus in this book quite intentionally on the *anthropology* of law. I have also tried to highlight important work from emerging voices in the field and, when possible, studies produced by colleagues working in languages other than English. Nevertheless, I have left some important topics aside, such as economics and religion (and likely others). The decision not to include a chapter on the anthropology of law and religion was in large part a recognition of the major contribution to the subject made by Fernanda Pirie in her 2013 book. I realize that colleagues will find many omissions in this volume and I can only beg indulgence in advance and hope that what does appear offers some measure of interest by way of recompense.

I had the good fortune to be able to refine different parts of this book through lectures and conferences over the last several years, and I must acknowledge the generosity and depth of engagement from faculty and students at a number of institutions: Martin Luther University Halle-Wittenberg (Department of Anthropology), University of Lucerne (Department of Ethnology), École des hautes études en sciences sociales (Laboratoire d'anthropologie sociale), Aarhus University (Center for Sociological Studies), University of Copenhagen (Department of Anthropology and the Danish Association of Anthropologists), University of Basel (Institute of Ethnology), University of Bern (Institute of Social Anthropology), Jagiellonian University (Faculty of Law), University of Ghent (Flemish Interuniversity Research Network on Law and Development), London School of Economics (Department of Anthropology and the Law School), Stanford University (Program on Human Rights, Center on Democracy, Development and the Rule of Law, Freeman Spogli Institute for International Studies), University of Coimbra (Centre for Social Sciences), University of Minnesota (School of Law, Institute for Advanced Studies), Stanford University (Stanford Archaeology Center and Department of Anthropology), University of Groningen (Institute for Multicultural Affairs), George Washington University (Department of Anthropology, Elliot School of International Affairs, Culture in Global Affairs Program), University of Macerata (Giacomo Leopardi School for Advanced Studies), and Cambridge University (Centre for Research in the Arts, Social Sciences and Humanities).

The list of people from whom I have learned much about anthropology and law is a long one indeed. Nevertheless, there are some whose influence on my work is notable—as mentors, as colleagues, as intellectual sparring partners, and as friends. At the risk of "implicating them in my confusions," as Clifford Geertz once put it, I would like to acknowledge the following: Franz and Keebet von Benda-Beckmann, John Bowen, Kamari Clarke, Rosemary Coombe, Jane Cowan, Eve Darian-Smith, Marie-Bénédicte Dembour, Daniel Goldstein, Carol Greenhouse, Anne Griffiths, Laura Nader, Ron Niezen, Barbara Oomen, Alain Pottage, Boaventura de Sousa Santos, and Richard Wilson. Colleagues who provided specific information about sections of the book, either with suggestions for references or points of historical clarification, or by way of helping me avoid embarrassing mistakes, include John Conley, Jessica Greenberg, Chris Hann, Robert Hayden, Jean Jackson, Lynn Meskell, and Bert Turner. Above all, I must thank Sally Engle Merry, who has taught me so much over the years, both professionally and personally. Sally's contributions continue to define and enlarge the boundaries of the field and I am deeply honored that her Foreword frames this book.

This book was written under the auspices of my new institutional home, the University of Lausanne, which has welcomed me with unfailing support and broad encouragement. I want to thank two colleagues in particular for the role they have played in the recruitment to and support of the chair I now hold: Professor Fabien Ohl, former Dean of the Faculty of Social and Political Sciences, and Professor Daniel Oesch, current Director of the Institute of Social Sciences. I also must thank my colleagues in the Laboratory of Cultural and Social Anthropology (LACS) who have gone out of their way to facilitate my integration, including Irene Maffi, Anne-Christine Trémon, and Yannis Papadaniel. Jérémie Voirol provided outstanding research assistance on the book, particularly for Francophone scholarship.

Important periods of writing were undertaken at the Max Planck Institute for Social Anthropology in Halle, Germany, and I am pleased to acknowledge the support and collegiality of the new Department of Law and Anthropology, of which I am also a member of its Consultative Committee. The Director of the department, Professor Marie-Claire Foblets, has a bold vision for the future of the field and it is my hope that this book reflects at least a small part of the anticipation and possibility that anthropologists of law will be associating with Halle in the years to come.

It is with both sadness and depth of feeling that I acknowledge the role that the late and incomparable Neil Whitehead played in my understanding of law at a particularly formative stage. Although not an anthropologist of law himself, Neil directed me for the first time to E. P. Thompson's *obiter dicta* on law in *Whigs and Hunters*, an intellectual discovery whose implications I continue to explore.

I want to extend a very warm note of thanks to my editor at NYU Press, Jennifer Hammer, who first approached me with the idea for this project and then provided encouragement and good cheer at every stage thereafter.

The book is formally dedicated to the late Simon Roberts, who both introduced me to the anthropology of law and supervised my master's thesis on the topic. My hope is that he would have found something of interest in the book and more generally in the way the field has developed in recent years.

As always, it is a pleasure to acknowledge the support and inspiration I receive from my muses, Isaiah, Dara, and Romana, and the lessons I've learned from Willow, particularly the importance of trusting my instincts.

For the rest: *Les jeux sont faits.*

# Introduction

## *From Status to Contract to Cosmopolitanism*

> Broadly . . . this [book] will seek to place the numerous theoretical devel-
> opments, methodological concerns, and changing ideological approaches
> in legal anthropology within a historical framework that further recog-
> nizes the necessity to address these fundamental elements with a view
> that is essentially integrative. Through the course of this analysis it will
> become obvious that the author does not stand on neutral ground vis-a-
> vis [sic] the various controversies and it is hoped that some small contri-
> bution to a more general theory can be made by analysing the relevant
> concerns both with a view to the past and a view to the future.

It is a particular kind of anguish to revisit one's writings not just from
an earlier period of life, but from an earlier self. Thus it is with some
trepidation that I begin this book with the opening lines from my 1991
master's thesis, memorably entitled "Legal Anthropology: An Historical
and Theoretical Analysis," which I wrote during that halcyon summer
seemingly permanently affixed to an aging green leather chair in the old
Reading Room of the British Library at the same desk—I was assured—at
which none other than Karl Marx had toiled away at *Das Kapital.*

I begin this text this way for two reasons. First, it serves as an illustration that some things have not—and perhaps never will—change. At a
structural level, this book also takes up questions of anthropology and
law in relation to a set of broader arguments about their various points
of conjuncture and disjuncture. At the same time, in offering a critical
introduction to anthropology and law, my own perspectives naturally
shape this volume's form, organization, inclusions and omissions, and
general claims about the extraordinary (if at times unrecognized) contributions that anthropologists continue to make to both the theory and
practice of law. In this sense, I am relieved in advance of the obligation

to produce an encyclopedic, globally comprehensive, account. On the contrary, what follows is an admittedly idiosyncratic examination of the many ways in which anthropologists have transformed—sometimes against their better judgment—the study of law into a cutting-edge domain of critical social science, engaged research, and ambitious social and ethical theory.

But second, to begin with language from a 1991 study of the anthropology of law is also a reminder of just how much the field has changed since then. Indeed, this fact is the reason for one of the book's central elements: its focus on developments during the various periods of the post–Cold War and beyond. As masters of the serendipitous, anthropologists found themselves confronting historical transformations in which law appeared to be playing a central, if contested, role. In my own case, I went to rural Bolivia in 1998 to conduct doctoral fieldwork on the (now painfully) naïve assumption that I would discover the secret to peaceful coexistence by studying what Karl Llewellyn and E. Adamson Hoebel had called, in *The Cheyenne Way* (1941), the "trouble cases," that is, those moments of conflict through which the contours of law become most visible. And although I did, indeed, study many trouble cases, mostly involving fights between young men during fiestas and "land invasions" by llamas left unattended by their very young shepherds, I did not, alas, discover the secret to peaceful coexistence.

What I did discover, unexpectedly, was a window onto the ways in which the end of the Cold War was transforming the relationship between law and society—a kind of transformation that anthropologists, particularly those in the field, could not ignore. By the late 1990s, rural Bolivia had become a hotbed of human rights activism; indeed, the broader rubric of development was being reconfigured by coteries of mostly Western European NGOs into a mechanism for the promotion of human rights ideology. Among the forty villages and hamlets in which I conducted research during that year, many of them had entered into transnational collaborations that blended human rights education with more traditional forms of assistance such as road building, microfinance, and agricultural investment. But it soon became clear that the idea of human rights was not being introduced primarily as a new kind of legal strategy that could be put to use in courts or within movements for social and political change. Rather, it was being taught—in the ubiquitous workshops that I frequently attended—as a new form of self-regard, a new form of being in the world, one that was anchored in a radical theory of human equality.

I was compelled, therefore, to adapt my research accordingly. From a more recognizable study of community dispute resolution, the relationship between state and local forms of law, and the ways in which law came to constitute an important "semi-autonomous social field" (Moore 1973), it shifted to a study of the practice of human rights as an emergent transnational legal and moral discourse, the influence of international and transnational norms in shaping ongoing social and political conflicts in Bolivia, and the resulting microprocesses of moral change and resistance that Sally Engle Merry (2006b) would later describe as "vernacularization."

But my experience was not an isolated one. These methodological shifts, as we would come to learn, were signaling the development of a new anthropology of law across a range of field sites as a response to a widening recognition that the post–Cold War landscape was one on which law and politics were being redefined in relation to each other (Wilson 2001); the practice—if not the principle—of state sovereignty was being challenged from both below and above (Coutin 1994); the coalescence of transnational legal networks was reshaping traditional understandings of global and local, inside and outside (Riles 1998); and, at least in the early and middle years, the spread of human rights and new rhetorics of justice was signaling the return of utopianism as a force in global politics (Niezen 2010).

Yet except for the visionary few, these seismic shifts, and their profound implications for the anthropology of law, were difficult to imagine back in 1991; our intellectual worldview was still very much shaped by a set of existing narratives about the history of the field, its potential and limitations, and its relation to other branches of the wider discipline. Even though Sally Engle Merry forecasted many of the changes to come in her 1992 *Annual Review of Anthropology* article, "Anthropology, Law, and Transnational Processes," it took more than a decade of research, trial and error theorizing, and institutional development for the shape of the new anthropology of law to come fully into view.

The nine chapters in this volume focus on these developments in the anthropology of law since the end of the Cold War. In this way, the book puts the emphasis on the ways in which anthropologists have responded to broader transformations through which the nature and function of law themselves shifted. In general, these shifts were associated with the growing importance and influence of certain kinds of law, particularly international and transnational law and domestically, constitution making. The political theorist Ran Hirschl (2004) described the emerging global hegemony of law in the post–Cold War period as a "juristocracy" and he worried that the growth of legal institutions and the dominance of legal logics of conflict resolution were changing the very terms of democratic politics in ways that made structural change less likely. As a response to these changes, anthropologists of law were forced to develop methodologies and theoretical questions that remained ethnographically coherent but also expansive enough to take in, and problematize, the implications of the growing legalization of social, political, and economic life.

In the process, anthropologists of law found themselves at the heart of some of the most important contemporary debates—in anthropology and beyond. As a disciplinary question, this represented a shift that in many ways mirrored the contested florescence of law itself as both a dominant form of social control and mechanism for "fabrication" (Pottage 2004). In making the study of "modes of action which are lodged in rich, culturally-specific, layers of texts, practices, instruments, technical devices, aesthetic forms, stylized gestures, semantic artefacts, and bodily dispositions" (Pottage 2004: 1) as much a part of the contemporary anthropology of law as the ethnography of court sessions and rule making, the field became central again.

This text offers a broad analysis of the consequential ways in which anthropologists have studied, interacted with, and critiqued the ways and means of law—as systems of enforceable rules, as ethical norms, as frameworks for political action, and as categories of identity. Since the early 1990s, anthropologists have found themselves confronting law in new forms (as with human rights) and in new cultural spaces in which law is the central mechanism through which problems like citizenship, indigenous movements, and biotechnology, for example, could be studied through anthropological research. This text explores these novel interconnections of law, politics, and technology and surveys the contributions that anthropologists have made to our understanding of them.

As we will see below, the anthropology of law began as a domain of inquiry that concerned itself with basic questions of social development, history, and political change. Over time, this concern with broader implications was lost as both the questions and methodological ambitions narrowed. The result was that the anthropology of law contracted for much of its disciplinary history. By contrast, although its concepts and categories are notably different from those of the nineteenth-century proto-legal anthropologists like Henry Maine, Lewis Morgan, Johann Jakob Bachofen, and John McLennan, the contemporary anthropology of law likewise sees the study of law as an opening to broader questions, for example, about the relationship between social conflict and economic inequality, the limits of law as a mechanism for structural change, and the potential of law to produce, shape, and protect categories of identity. In this sense, even if these kinds of questions and scope of analysis differ markedly from those of the nineteenth century, the tenor and expansiveness through which they are taken up suggest that the anthropology of law is coming full circle.

In focusing on the closing of this circle, this book is structured by two overlapping, though not coequal, rubrics. First, there is the *anthropology* of law. This is the now-open intellectual and ethical terrain on which key examples of leading-edge contemporary anthropology are being developed as both a response to, and critique of, the wider consolidation of the "neoliberal world order" (Ferguson 2006). In this way, the anthropological study of justice processes, financial regulation, human rights, international criminal procedures, constitution making, indigenous rights, and cultural heritage (among others), is nothing less than a critical anthropology of the present. This first rubric, or organizing principle, must be distinguished from the anthropology of *law*. This is a perspective that privileges law itself and considers the different ways in which anthropology as a discipline has developed methodologies and theories—both historically and comparatively—about law. This important branch of comparative legal studies has a long history and Fernanda Pirie's (2013) book continues this tradition of drawing from a wide range of substantive legal systems to arrive at a formal legal theory in which contemporary law is marked by a tension between "idealism" and "legalism," that is, between the "universality of law, on the one hand, and the conflicting, and particularistic, demands of equity and justice, on the other" (2013: 228).

But if this volume makes the *anthropology* of law, rather than the anthropology of *law*, its main focus, it also takes the measure of "the law's legal anthropology" (Niezen 2013a). In studying and analyzing law as a key mode of contemporary world-making, anthropologists have observed the ways in which a kind of disciplinary doppelgänger, "legal anthropology," has been employed by lawyers and others as a form of ideologically infused legal practice. Although, as will be seen in different places throughout the book, the law's legal anthropology has played an important role in more recent developments in transnational and international law in particular, this kind of appropriation has a longer history.

In a well-known example, the supposed informality and empathetic nature of traditional conflict resolution in small-scale societies was used as the point of reference by leading American jurists during the 1970s to create a new system to handle the backlog of court cases that resulted from the explosion in rights jurisprudence during the 1960s. As Laura Nader discovered while attending the 1976 Pound Conference that played a key role in the creation of the Alternative Dispute Resolution (or "ADR") movement, Warren Burger, the Chief Justice of the U.S. Supreme Court, himself turned to this imagined legal anthropology to find a way to dispose of what were seen as "garbage cases," even if the formal justification was about "access to law" (Nader 2002: 48–49). Although Nader remained "skeptical, if not contemptuous, of lawyers who claim the title of anthropologist merely because they are [appropriating] the law of everyday life or native peoples" (2002: 72), these forms of appropriation continue to shape the development of law and are worthy of our closest ethnographic scrutiny.

\*\*\*

The next three sections examine the intellectual history of the anthropology of law. Because the principal focus of this volume is more recent transformations, this survey is intended to provide just enough historical context to anchor what follows. Moreover, it is simply not possible, at least in the scope of an introduction to a single book, to write the kind of global history of *anthropologies* and law that perhaps could be mounted with sufficient cross-cultural, cross-historical, and cross-linguistic mastery of the materials—a project that would require a collective effort, in any case. Indeed, Sally Falk Moore went so far as to claim that it was "impossible to write a comprehensive history" of anthropology and law—and that was in 1969!

One final caveat should be lodged: the fact that much of the history of anthropology and law has been written by Anglo-American scholars for an Anglo-American audience. And within this historical and linguistic narrowness, a U.S. perspective has dominated to a large extent. This is partly due to the fact that British and American anthropologies of law developed in different ways, particularly from about the mid-1970s to the shifts of the post–Cold War (as we will see below). But this is also a result of the different ways in which the broader integration of social science and law took place in Anglo-American scholarship. In the United States, the creation of the Law and Society Association and then an academic journal, the *Law & Society Review*, during the mid-1960s, provided a new forum for anthropologists to participate in scholarship and debates about law and society apart from those that were taking place within the discipline of anthropology itself. Despite the fact that the law and society "movement" in the United States was initially—and, to a certain extent, still is—heavily influenced by scholars from sociology, academic law, and political science, anthropologists have nevertheless made notable contributions to law and society scholarship and institutional development (for example, two presidents of the Law and Society Association have been anthropologists, Sally Engle Merry [1993–1995] and Carol Greenhouse 1996–1997]).

In Britain, by contrast, as Reza Banaker has described across a number of critical histories (e.g., Banakar 2009), "socio-legal studies" developed within academic law schools without the same organic integration with the social sciences—including anthropology—and, as a result, has never had the same degree of legitimacy or influence as its U.S. counterpart. Indeed, in a somewhat bleak analysis of socio-legal studies in Britain, Max Travers (2001) argued that it was destined to remain marginalized as long as socio-legal researchers "believe that it should serve the latest government agenda for reforming or improving the legal system, rather than promote radical change," on the one hand, while, on the other, it abandons "any aspirations it once had to develop general theories" because of a rigid adherence to an applied "empiricism" (2001:

26; 29; referring also to earlier histories of socio-legal studies in Britain, including Campbell and Wiles 1976, and Willock 1974). Given the contested development of socio-legal studies in Britain as a branch of applied legal and policy research, it is not surprising that it did not provide an alternative means through which the anthropology of law could flourish.

Despite a heightened sensitivity to the problem of Anglo-American bias in many histories of anthropology and law, it is not possible to avoid the same perspective here entirely. Nevertheless, in the following sections and wherever possible elsewhere, an initial effort is made to reorient the intellectual historical map. Historically, alterative trajectories of anthropology and law were unfolding in many places outside the Anglo-American tradition, including France, Belgium, the Netherlands, South Africa, India, Spain, Portugal, and in some parts of Latin America (particularly in Argentina, Peru, and Mexico). In some cases, it is difficult to identify a distinct anthropology of law as such within histories that involve what would be recognized today as both theoretically and methodologically anthropological but which might have been undertaken in the name of, for example, sociology.

And even if the problem of Anglo-American bias in the history of the anthropology of law is adequately confronted, there is still the question of whether the broader relationship between anthropology, law, and colonialism has created a secondary bias—what Hounet and Lantin-Mallet (2017) have described as a "Eurocentric" perspective. This distortion leads even contemporary scholars, many working in French, to overemphasize the institutions and national laws of former colonies in studies that take place within bureaucratic settings that strongly discourage interdisciplinarity and the development of theories that are critical of the state. Of course, these forms of intellectual and institutional predisposition range much wider; in this sense, the case of anthropology and law is simply a microcosm of a more general trend. Fortunately, as the volume moves away from the narrative of history to focus on more recent developments, at least some of these biases become less pronounced. But without being able to produce a complete one here, the argument should be clear: an alternative global map of the anthropology of law in history would show additional points of prominence, different theoretical terrains, and alternative routes of circulation.

## From the Armchair to the Pile-Dwellings (1861–1926)

Although Alan Macfarlane (2000) makes a lively argument about the influence of Montesquieu's methodology in *The Spirit of the Laws* (1748) on later developments in anthropological studies of law and politics, a more grounded place to begin would be with a group of nineteenth-century scholars and colonial administrators who can be usefully thought of as proto-anthropologists of law. This first period was marked by two major developments, one theoretical, the other methodological. As we will see, although the transition away from the dominant methodology of the time would prove to be enduring among anthropologists of law, the theoretical approach would be one that would reemerge more recently, in form if not in content.

What distinguished this group was the fact that they viewed the comparative study of law, legal institutions, and legal history as an essential window onto social, political, and economic evolution. To study comparative legal history was to study the evolution of "civilization" itself because the social structures of law at any one time codified society—both in fact and ideally. Different scholars looked to different structures of law as a way to capture this duality; but each began from the premise that both the function and meaning of law went beyond its merely formal attributes as a mechanism of social control and sanction. Although the more recent anthropology of law has little interest in the early questions of social evolution and the relationship between law and civilization, an important continuity exists with the underlying epistemology—that is, the belief that the study of law reveals, perhaps uniquely, broader processes of history, politics, and economy. In this sense, in an odd shift in its intellectual history, much of the contemporary anthropology of law has returned to its nineteenth-century roots.

These roots have their most prominent beginnings in two books published in 1861—Johann Jakob Bachofen's *Das Mutterrecht: eine Untersuchung über die Gynaikokratie der alten Welt nach ihrer religiösen und rechtlichen Natur* ("Mother Right") and Henry Maine's *Ancient Law: Its Connection With the Early History of Society, And Its Relation to Modern Ideas* ("Ancient Law"). In *Mother Right*, the Swiss scholar Bachofen argued that the comparative literary and archaeological study of history revealed a process of cultural evolution through which an original period of female dominance, or matriarchy, was forced to give way to patriarchy as the development of property, state institutions, and social stratification was accompanied by the exercise of male power. In Bachofen's study, law both symbolized and made possible this world-historical shift from female to male "right." At the same time, Bachofen also meant his proto-anthropological analysis of the emergence of the "Apollonian," male-dominated, phase in cultural evolution—one marked by violence, inequality, and hyper-rationalism—to be read as a critical reflection on the ills of his own period (see Gossman 2000).

In the more well-known *Ancient Law*, the English classicist, legal scholar, and colonial administrator Henry Maine likewise used a historical and comparative method to develop a theory about the relationship between law and cultural evolution. Drawing from a range of sources, but particularly Roman law, Maine argued that the evolution from primitive to modern society was made possible by and through law. Among premodern societies, social norms regulated relationships between people, according to Maine, on the basis of different kinds of status—slave, son, the "Female under Tutelage." As societies grew and became more complex, status (ideally expressed by relationships within the family) was no longer an adequate social or legal principle. Instead, law developed as a mechanism for agency through which people—again, ideally—could choose how they related to others and therefore which sets of rights and duties they were obligated to recognize. Thus, the rise of these agreements, or contracts, marked a turning point in history, one that Maine believed continued to characterize his own mid-nineteenth-century world. Unlike Bachofen, however, there is no indication that Maine saw his proto-anthropology of law as a form of contemporary critique. The movement from status to contract, which also made the eventual development of the capitalist mode of production possible, was, as Maine put it, "progressive."

Among the proto-anthropologists of law, the Scottish lawyer John McLennan made perhaps the strongest argument for the evolutionary basis of law in his 1865 *Primitive Marriage. An Inquiry into the Origin of the Form of Capture in Marriage Ceremonies*. In it, he surveyed, among other sources, classical texts to support the hypothesis that accounts of "collusive abduction" in the historical period were the symbolic "survivals" of the older practice of marriage by capture, through which bands of men engaged in warfare in order to secure access to females. McLennan based this explanation for bride capture in a social and then legal extension of Charles Darwin's theory of evolution by natural selection, which had recently been published (in *On the Origin of Species*, 1859; see Stocking 1987). His argument went something like this: because of a general scarcity of resources in prehistory, there was conflict; because this conflict took the form of warfare, men were more valued than women; because women were a burden, female infanticide was widely practiced; but because of this, women themselves became a scarce resource over which men were forced to fight. Eventually, stealing and manipulative forms of bride capture evolved as a more sustainable alternative to constant warfare. According to McLennan, the first laws were laws regulating kinship—who could marry whom and how—and these laws were the direct result of the process of social evolution.

Lewis Henry Morgan's influence is perhaps the most complicated among the nineteenth-century proto-anthropologists of law. Part of the reason is the fact that he was the only real field anthropologist among this group. Although his biography is in many ways stranger than fiction (see, e.g., Moses 2009), the salient point here is that Morgan's long fascination with Native Americans, specifically the Iroquois, led him to conduct extended periods of fieldwork, often accompanied by the Seneca Ely S. Parker (born Hasaneanda, Moses 2009: 52). Yet despite the fact that two of his early books were based in part on these periods of fieldwork (the 1851 *League of the Ho-dé-no-sau-nee or Iroquois* and the 1871 *Systems of Consanguinity and Affinity of the Human Family*), his most important work, *Ancient Society* (1877), was not. In tracing the evolution of human society from "savagery" to "civilization," Morgan made the argument that the emergence of law marked the passage along a universal path of greater complexity and social differentiation. Mark S. Weiner (2006: 33) has described Morgan's intertwining of law and history's "ethna" as a "juridical-racial" theory of society and has drawn attention to the fact that property as a legal category looms large in Morgan's account of human progress.[1]

Finally, we turn to a group of Argentinian proto-anthropologists of law, members of the so-called Generation of '80, who came under the influence of the positivist school of Italian criminology. Italian criminologists like Cesare Lombroso had introduced the principles of empirical science and the field study of individual criminals into a discipline that had been traditionally influenced by metaphysical theories of criminality often linked to assumed cultural traits (see Gibson 2002). Lombroso's "criminal anthropology"—a phrase that comes down to us with a mischievous double meaning—was taken up by a group of young legal reformers and scholars in Buenos Aires who were concerned with rising levels of violence in the port city.

This group, which included Luis María Drago, Norberto Piñero, Francisco Ramos Mejía, and Rodolfo Rivarola, created the Society of Legal Anthropology (*Sociedad de Antropología Jurídica*) in 1888 in order to promote the anthropological study of crime in Buenos Aires and to shape public policy. (Navarro 2009; see also Guy 1991). Although the Society of Legal Anthropology itself was short-lived, the work of its members influenced the development of anthropological criminology in Argentina and Latin America more broadly, and, more important for our purposes here, represented one of the first sustained efforts to create an anthropology of law that was grounded in what later would be called "ethnography." In this sense, the members of the Society of Legal Anthropology in Argentina form a bridge between the so-called armchair anthropologists like Bachofen, McLennan, and Maine and the first of the dedicated ethnographers of law—Bronislaw Malinowski.[2]

## The Golden Age (1926–1978)

At the conclusion of his 1925 Frazer Lecture at the University of Liverpool, the Polish-British anthropologist Bronislaw Malinowski veered away from the main topic—"myth in primitive psychology." To lead into the *obiter dicta* that followed, he explained, "[a]s regards anthropological field-work, we are obviously demanding a new method of collecting evidence" (2002 [1926]: 126). Although he had both demonstrated and explained this new approach—ethnography—in his 1922 *Argonauts of the Western Pacific*, Malinowski felt the need to provide a more systematic justification to ground what he believed, with some justification, was a revolutionary advance for the "science of man." As he put it:

> The anthropologist must relinquish his comfortable position in the long chair on the verandah of the missionary compound, Government station,

or planter's bungalow, where, armed with pencil and notebook and at times with a whisky and soda, he has been accustomed to collect statements from informants, write down stories, and fill out sheets of paper with savage texts. He must go into the villages, and see the natives at work in gardens, on the beach, in the jungle; he must sail with them to distant sandbanks and to foreign tribes, and observe them in fishing, trading, and ceremonial overseas expeditions. Information must come to him full-flavoured from his own observations of native life, and not be squeezed out of reluctant informants as a trickle of talk. Fieldwork can be done first- or second-hand even among savages, in the middle of pile-dwellings, not far from actual cannibalism and head-hunting. Open-air anthropology, as opposed to hearsay note-taking, is hard work, but it is also great fun. Only such anthropology can give us the all-round vision of primitive man and of primitive culture (2002 [1926]: 126–127).[3]

For our purposes here, we can look beyond what is troublingly connoted in this "full-flavoured" justification for the ethnographic method, which would define and shape the course of socio-cultural anthropology more generally for roughly the next six decades. (*Writing Culture*, Marcus and Clifford's influential programmatic challenge to ethnographic method, representation, and the underlying history in which ethnographic anthropology was born, was published sixty years to the year after the publication of Malinowski's Frazer lecture.) Rather, what is important is to recognize the fact that the ethnographic method represented a profoundly different means of both studying and understanding social phenomena, one that insisted on the value in seeing and living these phenomena from the inside out. This "emic" epistemology also carried broader implications, particularly in an age in which the colonial anthropologist, comfortably ensconced on the verandah, was accustomed to summoning informants for a round of "hearsay note-taking"; as Malinowski suggested, this earlier approach was flawed both scientifically and ethically.

Thus it was that *Crime and Custom in Savage Society*—the first major book on anthropology and law based on the ethnographic principles of native language competence, immersion over time, and participant-observation—was published in 1926, based on Malinowski's research in the Trobriand Islands of Melanesia. What is most important about

*Crime and Custom* here is the fact that it established the anthropology of law as the empirical study of perhaps the most important relationship in any human society: the relationship between rules, or norms, and the complexities of social practice (see Conley and O'Barr 2002). Despite its apparent exoticism—for example, Malinowski memorably argued that the threat of suicide by leaping from tall palm trees, backed by occasional suicides, served as a normative sanction against defamation (see chapter 3)—the book's enduring legacy was to show how the "true problem is not to study how human life submits to rules; [but] how the rules become adapted to life" (1926: 127).

With the publication of *Crime and Custom*, the ethnographic anthropology of law entered its golden age, a period that would last until the late 1970s. The anthropological study of law developed into a subfield of the discipline; many of its practitioners were involved in major debates over key disciplinary concepts; and, over time, the focus among anthropologists of law moved away from the problem of "how the rules become adapted to life" to engage with basic questions of law itself. As we will see, however, the later shift toward fundamental debates about law based on anthropological research marked the beginning of a decline and eventual turning point in the anthropology of law's intellectual history. By 1969, Sally Falk Moore had to remind her colleagues that the "classical task of legal anthropology has been to understand the relationship between law and society" (1969: 294).

This shift from the social life of rules toward law can already be seen in Isaac Schapera's *Handbook of Tswana Law and Custom* (1938). The *Handbook*, which "few match . . . in quality" (Moore 1969: 261), was an extensive catalogue and description of the "traditional and modern laws and related customs of the Tswana tribes" (1938: XXV), produced at the request of the colonial administration. Although the *Handbook* was not written for anthropologists, it provided an early example after *Crime and Custom* of the way in which ethnographic study opened a window onto the diversity and prevalence of law outside the boundaries of conventional state institutions and control.

During this same period, a pioneering group of Dutch scholars was likewise studying law within the context of colonial administration. Even though their major purpose was to "improve the functioning of the administrative and legal system of the colony" (F. von Benda-Beckmann and K. von Benda-Beckmann 2002: 696), researchers like Cornelius van Vollenhoven, Barend ter Haar, and F. D. Holleman were using the study of native *adat* law to question the utility of making "sharp distinctions between law, custom, and morals" (2002: 697). Perhaps most significantly, F. D. Holleman and van Vollenhoven were developing an anthropological theory of law in the late 1920s and early 1930s that emphasized the role of "non-conflictive social practices" (2002: 699), as opposed to what Karl Llewellyn and E. Adamson Hoebel (1941) would later call the "trouble-cases." As the von Benda-Beckmanns convincingly argue, the critique of the limitations of focusing on trouble-cases, articulated decades later by scholars like Sally Falk Moore, was actually anticipated and developed by a group of Dutch ethnologists and legal scholars at least a decade before the publication of Llewellyn and Hoebel's influential *The Cheyenne Way* (see also J. F. Holleman 1973).

Nevertheless, whether focused on trouble- or "trouble-less" cases, the case study method emerged in the 1940s and 1950s as a major approach in the anthropology of law. As Moore has argued, Max Gluckman's 1955 *The Judicial Process among the Barotse of Northern Rhodesia* "was the first . . . to describe the proceedings before a tribunal in a technologically simple society from the point of view of an anthropologist who had actually seen . . . cases . . . as they were argued over, thrashed out, and ruled on" (1969: 263). Gluckman's study was followed two years later by Paul Bohannan's *Justice and Judgment among the Tiv* (1957) and thus began one of the most important debates in the history of the anthropology of law, one that, among other things, challenged the idea of an integrated "Anglo-American" perspective.

In *Barotse*, Gluckman used Western legal categories to explain the principles that Barotse judges applied in specific cases. The most well known, and controversial, was the category of the "Reasonable Man."[4] In *Justice and Judgment*, anthropology's "first casebook of dispute settlement in an acephalous society" (Moore 1969: 265), Bohannan drew a sharp epistemological distinction between "folk" and the kind of "analytic" explanations of law that were at the heart of Gluckman's study. Bohannan argued that analytic explanations trapped the anthropologist within Western legal categories that distorted the real nature of native *laws* (Bohannan claimed that the Tiv, at least, had laws but not Law). The solution to this dilemma, according to Bohannan, was to limit ethnographic research to the folk terms themselves.

Despite the "puzzling" fact that in the conclusion to *Justice and Judgment*, Bohannan does not offer a list of the "Tiv substantive-terminological-legal concepts with which so much of the book is concerned" (Moore 1969: 267), its fundamental challenge to Gluckman and the ensuing debate shaped the intellectual history of the field for at least a decade. Although the debate was ostensibly about the limits and possibilities of ethnography as a method to study fundamental questions of law, it also carried the seeds of disciplinary conflicts—within the anthropology of law and beyond—that wouldn't emerge until later, for example, over representation, the problem of ethnographic authority, and the role of anthropology as a scientific discipline capable of producing generalizable knowledge.

Even if these broader implications were always latent within the Gluckman-Bohannan debate, at the time, the intra-subdisciplinary conflict had the effect of narrowing the development of the anthropology of law even further away from the Malinowskian prescription to study "how the rules become adapted to life." Instead, the anthropology of law got bogged down in a debate about a particular category of rules themselves, law, and the best way to study and analyze them. With this debate becoming increasingly sterile and polarizing, it was not surprising that a new group of anthropologists of law sought to reinvigorate the field by moving away from questions of law as such toward those of dispute resolution, social order, and the relationship between law and social change (see, e.g., Gulliver 1963; Colson 1966).

A sense for how these intellectual and generational divides were transforming the anthropology of law at the time can be gleaned from Laura Nader's description of the two conferences she organized during the 1960s—one at Stanford in 1964 and the other in Austria in 1966.[5] Looking back on the 1966 conference, she explained that

> The conference . . . had been tumultuous. Clearly, the intellectual issues about ethnography and interpretation were all there simmering—whose categories do we use, the Other or the West? What is ethnography? When is ethnography ethnographic? Should we standardize data collection?

When do we include colonials and missionaries? . . . The political differences between us were there, but they were unmentionable. (Nader 1996: vii)

Despite the fact that as late as 1965 Laura Nader could argue that "empirical studies of law should be set in the general context of social control" (1965: 17), she was at the same time launching an ambitious collective project that would play a significant role in moving the anthropology of law back toward the study of law in society. Using her position in the anthropology department at the University of California, Berkeley as a base, Nader organized multiple generations of doctoral students to conduct ethnographic fieldwork on dispute processes "within the [broader] context of social and cultural organization" (Nader 2002: 39). The Berkeley Village Law Project collectively carried out research on dispute processes, rather than legal rules, across a wide range of field sites, from Liechtenstein to Papua New Guinea. In 1978, Nader and Harry Todd published a collection of essays based on over a decade of this organized research, *The Disputing Process*, which both explored conflict processes in ten societies and, more symbolically, reflected a wider flourishing of dispute studies within a reanimated anthropology of law.

## Chronicle of a Death (and Resurrection) Foretold (1978–1989)

Ironically, it was just at the moment when the disputing paradigm had firmly established itself, particularly among American anthropologists of law, when an ominous cloud appeared over the horizon. Simon Roberts, a law professor at the London School of Economics with dual training in both law and anthropology, published an article in the 1978 *Royal Anthropological Institute Newsletter* (*RAIN*) entitled "Do We Need an Anthropology of Law?" The freer format of *RAIN* gave Roberts the chance to make a bolder and more direct version of the argument against the anthropology of law that he was outlining more systematically during the same period in the pages of a book finished the same year, *Order and Dispute: An Introduction to Legal Anthropology* (1979).[6]

Roberts observed the evolution of the anthropology of law to the point at which Gluckman and Bohannan were aiming "polemical articles" (Fuller 1994: 3) at each other (see Nader 1969), and concluded that what was needed was to wipe the slate clean and redefine both the kind of research that was possible and the kinds of questions toward which it was directed. As he viewed them, the debates over the validity of generalizable legal categories versus folk categories expressed in their own linguistic and cultural terms was "mostly deadening" (Fuller 1994: 4) and was leading, in his judgment, to the decline of the anthropology of law, particularly in Britain.[7] For Roberts, the futility of these debates demonstrated the fact that a specific anthropology of *law*, one concerned with the problem of cross-cultural definitions of law and its institutions, was an intellectual and disciplinary dead end.

But in "pronouncing the death sentence on legal anthropology" (Fuller 1994: 2), Roberts had in mind a subsequent resurrection, one that would lead to the development of a branch of anthropology that was conceived in wholly different terms. Nevertheless, as Fuller has argued, Roberts's 1978 obituary for the anthropology of law captured—and perhaps accelerated—its fall into marginality, so that by 1994

> even the older classic texts of legal ethnography [were] no longer required reading for contemporary British anthropologists, as once they were. . . . The majority of British anthropologists—like the students taught by them—blithely ignore the subject, forget about its classic monographs, overlook new publications and do no original research on legal topics. (Fuller 1994: 4)

The resurrection that Roberts intended was one in which "law" itself disappeared as an analytical category for anthropologists, to be replaced by a *problématique* that was both ethnographically broader and theoretically more diffuse. As John Comaroff and Roberts argued in their pathbreaking *Rules and Processes: The Cultural Logic of Dispute in an African Context* (1981), disputes play an important role in constituting the social world. This happens through a dialectical tension between what they call the "sociocultural order" and the "normative repertoire." Individuals maneuver between and among the broader structures of society, which are formally and ideologically rule-governed but also open to challenge, change, and the exercise of even subversive autonomy. Although the innovation of *Rules and Processes* was in many ways independent of the coextensive development of the disputing paradigm in the American anthropology of law in particular, it gave new and expansive theoretical shape to it and thus served as a turning point as the "anthropology of law" (still framed in this way, despite Roberts's insistence) moved into the ambiguous and unsettling 1980s.[8]

The 1980s was a period of ferment, transition, and critique. At a political economic level, the winding down of the Cold War was accompanied by the emergence of a global-structural system that would usher in over the coming decade what the French economists Gérard Duménil and Dominique Lévy (2004) have called the "neoliberal revolution." At the same time, the politics of the traditional left in Europe and the United States was under attack; trade unions were being undermined in both the Global North and Global South; and many older revolutionary movements were being forced to reorganize on the basis of various forms of transnational criminality.

In the academy, a parallel process of transition was taking place. Unlike during the 1960s, however, the unrest in academia during the 1980s did not have an easily identifiable set of organizing principles. Across the humanities and social sciences, questions of power, history, the lingering effects of colonialism, and the politics of representation came together in a combustible mix. The resulting debates often broke along generational and disciplinary lines. Within anthropology, these conflicts sometimes led to institutional fractures. For example, at Duke University and Stanford University in the United States, warring factions decided—or were forced—to go their separate ways. The creation of separate departments of "cultural anthropology" and "anthropological sciences" was a response to widely divergent beliefs about the role of anthropology in public life, its ability to produce scientific knowledge, and the relationship between anthropology as a discipline and the history of colonialism.

This wider disciplinary upheaval and the resulting processes of questioning and critique had an important impact on the anthropology of law. What resulted was the introduction of a new set of theoretical and methodological questions just when the global geopolitical landscape was about to experience a seismic shift. For a signal example of how these wider disciplinary debates transformed scholarship and also laid the groundwork for the anthropology of law that would develop after

1989, we can look to the intergenerational meeting that took place in Bellagio, Italy, in 1985 around the theme of "Ethno-Historical Models and the Evolution of Law." Although the ostensible motivation for the conference was to explore ways in which a critical historical perspective could be integrated with the anthropology of law, what resulted was something much more far-reaching.

The organizers of the meeting, June Starr and Jane Collier, acknowledged that the anthropology of law was confronted by a "paradigm crisis" (1989: 5).[9] As they argued, despite the important advances that had come from the shift from a rule-centered to a process-centered orientation, both approaches still depended on a set of functionalist assumptions about the role of law, assumptions that had lost credibility. As they put it, "what is the anthropology of law if we doubt that legal systems settle conflicts?" (1989: 5). As a response to the "emerging idea that an anthropological understanding of legal processes needs to be based on a broader vision" (5), the fourteen essays in the volume demonstrated what it might look like to "construct[ . . . ] research questions that return to issues, and [formulate] research agendas [in the anthropology of law] that are important to social anthropology as a whole" (5).

The research questions and agendas that emerged revolved around four key themes: the problem that legal systems "encode asymmetrical power relationships"; the study of law over time as a set of "transformational sequences" that give "legitimacy to hegemonic groups" (reflecting the influence of the work of Raymond Williams, e.g., Williams 1977); the reinsertion of "law" back into culture as a "system" that is shaped by discourses of nationalism, ethnicity, and justice; and finally, the importance of studying legal change as a process through which "power and privilege are distributed through legal means" (1989: 6–14).

Taking *History and Power in the Study of Law* together with Comaroff and Roberts's *Rules and Processes*, the collective impact was to significantly enlarge the conceptual terrain of the anthropology of law at the moment in which wider geopolitical and political economic shifts were taking place. The anthropology of law had effectively come through its contested history in a position to respond both theoretically and methodologically to the coming "juristocracy," to return to Ran Hirschl's characterization of the way in which law would come to shape the contours of emergent and increasingly hegemonic processes in the subsequent decades. Although many of these new legal hegemonies could not be imagined in 1985 or even in 1991,[10] the anthropology of law would soon confront a transformed sociolegal landscape.

## The Three Domains of Contemporary Anthropology and Law (1989–Present)

At this point, the intellectual history catches up to the core of this book proper, which focuses on developments in the anthropology of law, and their implications for law, politics, and society more generally, since the end of the Cold War. Thus, an overview of the book's parts and chapters is also an introduction to the ways in which I conceptualize these developments and implications.

In examining the contributions of the post–Cold War anthropology of law up to the present (2017), three broad areas of debate and research can be identified and these three areas constitute the organizational logic of the book itself. Although they are described more fully below, they are, in brief: "law and the production of meaning," "law and agency, law as regulation"; and "law and identity."[11]

### Law and the Production of Meaning

Bronislaw Malinowski famously, if somewhat elliptically, described the ultimate purpose of the ethnographic method as the study of what concerns people "most intimately," that is, what gives their lives meaning—"the hold which life has" (1922: 25). Likewise, anthropologists of law have revealed the ways which law and legal processes can become intimately bound up with meaning—whether at the level of class consciousness (Merry 1990), legal education (Mertz 2007), or through the negotiation of cultural authenticity within intellectual property regimes (Crăciun 2012). The book's first part explores this most multilayered of frames through which anthropologists have studied the ways and means of law in the contemporary world.

Chapter 1 considers how the study of law and language has been among the most significant areas through which anthropologists have revealed the relationship between law and meaning making. From ethnographies of the "vulgar spirit of blogging in . . . Persian Weblogestan"

(Doostdar 2004) to the ways in which legal language can be used to "argue with" collective traditions (Richland 2008), anthropologists have developed a unique body of knowledge that combines linguistics, discourse analysis, and social theory, in order to trace the ethnographic contours of the "poetics of the law" (White 1985). This chapter surveys this important specialization in the broader anthropology of law and argues that linguistic legal anthropology has been a site of empirical research that has maintained a productive tension between anthropological theory and the methods of ethnolinguistics.

Chapter 2 examines the ways in which anthropologists have studied the linkages between law, colonialism, and contested history making. From the mechanisms through which international law both legitimates and excludes particular forms of "cultural heritage" (Meskell 2013) to the ways in which international criminal trials come to write history and even construct novel genres of history itself (Wilson 2011), law is revealed to be a dominant mode through which cultural and political narratives organize and authenticate collective action. The chapter argues that the juridification of the past can be understood as a form of myth making in which legal categories establish a set of baseline, implicit understandings that consist of common moral perspectives, historical sensibilities, and linguistic cross-references.

## Law and Agency, Law as Regulation

The chapters in Part II examine two major ways in which law shapes action. In the first, law provides a mechanism for exercising individual and collective agency—often with emancipatory consequences. Topics covered include anthropological studies of law and political reform, the role of law in transnational justice processes, and the use of law to promote broader development goals like access to health care and clean water, among others. In the second, anthropologists have studied the ways in which law regulates and often constrains social, political, and economic action. Here, the position of the state remains critical, even with the rise of new forms of international and transnational law after the end of the Cold War. In late-Westphalian politics, the state retains control over the exercise of national power and internal surveillance. As anthropologists have shown, the state has, if anything, become even more adept at using law to discipline groups and outliers who threaten its position within the broader neoliberal world order. But law-as-regulation also takes place beyond national borders, particularly within networks of global finance and commerce. Anthropologists have tracked these transnational forms of legal regulation in religious-based lending practices, the monitoring of gender relations, and the professionalization of truth and reconciliation processes

Chapter 3 examines the ways in which anthropologists of law have studied the contours of justice from a range of different angles as a distinct problem of law and society. This chapter surveys these contributions to the broader understanding of justice with a focus on the legacy of theorizing about justice based on ethnography, including recent studies of the International Criminal Court, research on the relationship between religious and state justice processes, and studies of the creative use of international legal mechanisms like the Alien Tort Claims Act to hold transnational corporations accountable for abuses against people and the environment. Innovative research on the gaps between state law and citizen security highlight the extent to which justice seeking involves basic dilemmas and compromises, particularly by people living on the margins. The anthropology of law demonstrates ethnographically that "justice" is an essentially open legal, cultural, and moral concept.

The discussion in chapter 4 focuses on anthropology's contributions to the study of the practice of human rights, contributions that have become one of the field's most notable markers of influence on law within international and interdisciplinary spheres. This influence has been multifaceted. The anthropology of human rights has developed innovative approaches in methodology, epistemology, and ethics such that an anthropological perspective is now a common, and even indispensible, presence within academic debates over human rights, within international institutional policy making, and among human rights practitioners. The chapter argues that anthropologists have made far-reaching contributions to the broader understanding of human rights that cover four distinct topics: human rights networks; moral creativity in the practice of human rights; the relationship between human rights and aspirational politics; and the role of economics in shaping human rights advocacy.

Partly influenced by wider theoretical developments around forms of regulation and governmentality, anthropologists of law have also examined the various means through which law constrains and shapes action through its logics and bureaucracies. Chapter 5 examines these forms of regulation as a marker of the ways in which legal forms of governance underpin wide areas of contemporary life, including international and transnational finance, health care, immigration and asylum seeking, intellectual property, and social change through constitution making. Anthropologists have emphasized the ways in which people who are subject to forms of legal regulation often subvert and modify them and the chapter explores the implications of this key insight.

*Law and Identity*

The third broad area in which contemporary anthropologists have developed new approaches to law is in the study of how different forms of identity—individual, collective, institutional, ethnic, gendered—either emerge through law, or, as one volume suggests, against it (Eckert et al. 2012). The three chapters in Part III take up the complicated production of identity through and against law as a form of "disambiguation" (Niezen 2013a): the need to separate, in this case, the anthropological study of legal identity from the forms of anthropology that are produced by legal identities. Doing so reveals the essential "polysemy" within categories of legal subjectivity. In addition, the book's final part examines the ways in which anthropological studies of law carry broader lessons for subject formation in conditions of social change, migration, violence, and resistance.

Chapter 6 considers how anthropologists have made wide-ranging contributions to the ethnographic and collaborative study of indigenous peoples. Much of the emergence of the indigenous peoples movement—even of the concept of indigeneity itself—has taken place in terms of forms of legal mobilization, from International Labor Organization Convention 107 (1957) to the United Nations Declaration on the Rights of Indigenous Peoples (2007). At the same time, anthropologists have worked closely with indigenous interlocutors at the boundaries of research and activism as a form of "emancipatory cultural politics" (Turner 1997). This chapter surveys the complicated ways in which the anthropology of law and the anthropology of (and for) indigenous peoples converge in the development of ideas about alternative dispute resolution, in postcolonial studies, and in the study of transnational social movements, among others.

As Sally Engle Merry's (2006a) seminal multisited ethnography of the international and transnational actors and networks that monitor the Convention on the Elimination of All Forms of Discrimination Against Women (CEDAW) demonstrates, the anthropology of gender and the law encompasses important questions of social class, ethnic identity, nationalism, and the (in-)capacity of law to regulate sexual identity on rapidly shifting social landscapes. Chapter 7 examines the ways in which anthropologists have studied the intersections of law, gender, and sexual identity, including the more recent ethnography of the transnational LGBT movement. Anthropological research across different regional and thematic domains shows how the law shapes and sometimes distorts moral economies of gender, with implications for the prevention of violence against women, the promotion of marriage equality, and efforts to identify and end forms of human trafficking.

Over the same historical period that anthropologists were tracking the emergence of human rights as a new form of transnational politics and expression of cosmopolitan identity, law was being deployed quite differently as the foundation for ethnonationalist projects in places like Central and Eastern Europe and for purposes of national reconciliation after mass atrocity in places like Rwanda. In this way, as anthropologists demonstrated, law became a tool to both unify and divide. For example, if the use of law to formally eliminate ethnic categories like Hutu and Tutsi was done to forcibly reshape the capacity of ethnic identity to fuel conflict, it did so by encouraging the formation of a vigorous new sense of Rwandan national identity. As the anthropology of the postgenocide period in Rwanda reveals, the legalization of nationalism carries the risk of underwriting new, potentially larger-scale conflicts. Chapter 8 explores the tensions in the use of law as the foundation for conflict transformation and national restructuring based on ethnic and religious forms of citizenship.

The book's Conclusion surveys a final group of emergent areas in the anthropology of law and uses these insights to reflect more generally about the limits of law in the face of existing transnational social and economic conflicts, and the likely emergence of new forms of collective violence, as human-driven climate and ecological change leads to massive migration and struggles over resources. In this sense, the final chapter considers what lies beyond the anthropology of law, since these imagined but likely future conflicts will arguably be beyond the carrying capacity of even the most transnational forms of law, that is, any form of law that is defined by the boundaries of human society and its interests. The Conclusion ends with a short exploratory section on what it would mean—for law and otherwise—to develop an ecological approach to these coming challenges, one based in new forms of solidarity and a postutopian pluralism.

## Conclusion: From Status to Contract to Cosmopolitanism

For the proto-anthropologists of law in the nineteenth century, the study of law was the study of fundamental processes of social development, historical change, and the causes of hierarchy. The methodological assumption, despite the thematic differences, was that law was a social ordering principle that involved the most critical aspects of human society such as conflict, gender and kinship relations, economic distribution, and political power. Over the intervening decades, the development of the anthropology of law undermined this assumption. This was partly the result of the rise of ethnography among "primitive" peoples as the dominant type of anthropological research, since for the most part, post-Boasian and post-Malinowskian anthropology was historically centrifugal: cultures, including legal cultures, were studied for how they revealed irreducible diversity rather than stages on a grand spectrum of unilineal cultural evolution.

But the narrowing of the anthropology of law away from broader questions of social, political, and economic importance can also be attributed to the trajectory of the subdiscipline's intellectual history, in which theoretical and methodological specialization and internecine disputes were, in some sense, the price of greater professional visibility and institutional development. Yet there was also a cost. By 1969, the year *Law in Culture and Society* was published, Richard M. Nixon had taken office as the U.S. president, vowing to end the disastrous war in Vietnam; the My Lai massacre by American troops had taken place less than a year before; and youth rebellion against established politics and economic and racial injustice was at its peak from Prague to Berkeley. And yet, beyond the "polemical articles" by Gluckman and Bohannan, the rest of the chapters in *Law and Culture and Society* were still focused—perhaps even more so—on "descriptive, functional analyses of [legal] systems both isolated and in contact situations," as Nader herself had described the trend in research from the mid-1940s to the mid-1960s. Even if Nader was highly critical of the state of the anthropology of law by this time (1965), her insistence that colleagues broaden "the angle of vision . . . to include descriptions that would explicate law as part of a many-threaded fabric" (1965: 17) was, by and large, not taken up for at least the next twenty years.[12]

Nevertheless, as we have seen, by the late 1980s anthropologists of law were forcing open the intellectual history in ways that would make it possible for the subdiscipline to respond to the coming changes in the "relationship between law and society" (Moore 1969: 294). As a consequence, with the growing influence of law as a key category of contemporary world-making, anthropologists once again found themselves surveying the ways and means of law for what they revealed about broader questions of historical change, cultural conflict, and the possibility of alternative futures. For Maine, it had been the emergence of contracts—agreements between individuals, enforceable by the state—that was the most important turning point in the relationship between law and society. Yet despite its historical methodology, Maine's proto-anthropological study of law was also, perhaps inevitably, a reflection of its times. His emphasis on contracts within the development of law was both rooted in and—intentionally or not—justified what Eric Hobsbawn (1975) has called the "age of capital," a time which brought the "triumph of a society which believed that economic growth rested on private enterprise, on success in buying everything in the cheapest market (including labour) and selling in the dearest" (1975: 13).[13]

As the years of the post–Cold War unfolded, a new pattern in the relationship between law and society emerged, one that was also deeply connected with wider political economies. At the same time that law continued to underwrite the consolidation of market fundamentalism as the engine of neoliberal expansion, it was also producing new forms of identity that challenged the concept of citizenship within bounded nation-states. These new "territories of citizenship," as they were described by the Swedish political theorists Ludvig Beckman and Eva Erman (2012), were often grounded in theories of cosmopolitan belonging that encouraged "thinking and feeling," as much as acting, "beyond the nation" (Cheah and Robbins 1998). From the explosion in human rights promotion to the development of international criminal justice tribunals to the emergence of "indigenism" (Niezen 2003) as a new transnational movement,[14] legal categories gave birth to categories of identity that ambiguously straddled the line between "mass-based forms of global consciousness, [and] . . . existing imagined political . . . communities" (Cheah 1998: 32).

The prevalence of legal cosmopolitanism reflected in part the search for new strategies of resistance during a time in which growing economic inequality was accompanied by the "dilemma of justice in a 'postsocialist' age" (Fraser 1995). The dominance of human rights, for example, within a wide range of political and social movements around the world, was the "politics of recognition" taken to its broadest and most consequential extreme. Nevertheless, as Fraser argued, any movement for justice that is based only in new forms of recognition and dignity, and not also on a "politics of redistribution," will be tragically incomplete. As the first decade of the post–Cold War period gave way to the second, and the second decade gave way to the third, Fraser's analysis has proven to be remarkably accurate.[15]

As the chapters in this book reveal, recent anthropological studies have examined the ways in which new categories of law have challenged existing categories of identity—particularly those bounded by the nation-state—without offering a credible means for undermining the relations of production that contribute to long-term and global forms of inequality. Indeed, there is some evidence that certain cosmopolitan legalities like indigenous rights are being used creatively as a new form of capitalist accumulation (Goodale 2017b). Nevertheless, in its concern with the shift from contract to cosmopolitanism (to playfully adapt Maine's sense of legal history), the contemporary anthropology of law confronts one of the most important of questions: the capacity of law, broadly construed, to facilitate radical social, economic, and political change. The answers to this question are still very much open even if, at one end of the spectrum, some have argued that the rule of law itself has become a form of "plunder" (Mattei and Nader 2008). But in reenvisioning the anthropology of law as the critical study of the linkages between law, identity, inequality, and power, scholars have infused the subdiscipline with some of its original ambition and have laid the foundations for its dynamic relevance in the years and decades to come.

## PART I

Law and the Production of Meaning

1

# Speaking the Law

The law can best be understood and practiced when one comes
to see that its language is not conceptual or theoretical—not
reducible to a string of definitions—but what I call literary or
poetic, by which I mean . . . that it is complex, many-voiced,
associative, and deeply metaphorical in nature.
—James Boyd White, *Heracles' Bow*

As we have seen, one of the most consequential periods in the intellectual history of the anthropology of law was the extended debate between
Max Gluckman and Paul Bohannan (see Bohannan 1957, 1969; Gluckman 1965, 1969). This "durable controvers[y]," which was also "very
good . . . academic business" (Moore 2001: 99) for the anthropology of
law, touched on many key themes that would shape the evolution of the
field over the next several decades: the relationship between generalized
analytical and culturalized "folk" categories in the study of law; the role
of ethnography as an empirical access point; the history of colonialism
in shaping indigenous legal identity; the place of politics and advocacy
in the anthropology of law; and the problem of representation—who is
entitled to speak the law?

In reflecting on the Wenner-Gren conference that took place in Austria in August 1966, where "[s]itting around that illustrious round table
were all [the twentieth] century's pioneers in [the anthropology of law],"
including Gluckman and Bohannan (who were frequently at logger-
heads), Laura Nader observed that the "political differences between us
were there, but they were unmentionable. Only later are we coming to
realize the tightrope that many ethnographers were walking between
advocacy and objectivity, between generalization and interpretation"
(Nader 1996: vii, x).[1]

Sally Falk Moore makes the convincing argument that Gluckman's
"dominant personality in law and anthropology" at the time, as well as

his "classical manner," obscured the fact that his interest in analyzing Lozi legal norms in terms of universal analytical categories "embodied a political position" (Moore 2001: 97, 98). As she puts it, "Gluckman wanted to show that indigenous African legal systems and practices were as rational in the Weberian sense as Western ones. . . . Embedded in his gloss on Lozi ideas was a splendid message about racial equality" (98). Even so, the nuances of this "splendid message" could get lost within some of Gluckman's more notable assertions, such as the fact that the "very refinement of English jurisprudence makes it a better instrument for analysis . . . than are the languages of tribal law" (Gluckman 1962: 14; quoted in Nader 1965: 11).

Yet from another perspective, the Gluckman-Bohannan debate was also about the relationship between language and law: Does language merely transmit legal norms or is it their source, or both?; Should one draw a distinction between legal languages that are embedded in particular cultures and histories and those that have become "universalized" by virtue of colonialism, economic power, or their "very refinement"?; If law is a "species of social imagination," does language occupy a unique position for the "unacknowledged poets of the world" (Geertz 1983: 232) who reveal it?; and How do legal languages articulate—and at times resist—broader structures of social power?[2]

Moreover, the Gluckman-Bohannan debate revolved around another problem that would come to occupy later anthropologists of law. If law can be understood as a distinct form of knowledge, what function do speech-acts serve in constituting and legitimating this knowledge? In her study of law, language, and conflict resolution among American Baptists in suburban Georgia, Carol Greenhouse argued that the domain of the anthropology of law had expanded beyond the boundaries of legal systems and legal rules to encompass "images of social structure and the language[s] that generate and convey normative knowledge and meaning (Greenhouse 1982: 70–71; see also Greenhouse 1986).

As she demonstrates, through an analysis of the ways in which American Baptists invoke norms in the process of building and maintaining a community that is as much epistemic as it is juridical (1982: 70), the speech-act is fundamental: it both highlights the differences between Baptists and non-Baptists and locates the speaker within a "system of social classification" (70).[3]

But if the study of the multiple relationships between language and law has played an important role in the wider history of the anthropology of law, this importance has expressed itself in different ways that reflect changing theoretical, ethical, and disciplinary preoccupations. A good example is the way in which the now-key concept of "discourse" was adopted and deployed by anthropologists of law. In the 1989 Starr and Collier volume on "history and power in the study of law," which was based on research conducted primarily in the 1970s and early 1980s, and articles written around 1985, "discourse" is used in ways that only gesture to the concept's future importance for anthropology. In the book's Introduction, the editors first and most obviously use "discourse" as a synonym for "dialogue" or "discussion": for example, "There is still much to discover from subdisciplinary discourse as we reach better understandings of how all legal processes are embedded in social relations" (Starr and Collier 1989: 6).[4]

Yet later in the same Introduction, the editors use discourse in a very different way that points to what was soon to come: "The contributors [to the volume] who use a cultural approach tend to treat laws and legal systems as elements of a discourse" (1989: 21). Here discourse is not simply another word for dialogue or even speech-act; rather, it invokes the meaning that was being introduced into anthropology via the writings of social theorists like Foucault, for whom discourse described an entire social and linguistic regime in which language itself constituted social objects as an expression of power (or, more precisely, power/knowledge).[5] And within this broader conception, some languages constituted power/knowledge more formally than others, principally those associated with key institutions of "biopolitical" control, such as prisons, universities, hospitals, and, of course, the institutions of law.

But if this key concept in the anthropological study of law and language had not yet been adopted by most scholars as of the mid-1980s, it certainly had been by the early 1990s, a shift that mirrors wider disciplinary realignments. For example, in the 1994 Lazarus-Black and Hirsch volume on "law, hegemony, and resistance," "discourse" is one of the most widely used theoretical concepts among the book's eleven contributors. At various points in the volume, evidence for a general shift toward a Foucauldian conception of discourse is clear: "power-laden discourse grounded in law" (Lazarus-Black and Hirsch 1994b:

29); "[l]aw is a discourse which interprets and conveys meaning, but it is a discourse with force behind it" (Merry 1994: 37); "meanings and practices form a discourse that both derives from and produces written law" (Coutin 1994: 284); and the "forbidden, revelatory quality of refugee testimonies gave these speeches a transformative power. According to Foucault . . . , knowledge that must be extracted is deemed more reliable than knowledge easily given. The testimonies publicized by the Sanctuary movement exemplify the confessional discourse that Foucault contends has become the authoritative method of producing truth in the West" (Coutin 1994: 298).

The one opposing perspective to the Foucauldian conception of discourse in the anthropology of law among the contributors is that of Susan U. Philips, who distinguishes "discourse at a distance" from the understanding of discourse used "by linguists and linguist anthropologists like [herself]," which is derived from "direct access" to speech and based on the use of "tape recordings or transcripts of speech of real people talking to one another" (Philips 1994: 62). Philips argues that while the Foucauldian approach to discourse is well-suited to historical interpretation, the "linguistic" approach provides a better set of tools to measure "how a given hegemony is constituted" in practice (1994: 62–63).

In a key early article, Elizabeth Mertz (1994) surveyed many of the most important intersecting developments in linguistics, legal studies, and critical anthropology and introduced a framework within which anthropologists of law could reground their approaches to legal practice and social power through sensitivity to such concepts as context in the structure of discourse, sociolinguistic creativity, language structure and social conflict, and the relationship between ideology and metalanguage within legal institutions. Her programmatic review also anticipated some of the tensions that would continue to shape the study of the relationship between law and language within the anthropology of law.

Mertz first draws a distinction within the broader study of linguistics between approaches to language that emphasize the structural aspects of language (often conceived in the abstract), those that focus on how language shapes social ends (instrumentally or functionally), and finally, those that study the ways in which language "embodies social creativity" (1994: 435–436). As Mertz argues, although these different insights from linguistics are not necessarily in opposition to each other, it is the relatively more recent strand of scholarship that explores "language as an active participant in social construction" that holds the most promise for the anthropology of law. As she puts it:

> If language is the key medium through which social exchange and under-
> standing are accomplished . . . then it becomes vital to develop a thorough
> analysis of the linguistic channeling and structuring of social life. This
> is particularly important in the domain of law, which is so often (par-
> ticularly in Western capitalist societies) a key locus of institutionalized
> linguistic channeling. . . . For this reason, legal language affords a key site
> for advancing the social-linguistic project of unpacking the social and
> creative character of language use and structure. (1994: 436, 441)

Mertz then turns to parallel developments in academic and critical legal studies that would provide many of the kinds of insights about legal "discourse at a distance" that, as we have seen, Philips distinguished from more fine–grained approaches to language use and structure. As Mertz explains, the approach to legal language by scholars within fields such as legal feminism and critical race theory was shaped by a belief that law was a key "site for struggle over social power" (1994: 441). Even though struggles for social power through law were most often won by those with more power to begin with, the languages of law could also be used as a resource for marginalized populations to resist these histori-cal structures of racial, economic, and political domination. Expressing some of the same concerns as Philips about this macroscopic approach to legal discourse, Mertz notes that critical legal scholars "could gain from anthropological insights about the power of detailed and system-atic aspects of language structure," but she concludes that anthropol-ogists of law in turn would benefit from a "more stringent sensibility about the relations of language, ideology, and power—particularly from the perspective of the disenfranchised" (1994: 442).

In retrospect, we can say that the convergence urged by Mertz—one that "combine[d] precise observation of the details of [legal] linguistic structure-in-use with consideration of the wider political and social forces at issue (1994: 448)—did indeed take place within the anthropol-ogy of law over the intervening decades, but only incompletely. In fact, as we will see in this chapter, research in the anthropology of law that "provide[s] a more acute understanding of the political dimensions of legal language" has remained somewhat distinct from research that focuses on the "texts that analyze legal language" (1994: 448). Although the reasons for this continuing division among anthropological studies of law and language are not entirely clear, three possible factors can be suggested.

First, as Philips's emphasis on "transcripts of speech of real people talking to one another" indicates, anthropologists who turn to law from a base in linguistic theory and methodology do so with a set of technical skills that revolve around close attention to speech-acts, the importance of coding, the nuances of linguistic partiality, and an awareness of "varying degrees of explicitness" (Philips 1994: 63). There can be a large gap between this utterance-level of analysis and the broader historical perspective that, according to Philips, allows the anthropologist's "urge to coherence to operate unchecked" (1994: 63).

Second, from the other side of the spectrum, that which focuses first and foremost on which hegemonies are reinforced (or resisted) by law and how, the preoccupation with the subtleties and partialities of particular speech-acts can be seen as an overly abstract exercise that can eclipse the broader intention, which is to understand how "legal language crystallizes the interplay of pragmatics, poetics, and social power with such clarity" (Mertz 1994: 448).

And finally, although the historical approach to the relationship between law, language, and power remains an important current in the anthropology of law, its reach has been tempered by a recognition that it often depends on a totalizing conception of discourse that can obscure as much as it reveals. In fact, this problem was recognized by Lazarus-Black and Hirsch themselves. Despite their emphasis on the historical approach to legal discourse, they also underscored the importance of "put[ting] the bite back into . . . concepts of power" (1994b: 4) by attending to both the discursive and material dimensions of law.

Thus, for these reasons (and likely others), the anthropology of law and language remains productively divided among what might be called discourse-near and discourse-far approaches. As we will see below, although this distinction has some heuristic value as a matter of intellectual history, in practice anthropological studies of law and language are diverse. The chapter surveys three broad areas within this diversity. The next section examines the different ways in which anthropologists transformed legal discourse into an object for ethnographic research. This move was itself an important innovation, because developments in reflexive ethnography and a concern with representation created linkages between the practices of legal discourse and the role of law in processes of "wider social change and reproduction" (Mertz 1994: 447).

The chapter then turns to anthropological research that has explored the relationships between language ideologies and legal power. As Mertz describes this area of scholarship, "[w]hat is the role of ideology . . . in the legal institutional regimentation and sedimentation of language—and in the linguistic regimentation and sedimentation of legal institutions?" (1994: 447). Following this, the chapter takes up the question of law's poetics, that is, the ways in which legal language can be understood aesthetically as much as instrumentally, or, to paraphrase Roman Jakobson (1960: 350), how legal language can also be a "work of art." This section explores revealing instances of legal-linguistic play, from parodies of the law in Papua New Guinea to the use of indigenous language swearwords in Mexico to resist the imposition of identities created by state law. The chapter concludes by considering the ways in which the anthropological study of law and language underscores law's heteroglossia: the fact that legal discourse always embodies many voices, many competing perspectives, many registers of power.

## The Ethnography of Legal Discourse

Through an important series of contributions that resulted from a collaboration that brought an anthropologically trained legal scholar together with a linguistic anthropologist, John Conley and William O'Barr developed a framework for studying legal discourse using the tools of ethnography and the theoretical underpinnings of interpretative anthropology (e.g., 1985, 1990, 1998). Conley and O'Barr conducted research in so-called informal courts in the United States in six cities in three distinct cultural and political regions. They studied a total of 466 cases in order to "build[ ] . . . models of lay people interacting with the legal system" through the ethnographic analysis of legal speech. This was complemented by post-trial interviews that were used by the research team to both confirm the linguistic analysis of court transcripts and to flesh out the outline of the eventual interpretation (Conley and O'Barr 1990: xi).[6]

Conley and O'Barr focused on small claims and magistrates' courts so that they would have more direct access to legal speech and legal storytelling within a form of dispute resolution that was relatively unstructured. As they explain, this focus on the use of legal language as a methodological end unto itself was not a common practice at the time (1990: xi). In fact, many scholars from the broader "law and society" movement, who were also studying legal language during the 1980s, were using quantitative techniques. As a result, early reactions to Conley and O'Barr's pioneering research were mixed; although colleagues from outside anthropology found the work interesting, they more often than not viewed it as necessarily preliminary to more formal statistical research (Halliday and Schmidt 2009: 123).

In developing the ethnography of legal discourse, Conley and O'Barr drew an important distinction between legal language as an object for research and legal language as a channel for meaning. As they described it:

> [O]ur guiding principle was to treat the language of litigants as the object of study rather than a mere instrument. Many other social science traditions . . . use language as a window through which other, presumably more important, things may be viewed. . . . Our premise has been that the window itself is often more interesting than what can be seen through it. As they tell their stories by giving their accounts, continually making decisions about structure, content, and forms of expression, litigants leave revealing fingerprints on the linguistic window. (1990: xi)

In applying this method to small claims legal practice, Conley and O'Barr discovered a "rules-relationship continuum," that is, a mode of legal practice in which legal actors move between rule and relational orientations to conflict in ways that are context dependent and marked not by formal principles of action, but rather by "subtle tendencies" (1990: xiii). And in an early argument against what was later described as the "seductions of quantification" (Merry 2016), Conley and O'Barr were careful to distinguish the ethnography of legal discourse from other linguistic approaches that required the "rigid categorization" of legal speech and "creat[ed] a misleading aura of precision" (1990: xiii).

In her study of legal discourse in Tonga, Susan U. Philips extended this conception of ethnography to include multiple sites at which the deployment of legal language shaped national identity "both in court and elsewhere" (2000: 230). Working in this particular study with both discourse-near and discourse-far perspectives, Philips analyzed the ways in which language references to Tongan cultural norms reinforced both traditional notions of national belonging and a system of hierarchy that required subordination and linguistic attention to public behaviors that were *tapu* (or forbidden). Her research showed that these strategies of normative language use operated at two levels within a "project of double legitimation" (2000: 236).

At one level, the performance of expected speech legitimated the contemporary project of nation making among a former colony of Great Britain marked by an imagined cultural and linguistic homogeneity. But at another level, the observance of tapu conventions through language worked to connect contemporary Tongan cultural and linguistic identity to a mythic past in which sister-brother relationships in particular formed the foundation of social life.

The ability of legal language to promote multiple social and political projects at the same time was also the focus of Larry Nesper's (2007) ethnography of legal discourse among the Lac du Flambeau Ojibwe, an American Indian tribe. Nesper studied a series of court cases that involved violations of recently codified tribal law regulating hunting and fishing rights. As Nesper explains, the creation of the tribal court itself in the early 1980s was a matter of some controversy. Tribal leaders were hesitant to introduce a powerful new legal institution into the community that would both supplant existing forms of dispute resolution and have the potential to shift the distribution of power among community members.[7]

At the same time, looking beyond the boundaries of the community, the tribe viewed the establishment of a court as an important symbol of self-determination and the marker of a capacity for self-governance through the rule of law as recognized by the state (2007: 679). In the end, the tribal court was composed as a legal hybrid, with members receiving training at a federal judicial college and yet implementing informal procedures that nevertheless did not lend themselves to a "distinctive jurisprudence reflective of community values and conceptions of justice" (679).

Nesper examines three illustrative cases through the methodological lens of the "pragmatics of court practice" (680). The first case involved a group of deer hunters who were accused of several violations, including transporting a loaded rifle in a vehicle, "shining" (the use of an artificial light to spot deer), and the use of an illegal spotlight ("a Halogen lamp encased in a twelve-pack beer carton with a lens painted blue") (683).

The second case involved what might be described as "deer decoy entrapment": a challenge by multiple defendants to the practice of tribal wardens setting up deer decoys to lure hunters into committing violations of the tribal code, such as shooting from vehicles. The third and final case revolved around a violation of the tribal code that prohibited the "unreasonable waste" of natural resources that tribal members were permitted to exploit in the "exercise of off-reservation treaty rights" (687). In this instance, a forty-year-old man was found with a "legally tagged" rotting deer carcass in his mother's yard, a fact for which the man explained that he had "already apologized to the Great Spirit . . . but that it was not intentional" (687).

In his linguistic analysis of these three cases, Nesper focuses on the ways in which language styles shape legal outcomes by encouraging the use of particular modes of expression that frustrate effective legal advocacy, including those that are embedded in "traditional conversational pragmatics" (681). As he explains, Ojibwe defendants tend to describe their circumstances in short, clipped sentences that reflect an emphasis on efficiency, a linguistic value that "recalls the traditional aesthetics of killing deer with a single shot to the head" (681).

In addition, because Ojibwe speakers "generally avoid asking direct questions," they prefer to use instead "either imperatives or indirection when asking for things" (681). As Nesper puts it, "[n]either of these orientations facilitates the work of cross-examination, a technical skill requiring considerable practice" (681). Finally, the Ojibwe tendency to use "nonstandard ordering of clauses . . . results in overlapping speech between defendants and their witnesses," something that further affects the capacity of Indian defendants to effectively represent their legal interests in the courtroom. Nesper concludes that the contrasting styles of language usage in the tribal court reflect wider struggles over representation and power in the community, in which different families and sectors struggle over how best to articulate tribal autonomy in relation to the state and themselves.

## Language Ideologies and Legal Power

A second major focus of anthropologists who have studied the relationship between law and language is the way in which language refracts wider ideologies through legal processes. As scholars have demonstrated, legal language becomes a key site of struggle over cultural identity, power, and the boundaries of rights protections in plural societies.[8] In an ethnographic reflection on language ideologies in the U.S. judicial system, John B. Haviland (2003) argues that certain conflicts over language reveal the extent to which "ideas about language rub off onto ideas about people, groups, events, and activities" in ways that shift between "theoretical and folk language ideologies" (2003: 764).

This dialectic is particularly notable in the area of language rights, which includes "bilingual education, rights to translators in the courtroom, minority language literacy, . . . [and protections against] linguistic oppression and extermination" (764). As he explains:

> Like all ideological products, the idea that "language" (whose integrity and individuality must be constructed, along with the related concept of "communities of speakers") can have "rights" (which, in turn, must be in principle threatened or at least contestable) at all must be historically grounded, and subject to institutional reproduction and modification. Moreover, . . . [i]deologies of language are not everywhere the same, nor, indeed, are they commensurably identifiable in all societies at all times.

Haviland develops this contingent approach to language ideologies through a consideration of language rights court cases in the United States in which he was a formal participant-observer as an expert witness. The most important case in which language ideologies shaped legal power involved a seventeen-year-old Mixtec-speaking Indian from the Oaxaca region of Mexico. The young man had been accused of murdering another Mixtec Indian in a strawberry field outside Portland, Oregon, during the time of the year in which undocumented migrant laborers lived and worked in crowded camps alongside farms. The trial

of the defendant involved a complicated interplay of language translations and mistranslations, since English was the official language of the
courtroom and of the judge, jury, and lawyers; Spanish was the language
used by the court translator to communicate with the defendant; and
Mixtec was the native language of the defendant, although he (and the
other Mixtec participants, including witnesses) were able to communicate at a level of Spanish that was "extremely limited" (769).[9]

The judge in the case followed a language ideology in which meaning can and must be rendered "verbatim" between what was said by the
defendant (or witness) and the language of the court transcript, which
was standard English. As Haviland explains, this language ideology in
court "interpenetrate[d] with a broader notion of personal identity, self-
presentation, and truth," which assumed that the "truth-functional core
of what someone says can be decoupled from the actual saying itself"
(768). In his analysis, this insistence on a particular language ideology in the courtroom led to confusion, frustration, and eventually the
breakdown of the legal process itself. At one point, after a long series of
misunderstandings along this English-Spanish-Mixtec chain of "propo-
sitional detachability" (768), one witness simply says in response to a
question, "I cannot talk" (769). In the end, the Mixtec Indian defendant
was convicted of murder and sentenced to life in prison before he had
turned eighteen years old.

As Haviland describes it, later research by investigators, Haviland
himself, and members of the defendant's home village in Oaxaca demonstrated that the killing had actually been committed by another person, who had fled the United States and was hiding in Mexico City (after
having received "shamanistic therapy for his crime" in his own village, a
fact that led to his discovery). Although this independent research did
not play a direct role,[10] the defendant was released from prison and later
went on to a varied professional career in the United States and Mexico,
including serving as a regular court translator for other Mixtecs. Haviland finds this "ironic," since this meant the man was "helping perpetu-
ate the linguistic ideologies that helped land him in jail in the first place"
(774).

In his ethnography of "language ideologies and legal power in Hopi
Tribal Court," Justin Richland (2008) similarly examines the interplay
of language codes and law in the courtroom. Except in this case, it is

not the language of the dominant society that exerts downward pressure but rather the tensions between different jurisprudential narratives that shape legal practice and open a window into struggles over identity, tradition, and authenticity. Like Haviland's, Richland's analysis of language ideologies and the law is also based on multiple perspectives; in addition to his ethnographic research on language use in Hopi courtrooms, he himself served as an appellate justice in the Hopi tribal court system.

As Richland explains, linguistic and cultural pluralism in the Hopi courts reflects a broader dynamic in which the micropractices of legal process stand in for a more fundamental struggle between the "federal oversight of tribal sovereignty and the demands of self-governance" (2008: 13). This is a struggle over the need to demonstrate legitimacy to the federal government in order to keep it at bay, while ensuring that the use of the "Anglo-American norms of justice" that establish this outward-looking-in legitimacy does not replace the cultural codes that mark off a distinctly Hopi jurisprudence.

In Richland's analysis, these tensions are never fully resolved in the legal practices of the Hopi justice system. Instead, they are precisely what characterize a form of jurisprudence that is constituted in part through legal discourse. The legal knowledge and identity that result are structured by "pragmatic paradoxes" (89). A key example of these for Richland is the case of a man who was brought up on charges by the governor of his own village for moving his mobile home into the village without a legal permit. After the tribal court had ruled against the man, he asked to address the court. In his emotional statement, he expressed deep sadness and shock at the fact that the village had turned against him, especially because his kinship ties with the village were long-standing. In his reply to the man's statement, the village governor acknowledged the social trauma involved in the case, but argued that the man "just didn't follow the rules that we tried to work out with him" (90).

As Richland explains, both the form and content of the man's statement were derived from Hopi cultural practices, in which "men gathered around the underground smoke circle always start [the ritual] by naming their ancestors and the kin relations they share with others around the circle" (90). By making his statement in the way he did, the man was in the process "indexing the unique constellation of traditional duties and obligations that he and his opponent [the governor] owe[d] each other" (90). Yet at the same time, the governor's response was also one that indexed Hopi traditions, which demand respect and obedience to authority and compliance with the rules formulated to protect and safeguard the village. Richland argues that these varying evocations of Hopi tradition in the courtroom reflect a pragmatic semiotics that "unfold[s] in complex iterations of native culture that constitute the emergent edge of indigenous governance practices" (92).

Finally, in her innovative ethnography of legal education in the United States, Elizabeth Mertz (2007) studied the ways in which the relationship between language ideologies and legal power that we have seen throughout this section becomes established at the moment at which law students pass through the discursive boot camp that trains them to "think like a lawyer." Mertz conducted ethnographic research in first-year Contracts classes at eight different law schools. Her study was motivated in part by the fact that—as in other countries—law provides the educational training for many leaders in government and beyond. To better understand, therefore, how lawyers are trained through "ideas that people hold about how language works" (2007: 3) is to understand more about the possibilities and limitations of democratic governance more generally.

Mertz's ethnography demonstrates that there are seven major features of legal language that shape legal knowledge and thus shape a broader worldview about the relationship between conflict and justice: that the law must focus on "form, authority, and legal-linguistic contexts rather than on content, morality, and social contexts" (2007: 4); that the use of a particular type of language for understanding conflicts determines how these conflicts can be understood; that legal language depends on abstract categories that emphasize specific details of cases, a focus that "conceals the social roots of legal doctrines, avoiding examination of the ways that abstract categories . . . privilege some aspects of conflicts and events over others" (2007: 5); that the "appearance of neutrality" in the language of law "hides the fact that [the] law continues to enact social inequities and injustices" (2007: 5); that the initiation to the language of law has different effects on people of "different races, genders, and class backgrounds" (2007: 6); that training in legal language ideologies reflects the social hierarchies of both the particular school and its students; and finally, that the apparent neutrality and abstraction of legal language reflect a "'double edge' . . . found in capitalist epistemology more generally," in which the erasure of context-as-social bias makes is less likely that the language of law will "permit in-depth understanding of social inequalities" (6). The end result, Mertz argues, is that the language of law creates a barrier to "law's democratic aspirations" (3).

## The Poetics of Law

Law is like . . . a language, but it is also like drama and poetry
and rhetoric and narrative . . . [T]he activity of law is at heart
a literary one.
—James Boyd White, *Heracles' Bow*

Full of merit, yet poetically, man
Dwells on this earth.
—Friedrich Hölderlin, *In lieblicher Bläue*

Anthropologists of law and language have also usefully drawn from the wider study of language and poetics to understand the ways in which forms of legal discourse reflect creativity, the play of emotions, ambivalence, and parody. In contrast to a certain extent with the sense of law that emerges from studies of language ideologies and legal power, those that focus on the poetics of law underscore the "unfinalized" nature of legal discourse, the fact that it is constituted by "'unmerged voices', . . . 'contrapuntal voices', [and] 'combined images'" (Lipset 2004: 64; quoting from Bakhtin 1984a: 32). As David Lipset puts it, in his ethnography of parody and legal pluralism in Papua New Guinea, a dialogic approach to legal discourse reveals the extent to which "metaphor, style, [and] intonation . . . struggle with and against each other [in legal argument] to compose an open-ended discursive field" (2004: 64).

Lipset's study took place against the backdrop of a long history of colonial rule in Papua New Guinea that was shaped by cultural and racial ideologies. As Lipset explains, Papua New Guinea was governed for almost a hundred years by the so-called Native Regulations, which imposed a set of strict rules on inhabitants, including prohibitions on alcohol, restrictions on freedom of movement, and even a requirement that clothes should cover upper and lower parts of the body (65).

But most important in Lipset's analysis was the fact that colonial Papua New Guineans were not subject to a formal system of indirect rule, one in which the colonial administration allowed the use of local law as a form of social and political control. Instead, the head colonial official "'vigorously opposed the setting up of tribunals composed of indigenes and administering customary law'" (65; quoting from Epstein 1974: 3) because it was believed, at least in the early years, that "indirect rule was impossible due to the barbaric nature of local-level authority" (65).

Nevertheless, in the waning years of colonial rule a hybrid legal system was installed in Papua New Guinea that used village courts overseen by local officials steeped in the norms of customary dispute resolution. This new justice system was problematic since the courts were often located in towns that were distant from many villages and because a "number of communities rejected the [hybrid] system because of its association with state control . . . [or] on the grounds that the village courts would serve only the interests of a rising, local elite" (66).

As a result, by the late 1990s "the legal system in PNG ha[d] been in persistent decline" due to a lack of legitimacy, "institutional ineffectiveness and lack of resources," and the inability to cope with the "polyphony of local-level values and processes to which the overwhelming majority of rural Papua New Guineans still adhered" (67). It was in this legal and social context that Lipset observed a parodic judicial process in the village of Darapap, a settlement "situated on the remote outer margins of [a] weak state and its overextended, deeply compromised legal system" (67).[11]

Lipset describes a mock trial that took place that included people playing the roles of judge, defendant, and witnesses. The case revolved around a supposed sexual relationship between the defendant and his wife's mother, a "shame-ridden" (74) accusation. The proceedings were characterized by complicated layers of dialogical play and sexual satire in which linguistic codes shifted quickly between comedy and metareferences to Papua New Guinean legal norms. In Lipset's analysis, the performance was both a form of cultural art and a critique of postcolonial justice; the use of comedic trials was a way for locals to assert equality with the absent state. As he puts it, the "act of metaphorization [was] an implicit nullification of difference: the one court of law . . . being held up as socially, politically, and conceptually equivalent to the other" (82).

In his ethnography of the "calligraphic state," Brinkley Messick (1993) analyzed the poetics of law through the aesthetic styles of documentary inscription that shape Islamic legal knowledge and moral identity. Messick's study was based in part on extended research on legal institutions and practices in the southern Yemeni town of Ibb. The core of Messick's analysis revolves around a consideration of the production, display, and use of Islamic legal documents. He argues that physical forms of legal texts themselves embody the law and convey its authority. But the transmission of this knowledge through the materiality of legal writing is not straightforward. Like any aesthetic object, the elaborately produced historical and contemporary legal texts in Messick's study also embody the unspoken (and perhaps, the unspeakable). As he puts it, the "power and mystery of the legal document resides in the nature of writing as human signature" (1993: 215).

In one particularly inventive methodology, Messick tracks the broader effects of changes in legal textual forms from the traditional calligraphy of earlier periods to more modern forms, which require linear strokes and the use of standardized colors like black and white. This creates a set of contrasts that reinforce the way in which legal texts, in Messick's study, come to form in themselves a kind of sociolegal performance: "the curving loops of Yemeni documents against the straight lines of printed forms, the rounded hand of the Imam's red seal against the lineal fonts of black-and-white administrative standard, and spiral against straight in the space of culture and power more generally," as Martha Mundy put it, in a review of Messick's research (1995: 355).

Finally, in her study of language, identity, and indigenous rights among the Cucapá in northern Mexico, a work whose title reflects its own dash of "grotesque realism" (Bakhtin 1984b) ("'Spread your ass cheeks': And other things that should not be said in indigenous languages"), Shaylih Muehlmann (2008) argues that languages associated with vulnerable minority populations can become a mechanism through which the state attempts to impose a tightly regulated legal identity. As she explains, among the various criteria through which international law recognizes indigenous people as rights bearers entitled to make claims on nation-states, language has become the most important and problematic.

The use of language to mark off (collective) legal personhood and agency in Mexico must be understood within a longer history in which indigenous peoples were historically marginalized for speaking pre-Columbian languages and otherwise resisting the dominant policy of assimilationism. With the transformations wrought by indigenous rights promotion beginning in the 1990s, however, the "very characteristics that . . . formed the basis of [indigenous people's] subordination—'backward' customs, a lack of fluency in Spanish, and isolation from modern conveniences—have now become the very characteristics that the state requires to recognize their rights" (2008: 35).[12] When Muehlmann asked one of her Cucapá interlocutors whether he thought this double-bind of language ideology was unjust or not, he replied, "Yeah, well, . . . that's the great contradiction. Now the government *wants* us to act like Indians" (2008: 35; emphasis in original).

Muehlmann's ethnography focused on a controversial speech genre in the linguistic anthropology of indigenous peoples: swearwords. Although linguists have studied swearing, slang, and dialect from various perspectives, for example as speech that creates solidarity among youth or as a way for working classes to acquire a form of "covert prestige" (Labov 1966), these forms of language among indigenous peoples are the subject of controversy among anthropologists. Muehlmann argues that scholars working in a broader context in which the socioeconomic and political status of indigenous people is closely associated with the capacity to speak indigenous languages "implicitly encourage[ ]" (42) the general assumption that "indigenous languages do not feature obscenity" by focusing on the ways in which such languages encode unique and irreplaceable knowledge about both the natural world and human relations.[13] As she puts it, "the ecological, medical, and spiritual vocabularies found in indigenous languages have been celebrated and enthusiastically recorded" (42).

By contrast, despite the fact that Muehlmann was uncomfortable adding her "list of Cucapá expressions like 'screw your mother' and 'spread your ass cheeks' to the more idyllic archives of indigenous languages, such as the Hopi vocabulary, which can still imagine time in superior ways . . . , or the O'odham words for the plants and animals integral to their cultural traditions" (42), her ethnography nevertheless shows that the use of swearwords among the Cucapá was a way to subvert the legal and political expectations associated with the image of the "hyperreal Indian" (Ramos 1994).[14]

Muehlmann describes a complicated sociolinguistic landscape on which swearwords function as an implicit critique of projects of indigenous authenticity, which are often associated with NGO and state initiatives that can bring significant resources to the community. As Muehlmann argues, Cucapá youth "curse the unknowing outsider" (45) as both a recognition that they have no control over the social and ideological forces that seek to encapsulate them in (or exclude them from) an imagined indigenous identity, and as a protest against it. She concludes her study with a hypothetical question: How would her Cucapá interlocutors respond to the legal assumption that their language is what makes them "inherently valuable to all of humanity? I think, by now, one can guess how they might respond" (45).

## Conclusion: The Heteroglossia of Law

In his essay "Discourse in the Novel" (1934–35), Bakhtin argued that language is characterized by "heteroglossia," that is, by struggle, contradiction, lack of discursive authority, and the simultaneous presence of multiple "axiological belief systems" (1981 [1934–35]: 304). As he put it:

> Within the arena of almost every utterance an intense interaction and struggle between one's own and another's word is being waged, a process in which they oppose or dialogically interanimate each other. The utterance so conceived is a considerably more complex and dynamic organism than it appears when construed simply as a thing that articulates the intention of the person uttering it, which is to see the utterance as a direct, single-voiced vehicle for expression." ([1934–35] 1981: 354–55)

As the anthropological research surveyed in this chapter has revealed, the languages of law are perhaps quintessentially heteroglot. Although Bakhtin derived his broader philosophy of language from the study of the novel, one can argue that legal discourse is equally constituted by "intense interaction and struggle," the play of competing ideologies and belief systems, and "plural versions of authority" (Lipset 2004: 64). And because the language of law is most often deployed in situations of conflict, resistance, challenge, and even social threat, it is characterized by what might be thought of as a double heteroglossia: the first, internal to legal discourse itself; the second, in the nature of the broader framing context that demands the use of legal discourse while at the same time excluding the use of others.

Finally, anthropological insights into the structures, contexts, and poetics of legal language also carry significant implications for the wider understanding of what E. P. Thompson called the "forms of law" (1977: 262). Although Thompson concluded that the law in Walpole's England was the primary means through which the "hegemony of the eighteenth-century gentry and aristocracy was expressed" (262), there were times in which something internal to the law kept it from being manipulated as a naked instrument of class power. Thompson attributes this to the fact that the law "has its own characteristics [and] its own independent history and logic of evolution." As he puts it, "the law may be rhetoric, but it need not be empty rhetoric" (263).[15]

But the anthropology of law and language points to yet another explanation for the kind of contingency and unpredictability that Thompson describes. If legal discourse is as deeply and essentially heteroglot as contemporary anthropological research suggests, then its capacity to "contain multitudes," to paraphrase the American poet Walt Whitman, is not necessarily the result of an abstract "logic of justice" (Thompson 1977: 263) expressing itself through a particular language of governance. Rather, the law's capacity to embody both hegemony's imperatives and the kind of "carnivalesque revelry" (Lipset 2004: 82) that depends on mockery, irony, and linguistic subversion, is structural, and holds the key to better understanding legal pluralism, the limits of law as a mechanism for social change, and law's unexpected poetry.

# 2

## History, Heritage, and Legal *Mythoi*

In his influential demonstration of the proposition that "anthropology needed to discover history," Eric Wolf argued that "the world of human-kind constitutes a manifold, a totality of interconnected processes, and inquiries that disassemble this totality into bits and then fail to reassemble it falsify reality" (1982: 3). But if "history is the working out of a moral purpose in time" (1982: 5), then it is also true that the law, broadly conceived, plays a key role in defining and regulating the normative rendering of this history. As we saw in the Introduction, the study of history was a fundamental method in the early years of the anthropology of law. Proto-anthropologists of law like Bachofen, Maine, and McLennan viewed the evolution of law over the centuries as a window into both the development of a particular "civilization," and human society more generally. Law and legal institutions, in this sense, were believed to crystallize society, to express its essential characteristics as these developed and were transformed over time.

With the rejection of theories of unilineal evolutionism and the introduction of the ethnographic study of "primitive" peoples, however, the status of history within the anthropology of law was greatly diminished. At a theoretical level, functionalists like Malinowski believed that rules regulating crime and custom were distinct to each culture and were interconnected with other rules, other institutions, all of which functioned interdependently to bind a culture together and distinguish it from all others. As Malinowski put it, in "each culture, we find different institutions in which man pursues his life-interest, different customs by which he satisfies his aspirations, different codes of law and morality which reward his virtues or punish his defections" (1922: 25).[1]

And at a methodological level, early ethnographers of law conducted research with the assumption that primitive societies passed from one year to the next cyclically, each point in a particular year appearing very much as it did the year before and as it would during the next. This was a way of understanding societies that the structuralist Claude Lévi-Strauss described in 1959 as "cold": they "produced extremely little disorder, which physicists call 'entropy', and they tend to preserve themselves in their initial state. Incidentally, it explains why they seem to us as societies without history or without progress" (quoted in Charbonnier 1969: 33).[2]

Thus, despite the later recognition that the synchronic approach to the anthropology of law was deficient, it nevertheless shaped the intellectual history of the field until the 1970s, when scholars began to look beyond atemporal concerns with tribal codes, dispute resolution, and social control toward questions of regional and global interconnectedness, legal change over time, and the impact of Western capitalism on conflicts. In moving toward a "theoretically informed history and a historically informed theory" (Wolf 1982: 21) of the place of law within processes of change, anthropologists during this period underscored "the relationship of law to wider systems of social relations" (Starr and Collier 1989: 2). By reorienting the anthropology of law toward history, political economy, and the relationship between law and enduring structures of global power, anthropologists moved the focus of the field definitively away from the "limited . . . analytic dichotomies" of the preceding decades in favor of a macroscopic perspective that viewed law as a central locus of change "within world historical time" (Starr and Collier 1989: 4, 3).

Nevertheless, even if a concern with history as such did not take epistemological root in the post-Malinowskian anthropology of law until the 1970s, problems of history had figured prominently in other ways throughout the twentieth century. First, and most importantly for the anthropology of law, was the fact that much of the research occurred during *la longue durée* in which Western colonialism formed the geopolitical and ideological logic through which much of the world could be said to constitute a "totality of interconnected processes." Anthropological studies took place within a wider historical context in which field sites were located in regions that were often on the front lines of colonial wars.

Although some scholars elided this fact and, even more, failed to account for it as an analytical problem, others acknowledged it—at least in sections of writing that set the background to the conventional typological description of "a people" that would follow. For example, in the introduction to his account of the "modes of livelihood and political institutions of a Nilotic People," E. E. Evans-Pritchard (1940) includes a startling passage that evokes the violent colonial context in which his research among the Nuer took place:

> A Government force surrounded our camp one morning at sunrise, searched for two prophets who had been leaders in a recent revolt, took hostages, and threatened to take many more if the prophets were not handed over. . . . It would at any time have been difficult to do research among the Nuer, and at the period of my visit [1930] they were unusually hostile, for their recent defeat by Government forces and the measures taken to ensure their final submission had occasioned deep resentment. (1940: 11)[3]

Beyond the fact that much of anthropology itself developed within a broader historical period of colonial rule, the twentieth-century anthropology of law was closely associated with colonialism in a more specific way. Among the various means through which anthropological knowledge was valuable to colonial administration, it was the knowledge about local legal systems and practices that arguably proved most useful to the form of governance known as "indirect rule." This was a mode of administration in which colonial powers—notably Britain and France—coopted traditional (actual or invented) legal structures, and empowered traditional rulers (existing or installed for the purpose), as a cost-saving and bureaucratically more efficient means of extending imperial territory and ensuring continued access to raw materials and labor. Although indirect rule, which Mahmood Mamdani (1996: 37) has described as "decentralized despotism," did not turn out to be the governance panacea that empires like Britain, in particular, imagined, it did create the milieu in which several influential anthropological studies of law were produced.[4]

An important example of this genre is Isaac Schapera's *A Handbook of Tswana Law and Custom* (1938), which was, as the book's subtitle acknowledges, "compiled for the Bechuanaland Protectorate Administration," yet another British colonial possession, which became Botswana upon independence in 1966. *Tswana Law and Custom* was commissioned by Charles Fernand Rey, Resident Commissioner of the Bechuanaland Protectorate (1930–1937), whose introduction to the book observes that:

> Whether from the point of view of the anthropologist or the administrator, it is surely a desirable thing in any African Territory that all available information bearing on the matter of Native Customary Law should be collected with such measure of accuracy as may be possible, and recorded in permanent form. (Schapera 1938: vii)

Yet despite the fact that Schapera's monumental study had its origins as a tool of colonial rule, its compendious accounting of Tswana legal history and tribal constitution, and its thick descriptions of Tswana family, property, commercial, criminal, and procedural law, proved highly influential as a model for how an anthropologist could document a non-state, non-Western, legal order through analytical categories adapted from general (largely Western) jurisprudence.[5] And in a surprising turn of history, Schapera's work became an important legal authority on matters of customary law in postcolonial Botswana, being cited by the country's high court as recently as 2000.[6]

If a concern with history played a role in instrumental studies of law by anthropologists working under conditions and in support of indirect rule, so too did history figure in anthropology conducted within colonial structures that mixed indirect rule with more robust and direct forms of legal governance, such as the Dutch colonial regime in the Dutch East Indies. As Franz and Keebet von Benda-Beckmann (2002) explain, in an overview of the history of the anthropology of law in the Netherlands, Dutch scholars played a key role in both producing knowledge about the "folk law" of the Dutch colonies and in using such knowledge to influence colonial legal policy and to design colonial legal institutions (see also Trouwborst 2002). The focus of research in the early colonial period was on the widespread customary system of *adat* law. This concentration developed into a full-fledged tradition in the anthropology of law in the Netherlands, the legacy of which had important consequences for the study of legal pluralism more generally.[7]

Nevertheless, despite the fact that the early Dutch anthropology of law developed essentially as a form of bureaucratic knowledge adapted to colonial governance, there were key differences among researchers that would prefigure later debates about the relationship between legal knowledge and government policy. Although most Dutch scholars of *adat* during the colonial period shared the "objective . . . to improve the functioning of the administrative and legal system of the colony" (F. von Benda-Beckmann and K. von Benda-Beckmann 2002: 696), some (e.g., Cornelis van Vollenhoven)[8] took a more academic approach, in part based on "[s]ympathy for the native peoples and their legal ideas" (2002: 696), while others (e.g., Barend ter Haar) worked more instrumentally to "find[ ] th[e] unwritten law in order to help colonial judges" (2002: 697).

As we will see below, the complicated relationship between the anthropology of law and colonialism continued to shape the development of the field well into the postcolonial period. On the one hand, the legacy of this history was eventually taken up as an example of how legal knowledge often constitutes the basic framework for structures of governance that can be exploitative, ethnocentric, and exclusionary. But on the other hand, the colonial anthropology of law contributed to the destabilizing—and potentially empowering—concept of legal pluralism: that is, that multiple legal systems can dynamically coexist in practice in the same sociopolitical space, despite the official orthodoxy that law is the privileged domain of the state.

In the next section, the chapter surveys works in the anthropology of law that examine these colonial legacies of history and law most directly, from the history of Aboriginal title legislation in Canada to conflicts over territory and traditional land rights in postcolonial West Africa. The chapter then shifts to consider new ways in which history has come to frame the contemporary anthropology of law as an analytical and methodological problem. For example, with developments in international law around rights to material culture, the protection of areas of "outstanding universal value," and rights to the return of "cultural property" to countries of origin, anthropologists turned their attention to the relationship between law and history as a site of ideological conflict.

Moreover, it was through the study of the contested legal concept of "heritage" that archaeologists made important, if often unacknowledged, contributions to the anthropology of law. Following this, the chapter examines how anthropologists have studied the various ways in which history is imagined through the law. As anthropologists have demonstrated, the unfolding of law in the course of legal arguments and judicial decision making is also a means through which history, which is essentially in dispute, is constructed. Indeed, from a certain perspective, the law itself can be seen as a genre of history. The chapter concludes by considering how an anthropological understanding of myth helps explain why narratives about the past are essential to the resolution and meaning of conflicts in the present.

## Colonial Legacies

In their study of the relationship between social, political, and ideological transformation and different forms of violence, John Comaroff and Jean Comaroff (2006) argue that law has a close relationship with "disorder in the postcolony." As they put it, "[w]hether or not there is a necessary relationship between the lethal and the legal . . . their historical affinity seems beyond dispute" (2006: 2). As they explain, law is involved in a paradox in regions that were subject to the yoke of colonial rule. At the same time that assemblages of disorder seem to be proliferating on the "schizophrenic landscapes of many postcolonies" (20), these landscapes are also marked by a pervasive fetishism of the law, its institutional contours, its historical assurances, its mythological *esprit*.

But this dialectical constitution of the postcolony, in which "law and lawlessness . . . are conditions of each other's possibility" (21), is as much a reflection of the past—of colonialism and its reliance on "lawfare"[9]—as it is a response to present contradictions. And here is where colonial legacies continue to haunt contemporary legal imaginaries. Indeed, colonialism itself becomes caught up in the paradoxical twining of law and disorder. As they put it, "[h]auled before a judge, history is made to break its silences, to speak in tongues hitherto unheard and untranslated, to submit itself to the scales of justice at the behest of those who suffered it, of its most abject subjects" (29).

As other anthropologists of law have shown, when history is "made to break its silences," what results can reproduce the violence of colonial legal ordering as often as it subverts it. In her sweeping ethnographic and historical study of Aboriginal title litigation in British Columbia, Canada, for example, Dara Culhane (1998) argues that the adjudication of claims over Aboriginal lands in court opened a window onto centuries of European cultural ideology translated into law, in which relationships to land were filtered through racialized juridical categories.

On this reading of legal history in the Canadian courts, only white settlers possessed the capacity to exercise their Lockean natural right to mix their labor with the fruits of *terra nullius* and thereby own what resulted. "Indians," by contrast, traditionally lived within forms of social organization that were not, and could not be, recognized under colonial/Western law, since they did not privatize and codify rights to territory; they did not systematically seek to "improve" (that is, commodify) the bounty of nature; and most critically, they did not create market economies and modes of production based on consumption, at least before the arrival of European traders and settlers.

Culhane's study follows the arc and transformations of a single Aboriginal land title case from trial during 1987–1991 to its appeal from judgment and final decision in the Supreme Court of Canada in 1997. As she puts it, the

> Landmark case of *Delgamuukw v. The Queen* heard in British Columbia during 1987–1991 represented a crystallizing moment in the history of Aboriginal peoples and the law in British Columbia. . . . History followed [the parties] into the courtroom, and they carried the future out with them when they left. (1998: 17)

The case was based on claims filed by the Gitksan and Wet'suwet'en Nations over ownership of 58,000 square kilometers of land in northwestern British Columbia, a region that had been subject to intense clear-cut logging by large companies. Nevertheless, "immense forestry reserves [remained] throughout the territory which are of great economic value" (from the "Reasons for Judgment," quoted in Culhane 1998: 235).

During the trial in the Supreme Court of British Columbia,[10] anthropologists (including Hugh Brody, who figured briefly in chapter 1) appeared as expert witnesses to explain to the court that the oral history presented during testimony by Gitksan and Wet'suwet'en chiefs and elders should not be considered inadmissible hearsay because the knowledge expressed through the *adaawk* and *kungax* traditions was

sacred and thus subject to its own "rigorous demands through valida-
tion" (1998: 121).[11]

In the end, the court (Chief Justice Allan McEachern, in a "judgment
that rambled over 394 pages," Times Colonist 2008) rejected the plaintiffs' claims based on the legal theory that aboriginal rights, to the extent
to which they can be said to exist, do so at the "pleasure of the crown,"
and thus can be extinguished whenever the Crown so desires. Based
on this rule of law, the court held that Gitksan and Wet'suwet'en rights
to the claimed territory had been extinguished by virtue of centuries
of European colonization of North America, which demonstrated the
requisite intent to terminate any Aboriginal rights to the same lands.

Moreover, as Chief Justice McEachern explained, the taking of Gitksan and Wet'suwet'en territories by the colonial government in the
course of its westward expansion was a way to bring the benefits of civilization to the not-so-noble savages. As the honorable justice put it, "it
would not be accurate to assume that even pre-contact existence in the
territory was in the least bit idyllic . . . there is no doubt, to quote Hobbs
[sic], that aboriginal life in the territory was, at best, 'nasty, brutish and
short'" (quoted in Culhane 1998: 236).[12]

But as Eve Darian-Smith (1999) shows, in her study of "English legal
identity in the new Europe," the shadow of the colonial legal imaginary
could be seen even at the heart of the empire itself. Indeed, her ethnography of the sociolegal consequences of the Channel Tunnel connecting
mainland Europe and the United Kingdom suggests that debates over
colonialism, law, and culture take place even within nations that have
made law both a rubric of conquest and a "potent figure of national
identity" (Fitzpatrick 1992: 117; quoted in Darian-Smith 1999: 194).

Darian-Smith conducted ethnographic research from her base "in a
very small apartment above a health-food shop and a 'fish-and-chippy'"
(1999: xv) in the last year leading up to the opening of the Channel Tunnel in 1994. She focused on Kent, the "home county" region that would be
the point of entry for the rail link from France and thus the open door to
the wider world that England had kept itself isolated from for centuries.
As she explains, Kent occupied a conflicted position in English national
mythology. As the "Garden of England," it "embodie[d] certain features
of an idealized English heritage. Rolling green hills in an idyllic pastoral
landscape embod[ied] profound and fiercely defended icons of a time-

less, Anglo-Saxon imperial power brimming with class hierarchy and feudal patronage" (1999: 44). At the same time, however, because of its location as the "corner of the island continent" (46) separated by just over forty kilometers from Calais in France, Kent had always been one of the most cosmopolitan regions of England—even its most "European" (48).

Despite this actual history of deep interconnection with mainland Europe, Kent became a more modern symbol for wider shifts that were taking place at a time in which the United Kingdom was negotiating the legal, political, and economic terms of its association with the emerging European Union. Law played a particularly important role in these debates. If English law, as we saw above, formed the basis for colonial expansion and the imposition of a cultural ideology translated into legal categories, this history was suffused with the belief that English law was *sui generis*, coextensive with English identity, and as rooted in the English soil as the emblematic oak tree (1999: 17).

With the opening of the Channel Tunnel, however, and the impending absorption of the United Kingdom into the wider legal universe of the European Union, this linkage between law and national identity was undermined. Moreover, the fact that it was a railway that symbolized this challenge to English legal identity was a historical irony, since the railroad had always been—from India to Egypt—a mark of British colonialism. The implication was that one of the world's most prolific colonial powers was finally being colonized itself with the master's tools—the law and the train. As Darian-Smith concludes, the "Tunnel calls into question concepts of sovereignty, territorially based democracy, and the exclusivity of nationalism that have historically been critical in the legitimization of modern principles of law" (193).

Finally, in her ethnography of law and border conflicts in postcolonial West Africa, Carola Lentz (2003) argues that the colonial construction of legal space continues to shape more recent conflicts *within* the postcolony. Lentz studied "a certain event [that] took place on the banks of a pond in the village of Kyetuu, which straddles the international border between Ghana and Burkina Faso" (2003: 273). The event in question was a fight between a group of earth priests, who historically had controlled the pond and had regulated the fishing that took place on its shores, and a group of farmers, who had settled in the region more recently. The conflict began when the farmers disregarded the earth priests by bringing modern fish-

ing equipment to the pond and turning fishing into a "profitable individual enterprise" (273). This represented a troubling challenge to traditional
practices, in which "fishing was a communal activity, undertaken toward
the end of the dry season after the earth priests had performed the necessary sacrifices to the spirits of the pond" (273).

As Lentz explains, the problem of legal boundaries intersected in
complicated ways with interethnic conflict, competition over a valued
economic resource, and age hierarchies. Traditionally, the region's territory had come under the jurisdiction of different "earth shrine areas,"
which were defined as the spaces that were protected by different local
earth gods ("*tebuo* in Sisala; *tengan* in Dagara, lit. the crust or skin of the
earth" [275]). In this jurisdictional system, the earth priest, or "master of
the shrine," played a paramount role: he was "responsible for sacrifices
to the earth. . . . He also allocate[d] land to new settlers, allow[ed] them
to 'open' their houses and bury their dead, and open[ed] the annual fishing and hunting parties" (275).

However, with "[c]olonial pacification and the introduction of chief-
tancy in the formerly 'stateless'" (275) region, a new system of land
boundaries was introduced that was organized around a completely
different logic. Nevertheless, as Lentz shows, the earth shrine system
continued to operate at an unofficial level even as colonial international
boundaries gave way to postcolonial ones that had as little regard for the
traditional jurisdiction as those they replaced.

But as Lentz argues, the ethnography of the fishing pond conflict
problematizes simplistic dichotomies between colonial and postcolonial,
traditional and modern, because the actors in the conflict themselves mobilized different conceptions of legal and political space depending on cir-
cumstance and interest. As she puts it, "it has become increasingly clear
that even if African borders were originally 'artificial' creations, they have
long since become an integral part of the lives" (274) of the people for
whom the border is both a fact of everyday life and a potential resource
in the struggle for livelihood and ethnic, national, and religious identity.

## Making the Present with the Past

Despite the fact that most anthropology of law has developed within
the traditions of social and cultural anthropology, archaeologists have

recently made important contributions to the study of history and law through a critical engagement with the international legal regime that has emerged to regulate "global heritage," which Lynn Meskell has defined as the "set of politically inflected material practices" that reveal, classify, and give meaning to the "many things that remain from the past in the present" (2015: 2).

This domain of research focuses on the implementation of the controversial 1972 UNESCO World Heritage Convention, which establishes a regulatory process through which cultural and natural heritage that is considered to be of "outstanding universal value" can be nominated to be designated as a "World Heritage Site." Although, according to the Convention, the world is filled with cultural and natural heritage that constitutes the "priceless and irreplaceable assets, not only of each nation, but of humanity as a whole," only a tiny subset of this irreplaceable heritage is considered "worthy of special protection against the dangers which increasingly threaten [it]" (UNESCO 2015: 1).[13]

Yet as scholars have shown, the application of these normative criteria, this attempt to conceive a framework of universal value from a vast cultural and natural global diversity, has in practice been marked by political exclusion, ethnocentrism, and sheer folly. For example, at the same time that the country of Bhutan has no listed heritage properties, despite having some of the most important religious sites in Himalayan Buddhism (such as the iconic seventeenth-century Taktsang Palphug Monastery), Uruguay managed (in 2015) to have a meat-packing plant recognized as having "outstanding universal value," even though it is most well-known in history for its production of canned corned beef. And although Eritrea also does not have a single listed property despite being home to many important sites from the time of the Aksumite Kingdom (such as the ruins of the ancient city of Qohaito), a single house in the Netherlands (the Rietveld Schröder House) built in 1924 is on the list because it epitomizes "De-Stijl," or open design, within modern architecture.

Across a range of key interventions (e.g., 2013, 2014, 2015), the social archaeologist Lynn Meskell has subjected the UNESCO world heritage regime to critical scrutiny from a number of angles. As she argues, archaeologists have a unique role to play in the study of what one collection of essays calls "The world according to UNESCO" (*Le monde selon l'Unesco*).[14] As she puts it:

> While not underestimating the intangible aspects [of UNESCO's global heritage regime], it is the material dimension and its ramifications that scholars, particularly those with archaeological training, are adept at tracing. The material constitution of sites, their management, conservation, insertion into tourist economies, mobilization within national and global imaginings, and their many connected communities are all processes in which archaeologists are well versed. (2015: 2)

Meskell's global heritage research comprised a wide range of methodologies and sites: she conducted ethnographic research at UNESCO headquarters in Paris; she was an official observer at meetings of the committee charged with implementing the 1972 Convention; and she worked at World Heritage Sites in Turkey and South Africa (Meskell 2013). Meskell argues that the UNESCO global heritage regime faces three critical challenges. First, her research revealed that there was a widening gap between the recommendations of scientific experts regarding what are called "inscriptions" on the heritage list, and the list of sites eventually adopted by the World Heritage Committee. Meskell found that political differences between the two internal bodies reflected a broader conflict over what has been viewed as the Global North's domination of the global heritage process. As she notes, one Senegalese participant argued that "UNESCO largely began as an organization to preserve European architectural achievements after the devastation of World War II," while the German ambassador to UNESCO, in response to such postcolonial critiques, claimed that European countries had the vast majority of sites because "'[o]ur countries build in stone'" (Meskell 2013: 488, 489).

Second, Meskell's research uncovered the presence of powerful voting blocs on the World Heritage Committee, which create a "marketplace" of alliances in which "national imperatives and economic necessities" (2013: 489) shape the evaluation of potential heritage sites rather than the criteria of the Convention itself. For example, the members of the so-called BRICS countries (Brazil, Russia, India, China, and South Africa) forged a "formidable geopolitical alliance" that included the mutual promotion of each others' interests on the Committee, the repaying of debts by shielding existing sites that were threatened by important industries and, in general, the use of "palpable degree[s] of duplicity" (2013: 490).[15]

And third, Meskell's study showed that the UNESCO global heritage regime, and indeed UNESCO itself, came under intense financial pressure because of the decision, first to admit Palestine to UNESCO, and then, in 2012, to recognize a World Heritage Site in Palestine, the Church of the Nativity in Bethlehem.[16] As Meskell explains, these manifold conceptual, political, and economic crises in the system to recognize sites of "outstanding universal value" came to a head when civil war threatened the destruction of Timbuktu in Mali. Despite calls to act, the World Heritage Committee was "powerless to protect" Timbuktu and thereby fulfill the intent of the Convention because of legal and political constraints and bickering among officials.

Yet as the Bangladeshi scholar Lala Rukh Selim (2011) shows, in her study of the 2007 "Guimet Affair," the perils and contradictions of making the present with the past under the sign of law are often felt more indirectly, as much through missed opportunities to reconfigure forms of international collaboration as through neglected or desecrated sites of irreplaceable heritage. The Guimet Affair was a conflict that erupted around an international agreement, signed between Bangladesh and France in 2007, to allow the Musée Guimet in Paris to host a blockbuster exhibition that was to be called "Masterpieces of the Ganges Delta."

This planned event in Paris was meant to be the culmination of a much longer process of joint archaeological cooperation that began with excavations in the early 1990s at sites of undisputed archaeological significance. This research had produced nearly two hundred Buddhist, Hindu, Jain, and Islamic artefacts that had been exhibited in the Bangladesh National Museum since 1999. The idea was to continue and extend the exhibition by transferring the artefacts to Paris, where a joint team of French and Bangladeshi curators would oversee the display. With respect to the Bangladeshi staff, they had received training in techniques of museum display and artefact preservation from their counterparts from the Guimet in anticipation of the exhibition in Paris.

As Selim explains, the justification for displaying the Bangladeshi artefacts in Paris was the fact that some museums were seen as "universal," that is, they transcended in both their holdings and audiences the merely "cultural," while other museums—by implication the Bangladesh National Museum—were trapped by a "nationalistic" perspective and thus incapable of displaying items in a way that represented their universal significance (2011: S179).

This distinction between "universal" and "national" museums was in part an outcome of the growing pressure from the repatriation movement among governments and museums from "source" countries. In 2003, a group of museum directors from many of the largest and wealthiest museums in Europe and the United States promulgated a "Declaration on the Importance and Value of Universal Museums." In it, the directors argued that despite the fact that many objects in their collections were obtained under dubious circumstances that were nevertheless "reflective of [an] earlier era," their long-term display had played a key role in the development of universal knowledge and an appreciation for global history. However, somewhat contradictorily, the directors also asserted—in a way that perhaps reveals the economic undercurrents of the Declaration—that their "universal" museums should also be valued differently because their collections "have become part of the museums that have cared for them, and by extension part of the heritage of the nations which house them" (International Council of Museums News 2004: 4).

Yet as Selim acknowledges, despite the broader controversy around the distinction between universal and national museums, the fact remained that the Guimet Affair unfolded against a historical background in which Bangladesh had been the site of centuries of material cultural appropriation, theft, and commodification. The regular and extensive looting that took place during the colonial period was replaced by the appropriation of artefacts by diplomats and aid workers more recently, who "acquired objects as emblems of their virtuous mission abroad to help the poor" (S181).

For example, Selim's study discusses the case of David Nalin, a distinguished American doctor who worked in Dhaka as part of the U.S. National Institutes of Health's Cholera Research Laboratory. Apart from his medical work, he amassed one of the most extensive private collections of South Asian antiquities. On his biographical page at the Rubin Museum of Art in New York City, where he is on the Board of Trustees, it notes that "[w]hile in South Asia, Dr. Nalin became captivated with local cultures. Realizing ancient sculptures were being scrapped for their metal and destroyed in ethnic conflicts, he became committed to preserving the visual arts of the region" (Rubin Museum of Art 2016).

Although, according to Selim (S181), Nalin later claimed that his Bangladeshi collection was acquired legally, there remained some dispute about how such a large collection (more than a hundred items) could have been transported out of the country even though Bangladesh's Antiquities Act of 1968 imposes a total ban on the export of antiquities. However, apropos of the Guimet Affair, the Antiquities Act creates an exception to the ban in cases in which the Director of the National Museum's Department of Archaeology has granted a license, but only for the "*temporary* export . . . for the purpose of exhibition" (quoted in Selim 2011: S183; emphasis added).

Thus it was in light of this fraught history that a diverse coalition of Bangladeshi "archaeologists, anthropologists, artists, architects, senior citizens, intellectuals, and cultural workers" (S183) mobilized against the planned Guimet exhibition in late 2006 and early 2007. Despite the arguments of a group of local supporters, who maintained that the display of "Masterpieces of the Ganges Delta" in Paris would bring prestige and respect to a country known more for its "floods, cyclones, and corruption" (S177), the opposition forces gathered steam. A lawsuit led to an injunction against the planned shipment of artefacts. However, when the injunction was lifted soon after, violent protests broke out at the National Museum and at the airport, where some boxes were waiting to be sent to France. In the chaos, boxes were broken and some artefacts were destroyed. Some boxes, including one that "contained two Gupta-era terracotta sculptures of Vishnu, a bust and a full figure, dating back to the seventh century" (S187), were never found. And to make matters worse, the French company responsible for insuring the entire consignment had dramatically undervalued the shipment (at about 10 million euros). Indeed, some items were assigned no value at all in legal documents, further reinforcing the protestors' claim that the entire exhibition was really a money-making proposition for the Musée Guimet and a "feather in [its] cap," as one German scholar put it in a letter to the French ambassador (S188).

Selim concludes that the Guimet Affair demonstrates the inherent tensions between different approaches to history, cultural heritage, and universal values that are promoted against a backdrop of colonialism, structural poverty, and legal ethnocentrism. Yet despite the competing positions, Selim argues that "cultural heritage is most significantly studied in its context. Artefacts are not value-free, empty museum pieces. . . . [Those involved here] invoke the wealth of Bengali culture and a wider interpretation of . . . Bengali Muslim identity which has embraced with pride its syncretic past to foster a secular Bengali nationalism" (S188).

## Imagining History through the Law

In addition to examining the enduring legacies of colonial legal governance and the processes through which ideological understandings of the past are translated into legal categories, anthropologists have also studied the ways in which law making becomes a problematic genre of history making. Here, we must distinguish the more mundane forms of documentation used in law—the procedural history of a case, witness testimonies that discuss past events, even the way contracts mark a point in the past (for example, the beginning of a commercial relationship)—from another sense in which history is implicated in law. This is the way that history writ large is crafted—sometimes deliberately, sometimes not—in the course of legal processes whose scope and subject matter encompass major traumas that threaten society itself: genocide, crimes against humanity, civil war, war crimes.

Important new legal tribunals were created in the post–Cold War that developed hybrid rules of evidence; occupied an ambiguous position in relation to the nation-state (and the principle of state sovereignty more generally); and, in the case of the International Criminal Court (ICC), became enmeshed in a postcolonialist politics that threatened to ride roughshod over questions of impunity, abuse of power, and justice for victims of ruthless political leaders and ethnic warlords.

But as Richard A. Wilson (2011) has argued, in a study of the changing relationship between history and law in international criminal tribunals, it has been the very open, dynamic, and supranational nature of international legal forums that has permitted courts to address the historical context of conflicts in new and potentially far-reaching ways. In comparing the role of history in the two early *ad hoc* tribunals (the International Criminal Tribunal for the Former Yugoslavia and the In-

ternational Criminal Tribunal for Rwanda) and in the ICC with its role
in domestic trials, Wilson underscores the structural and political differences. As he puts it

> The most obvious contrast between domestic courts and international tri-
> bunals is that the latter are not constituted in the institutional framework
> of the nation-state. As a result, international courts do not face mate-
> rial conflicts of interest [in the same way]. Although they do experience
> political pressure as overbearing as might be experienced by a domestic
> court, the external intrusions are of a dissimilar nature and do not affect
> historical inquiry in the same way. Because the nation-state is not in its
> usual place, the compulsion to engage in nation-building rhetoric or in
> nationalist mythmaking is not as acute as in national settings. (2011: 37)[17]

Moreover, at the level of jurisprudence, "international tribunals are
not bound by the legal conventions of any nation-state, which gives them
more freedom to develop their own rules of procedure and evidence"
(2011: 38). Wilson's research gave him unprecedented ethnographic access to "what actually goes on behind the scenes, as researchers and
prosecutors develop their cases, and in the Trial Chamber when historian expert witnesses give testimony" (18). The result is an analysis that
goes against the grain of much of the non-anthropological critique of
the relationship between history and law.

As he argues, international tribunals "write history" in two important
ways. First, the open and liberal rules of evidence in international courts
have permitted a wide range of accounts and testimony about the causes
of armed conflicts and violations of humanitarian law to enter the public record in ways that would not have been possible within domestic
courts. Even more, new legal doctrines like genocide create "specifically
legal imperatives to write history and include social and political context" (18) within an adversarial process that tests the evidence in ways
that approximate the production of scientific knowledge.

And second, even when the process of writing history in courts fails
to produce a comprehensive accounting of the conflict, enough detailed
and unique evidence has usually been introduced to form an incomparable source of information for future historians and researchers. As
Wilson explains, "in that sense, their impact as producers of history lasts

long after the trials are completed" (18). Wilson concludes that the ethnographic study of international tribunals suggests a wholesale reconsideration of the relationship between history and law. As he puts it, "there is a compelling case for rethinking the long-standing view that the pursuit of justice and the writing of history are inherently irreconcilable" (19).

## Conclusion: Law's Mythologies

Myth is neither a lie nor a confession: it is an inflexion.
—Roland Barthes, *Mythologies*

As we have seen, anthropologists have explored the historical inflections of law and the legal inflections of history in ways that reveal both deep interconnections and points of contrast, as well as the enduring impact of moments in time in which "configurations or syndromes of material relationships" (Wolf 1981: 21) were based on the "exploitative relation between metropolis and satellite," a relation that was moreover "repeated within each satellite itself" (Wolf 1981: 22).

In addition, ethnographic research has produced a spectrum of case studies that offer different responses to the question of whether or not the law can (re-)write history so that reckonings with the past are compatible with the development of what the Norwegian scholar Johan Galtung (1964) once described as "positive peace," that is, long-term structural transformation that makes large-scale violence less likely to occur. On one side of the spectrum, there are studies like Culhane's, in which the use of (domestic) law to confront the legacy of colonial injustice is circumscribed by the boundaries of the modern state itself, particularly one founded on and justified through ideologies of racial and cultural superiority. But on the other side of the spectrum, there are studies like Wilson's, in which the use of (international and hybrid) law opens up novel epistemological spaces in which historically informed theories of conflict can be mooted, passed through the crucible of critique, and in certain cases made the basis for a deeper understanding of the past.

Yet across the spectrum of history and law, anthropological studies reveal a common theoretical denominator, which is the fundamental importance of myth as a basis for legal knowledge. By myth I do not mean something like "false story." Even less do I use myth in the sense associated with critical theorists like Horkheimer and Adorno, for whom myth represented a moment in cultural-intellectual development in which structures of "false clarity" were deployed because of "the fear of truth which petrifies enlightenment itself" (2002 [1947]: xvii, xvi).

Rather, as an insight into the relationship between history and the production and diffusion of legal knowledge, I am referring to the importance of *mythos* in its earlier conception. As Jeffrey Walker (2000) explains, in his study of rhetoric and poetics in antiquity, mythos (usually translated as "plot") was an important characteristic of public discourse through which the civic performance of a story "persuade[d] and t[aught] its audience how things can and do happen in human life. . . . A *mythos*, then, is a sort of 'case' that demonstrates the ways things are, or could be, in a particular set of circumstances" (2000: 280; emphasis in original).

But crucial to the effectiveness of mythos was the fact that the public had to share a set of baseline cultural and normative understandings in order to be persuaded and taught. Indeed, much like the preconditions that Habermas assumed for a public sphere in which "communicative action" could take place, mythos likewise required the cultivation of a public that was both ready and willing to be "enveloped . . . in a narrative representation of the vital motifs of cultural identity—the emblems of origin, legitimacy and community," as Alain Pottage (1993: 615) put it, in a review of Peter Fitzpatrick's *The Mythology of Modern Law* (1992).[18]

Yet if it is true that "the oldest stories are, after all, the best" (Pottage 1993: 615), then how does this originary conception of myth cast the relationship between history and law in a different light? First, it suggests that law embodies a series of cultural and normative "plots" that are meant to both represent a society's "vital motifs" and encourage—or more directly, compel—people who live within a particular jurisdiction to act in their name. In this way, the question becomes not whether history and law are compatible, because history is always *in* law, but rather which history, which "sort of 'case' that demonstrates the way things are, or could be."

Second, an anthropological account of the mytho-logics of law provides an alternative perspective on law's resistance to change, which

Stanley Fish has described as "law's conservatism, which will not allow a case to remain unrelated to the past, and so assures that the past . . . will be continually rewritten" (Fish 1989: 94). Thus, as we have seen throughout this chapter, the inertia of law comes not from its procedural complexity or because it is a system trapped within the paradox of autopoiesis—that is, the fact "that the application of a legal rule is also the creation of a legal rule" (Goodrich 1999: 198), a paradox that has been called the "violence of an arbitrary distinction" (Teubner 1997: 765). Rather, it is because law is in part an embodiment of myth that it is also in part an embodiment of society, even if the vital motifs expressed through law are obsolete, exclusionary, and ripe for challenge.

And finally, a mythological framing of history in law suggests the possibility for something like the opposite of law's inertia. As Pottage (1993: 618) has argued, "the radical energy of 'myth,' . . . its productive quality," is essentially subversive, even as it shapes the emergence of a public that is prepared to hear "the way things are." This means that law's mythologies are always open to revision, to reinscription within more just social and political projects, to a sharper bend in the arc toward justice.

PART II

Law and Agency, Law as Regulation

3

## Justice between the Devil and the Deep Blue Sea

> This methodological anecdote teaches us [a] lesson. In a community
> where laws are not only occasionally broken, but systematically circum-
> vented by well-established methods, there can be no question of a "spon-
> taneous" obedience to law, of slavish adherence to tradition. For this
> tradition teaches man surreptitiously how to evade some of its sterner
> commands—and you cannot be spontaneously pushed forwards and
> pulled back at the same time! (Malinowski 1926: 81)

The anecdote that precedes this reflection in Malinowski's *Crime and
Custom in Savage Society* is the notable ethnographic description of
Kima'i's suicide. Kima'i, "a young lad of my acquaintance, of sixteen
or so" (1926: 77), had been accused of committing adultery by the
"discarded lover" of the daughter of his mother's sister. Although the
relationship was widely known, the social prohibition against it did
not crystallize until the jilted boy denounced Kima'i in the center of
the village along with "hurling at him certain expressions intolerable
to a native" (1926: 77–78). Because the accusation had been put in front
of the community in this way, "there was only one remedy; only one
means of escape" (78). The next morning, Kima'i "put on festive attire
and ornamentation"; climbed to the top of a nineteen-meter palm tree;
delivered a long oration in which he explained his actions and "launched
forth a veiled accusation" against the boy who had accused him; "wailed
aloud, as is the custom" (78); and then leaped to his death.

Malinowski interprets this ceremonialized suicide as a form of justice
making. However, the wrong that called for justice was not the adul-
terous relationship; it was the act of public shaming by the "discarded
lover" of Kima'i's "sister."[1] Or, to be more precise, the ritual suicide was
the application of justice for two separate wrongs. There was no question
that the commission of adultery with a totemic sister was a "pronounced

crime" at a normative level, as an "ideal of native law" (78, 79). But because the community took no action, because it chose to disregard the
act of adultery as a concession to the subtleties of village life, Kima'i had
to "carry out the punishment [against] himself" (79). Yet this was not
necessary—that is, the abstract crime of adultery did not become a real
crime that demanded sanction—until something out of the ordinary
happened, something that could not be explained through simplistic
accounts of law as a mechanism of social control. It was only when the
community was forced to confront its quotidian compromises with its
own normative ideals that Kima'i was compelled to act. But in so doing,
in depersonalizing and then punishing himself, he also punished the
discarded lover for *his* transgression, which was to take the flexible practice of everyday life, suited to the complexities of sexual relations, and
make it suddenly inflexible. Indeed, during his oration from the treetop,
Kima'i called upon his clansmen to take revenge beyond the punishment
of calling out the rival; according to Malinowski, this followed immediately, as a fight broke out "in which the [boy] was wounded" (78).

So this is a complicated web of action and intention, symbolism and
affect, one that could be made even more complicated if it were recalled
that suicide justice making by leaping off tall palm trees (*lo'u*) is only
one of three such forms described by Malinowski, the other two being
the eating of poison extracted from the gall bladder of the globefish
(*soka*) and the eating of vegetable poison (*twa*), which is more ambiguous, since the effects of the latter can be easily reversed by a "generous
dose of emetic" (94). Yet with all three, their use reveals a cultural-legal
consciousness in which the "desire of self-punishment, revenge, rehabilitation, and sentimental grievance" (95) come together—with un-
predictable consequences.

I begin this chapter on the anthropology of justice with this problematic, if classic, reference for two reasons. First, it underscores something
about the anthropological approach to justice that has remained constant, even if, as we will see, the thematic questions and ethnographic
contexts have changed dramatically over the last twenty years. With few
exceptions, anthropologists have approached questions of justice from a
deeply emic perspective. This is not necessarily the same thing as saying
that the anthropology of justice has developed in terms of "folk categories," although the relationship between local conceptions of justice and

language is clear enough. Rather, it is that the ethnographic study of justice has taken place at a well-defined remove from the normative implications that might or might not be derived from what can be thought of as the practice of justice making. Of course, this epistemological separation is present in much of anthropology, but it is particularly striking in studies of justice, where research takes place in normatively charged ethnographic contexts that—especially recently—are also intensely politicized.

And second, Malinowski's willingness to accept, both ethnographically and conceptually, the counterintuitive and even bizarre possibility that ritualized suicide can be an important form of justice making points to a disciplinary pattern in anthropology that takes seriously the diversity of ways through which societies accommodate their own moments of fracture, social suffering, and repair. In his 1989 *The Anthropology of Justice*, Lawrence Rosen described this as a "course that seeks to reduce neither difference to universals nor uncertainty to utter precision but rather tries . . . to glimpse a culture and a law that bespeak other ways of working through the conflicts of everyday life that seem at once so very exotic and yet so very human" (1989: 19).

Taken to its most capacious limits, this pattern in the anthropology of justice has led scholars to ask questions like "Why did you kill?" to the perpetrators of genocide and then take the answers seriously in order to reveal meaning in even the most horrific of human histories (see Hinton 2004). This approach to justice has given anthropologists the ability to encompass analytically everything from "resentful silences" (Theidon 2010) to "hypocrisy and the violence of local/global 'justice'" (Casey 2011) without reducing them to preexisting political or theoretical categories. In this way, the anthropology of justice has become an innovative, if often unacknowledged, source of uncomfortable insights within broader debates over genocide, truth and reconciliation, international criminal law, and the relationship between the state and citizens who have become "outlawed" (Goldstein 2012).

To this end, this chapter examines the anthropology of justice as a key specialization within the anthropology of law. Anthropologists have tracked the politics, praxis, and meanings of justice within a wide range of ethnographic case studies; this chapter focuses on more recent and illustrative developments. The chapter first considers the rise and possible fall of international criminal law in the post–Cold War period. Anthropologists have conducted important research on international criminal justice and the broader tendency toward the "tribunalization of violence" (Clarke 2009: 45). For at least the first decade of the 1990s, international criminal tribunals were seen as a major advance in the struggle for justice against hostile states and political leaders who conducted war against their own citizens during times of ethnic conflict and the struggle for natural resources. But as anthropological research revealed, the development of international criminal law exposed deep flaws in the idea of universal jurisdiction and in the potential for justice beyond national borders.

The chapter then turns to two closely connected developments in the anthropology of justice: the study of truth and reconciliation commissions and the problem of state-sanctioned violence as a form of politics by other means. When justice processes moved outside courtrooms and into less formal settings like Rwanda's *gacaca*, anthropologists observed the ways in which culture, power, and the influence of international and transnational elites shaped responses to mass violence and the struggle over memory. At the same time, the intervention of powerful state and nonstate actors was often riddled with ethical contradictions, as anthropologists discovered through studies of debates over, for example, the prohibition against torture (see, e.g., Kelly 2011).

Next, the chapter surveys the ways in which anthropologists have problematized justice as discourse and practice in the face of structural violence, chronic poverty, and institutional racism.[2] Scholars have drawn important contrasts between justice and security as an ethnographic problem. They have found that there is often a wide gap between visions of justice promoted by state agencies and international and transnational donors and local citizens, who are forced to construct their own systems of justice making outside the boundaries of the law. Following this, the chapter examines the ways in which anthropologists study justice processes as a form of public representation. As Ronald Niezen has argued, many of the recent justice mechanisms that have been celebrated can also be understood as an effort at "civilizing a divided world" (2010: 137). This section surveys the way scholars have conceptualized the practice of justice as a site of invention, production, and (collective) self-making.

The chapter's conclusion draws together the preceding discussions to consider what contemporary anthropology has to say more generally about "justice" as an enduring framing device within some of the most consequential moments of conflict, inequality, violence, and resistance.

## The Banality of Justice

What are we going to say if tomorrow it occurs to some African state to send its agents into Mississippi and to kidnap one of the leaders of the segregationist movement there? And what are we going to reply if a court in Ghana or the Congo quotes the Eichmann case as precedent?
—Hannah Arendt, *Eichmann in Jerusalem: A Report on the Banality of Evil* (1963)

In the aftermath of the Nuremberg and Tokyo war crimes trials (1945–1948), the development of international criminal tribunals came to a standstill. What distinguished these important early postwar international legal forums is the fact that they provided a mechanism through which individuals could be prosecuted for acts that went beyond the violent ordinary to violate humanity itself. Despite this abstraction, it was important that individuals—typically those with "command and control" authority—were held accountable for histories of mass atrocity that were rationalized by political or racial ideologies, devotion to the state, or the lingering effects of earlier periods of economic pressure. As a judgment of the Nuremberg Tribunal put it, "crimes against [humanity] are committed by men, not abstract entities" (quoted in Eltringham 2010: 208).

And yet, the countervailing logics of the Cold War made it difficult for the international community to establish permanent tribunals during the decades in which the violence of colonialism gave way to resistance and the possibility of independence; major Western powers like France and the United States fought brutal wars against peasant and revolutionary forces in places like Algeria and Vietnam; the NATO and Soviet bloc countries were locked in a cold and proxy war over global influence and ideology; and faith in the progressive potential of governmental institutions was, particularly in the centers of global power, at a low point. This is not to say that no supranational courts were created during this time. But from the International Court of Justice (1946) to the European Court of Human Rights (1959) to the Inter-American Court of Human Rights (1979), limitations and weaknesses in jurisdiction, regional scope, political bias, and enforcement of judgments meant that war crimes, crimes against humanity, and the "new" crime of genocide, the so-called crime of crimes (Schabas 2009), went unpunished in international law until the 1990s.[3]

The establishment of the International Criminal Tribunal for the former Yugoslavia (ICTY) in 1993 and the International Criminal Tribunal for Rwanda (ICTR) in 1994 began a new era in international justice seeking. Like their early postwar predecessors in Nuremberg and Tokyo, the ICTY and ICTR were also "ad hoc" tribunals, meaning that they were created (in this case by UN Security Council resolutions) in order to prosecute individuals for committing mass atrocities within specific conflicts. The creation of these tribunals in the early 1990s was followed by others, including the East Timor Tribunal (2000), the Special Court for Sierra Leone (2002), and the Khmer Rouge Tribunal (2006), all three "hybrid" courts that combined domestic and international law and personnel, often within the terms of a peace treaty or international resolution. Finally, and most significantly, in 2002 the first permanent international criminal court was established. The International Criminal Court (ICC), based in the Hague, the Netherlands, has jurisdiction over the crimes of genocide, crimes against humanity, and war crimes committed by individuals in states that are members of the 1998 Rome Statute.[4]

From the creation of the ICTY to the most recent investigations involving the ICC, anthropologists have conducted innovative research within this emergent sphere of law that "takes place at the intersection of the often contradictory practices of petitioners, litigants, bureaucrats, lawyers, victims, witnesses, accused, judges, and third parties" (Kelly and Dembour 2007: 2). But the anthropological study of international justice has also been concerned with what the critical legal scholar David Kennedy (2004) would call the "dark side of [its] virtue": its political silences and manipulations; its "fictions" (Clarke 2009); its clouded "mirrors" (Clarke and Goodale 2010); and the "increasing disenchantment" (Kelly and Dembour 2007: 5) that results when the promise of justice beyond the nation-state must confront the reality of its limitations.

Several themes stand out in this body of research. In his study of the effects of the ICC on internal conflicts in Côte d'Ivoire, Mike McGovern (2010) argues that the threat of prosecution amounts to a "judicialization of international politics" that leads to unintended consequences— sometimes on the side of justice and sometimes not. As he explains, because the international focus on Côte d'Ivoire waxed and waned over the years, "Ivorians found moments of tactical possibility, during which they could take advantage of international inattention, discord, or duplicitousness to forge ahead in sometimes violent fashion" (2010: 86).

In her study of a series of cases brought by Gypsies [sic] in the European Court of Human Rights, Sal Buckler (2007) explores the way in which international courts depend on legally defined identities of victims and claimants that can be both at odds with lived identities and at the same time deny them the right to exercise moral agency. As she puts it, we must "recognise that the decisions made by courts . . . impact upon cultures differently and privilege certain mainstream and hegemonic ways of being-in-the-world. . . . [T]he exercise of the law is not culture-neutral" (2007: 259).

Finally, anthropologists have used the ethnography of international justice to reflect on and contribute to broader debates over key concepts like culture, religious identity, neocolonialism, and legal pluralism. In her study of the controversies over ICC prosecutions in Africa, Kamari Clarke (2009: 88) argues that international law—and perhaps law more generally—is produced through an "odd combination of morality-driven ambitions and [a] political economy" that determines when and where prosecutions take place, which violations of rights form the basis of action and which do not, and how funding linked to "donor capitalism" (2009: 81) gets allocated strategically in ways that reinforce the priorities of institutions such as the World Bank and the IMF.

In studying the tensions between the demands of international law and the "religious politics of incommensurability" in Sub-Saharan Africa, Clarke demonstrates that the meanings and practices of international justice are intimately bound up with broader policies of development, geopolitical security, and cultural power. Within this broader context, a set of "liberalist" logics predetermine which understandings of justice will "thrive" and which will not. In this way, "justice" loses its grand connotations and abstracted associations with emancipation and with making broken societies whole again. Instead, as Clarke argues, the pursuit of justice in Africa through international courts has become in part a mechanism for promoting the values of "private property, the rule of law, and individual liberty and freedoms" (2009: 235).

As we will see in the next section, anthropologists of law have uncovered similar tensions and inconsistencies when the pursuit of justice moves outside formal tribunals after periods of mass violence and armed conflict.

## Bare Justice

Over the same years in which the institutions of international criminal justice were being created, another form of justice making was emerging. As early as the Nuremberg and Tokyo trials, it was clear that the process of retributive justice, centered on legal tribunals and a small number of prosecutions, had its limits in the face of massive trauma, political transition, and "social suffering" (Kleinman, Das, and Lock 1997). In 1964, the Norwegian peace theorist Johan Galtung had already given shape to the broader and more ambiguous nature of postconflict recovery by drawing a distinction between "negative" and "positive" peace. The first simply described the absence of violent conflict. The second, by contrast, referred to an extended period of fundamental and wide-ranging change in which—ideally—social, economic, and political conditions are reconfigured so that new periods of violence become much less likely. In this way, according to Galtung, even the most horrific histories of mass violence can form a turning point for societies that have suffered under conditions of structural violence, racism, and inequality.

Beginning in the 1990s, anthropologists turned to this more ambitious scope of action when justice making moved outside courtrooms to be woven into the very fabric of nation building in an era of prevailing "democratization." An early and important example of how truth and reconciliation commissions (TRCs) came to serve as key markers for democratic transition was the experience of South Africa. In his ethnography of the South African TRC, Richard A. Wilson examined the ways in which the TRC expanded beyond its original functions to symbolize the importance of "transnational validity as one of the main mechanisms for announcing a new democratic order" (2001: xviii). As a nonjudicial forum that was established as a linchpin of the transition to a postapartheid state, the TRC, as Wilson explains, was given two tasks: first, to provide a means through which the truth about South Africa's violent and racist past could be acknowledged and legitimated; and second, to make this form of collective witnessing the basis for national reconciliation.

Wilson's nuanced study carefully parsed the relationship between the working of the TRC in all its bureaucratic specificity and the wider effects of the TRC on local processes of justice making, legal pluralism, and human rights activism. Critically, Wilson's ethnography resisted the formal and abstracted claims of truth and reconciliation during the South African transition by placing his findings in a longer historical context that stretches back into South Africa's colonial past. Doing so led him to view the South African TRC with deep anthropological skepticism. Although the "literature evaluating the achievements of the [South African] truth commission[ ] has mostly been positive and laudatory, claiming th[is] commission[ ] heal[ed] the nation by providing therapy for a traumatized national psyche" (2001: xix), Wilson's ethnography came to a very different conclusion. As he argues, "the TRC should be seen [instead] as part of a continuous history of state efforts to centralize and reduce legal pluralism and to transform local notions of justice" (213). Because of its denial of problematic forms of local justice shaped by a discourse of vengeance, the South African TRC ended up creating a justice gap between the centralized state and local communities, a gap which, on Wilson's reading, led to enduring difficulties in the broader mission to forge a unified postapartheid nation.

Yet other kinds of gaps were created in the course of the transitional justice process in postgenocide Rwanda. These processes were developed partly in response to what was seen as the inadequacies of the South African TRC, including the dominant role of the state, the relatively small number of participants in relation to the actual number of perpetrators, victims, and witnesses, and the absence of traditional conflict resolution techniques. Instead

Rwanda resurrected and transformed an ad-hoc, local-dispute resolution mechanism (*gacaca*) into a formalized system of more than 11,000

> community courts. . . . Gacaca was a proudly homegrown response to
> mass violence . . . that explicitly contested the international community's
> preference for international criminal tribunals and national truth com-
> missions. (Waldorf 2010: 183)

This homegrown response became the "most ambitious experiment
in transitional justice ever attempted: mass justice for mass atrocity"
(Waldorf 2010: 183). But as Jennie E. Burnet (2011) has shown, in an
ethnography that spanned the entire course of the gacaca process, it
eventually evolved into a mechanism for the consolidation of Tutsi state
power through a series of procedural steps and normative erasures that,
in her analysis, were focused as much on revenge as on the development
of an innovative platform for transitional justice. In perhaps the starkest example of the politicization of gacaca by the postgenocide Kagame
government, a new law was passed in 2008 that changed the official
phrase that designated the 1994 violence from the broader "genocide and
massacres" to the much more restrictive "genocide against the Tutsis"
(2011: 103).[5]

This change in state terminology profoundly altered the course of
truth and reconciliation in Rwanda even fifteen years after the genocide,
since it discursively and legally removed Hutu victims from the category
of people entitled to participate in "national mourning activities" (2011:
103). Much like Wilson's analysis of the South African TRC, Burnet's
evaluation of Rwanda's gacaca is equally guarded. Despite its novel ambitions, the gacaca process in Rwanda has only "delivered justice for some
and established at least a partial truth, but it has undermined the rule of
law and underscored the impunity for . . . crimes" (115) committed by the
forces that ended the genocide and established the postgenocide regime
that still governs Rwanda (as of 2016). In trying to explain the ultimate
failure of gacaca to meet its broad objectives, Zarir Merat, the head of
Avocats Sans Frontières-Rwanda, reflected that perhaps "genocide is too
heavy for the shoulders of justice" (quoted in Waldorf 2010: 195).

Finally, anthropologists have studied what happens to a society in the
aftermath of mass atrocity when it resists the call to establish a national
truth and reconciliation commission as part of state efforts to shape the
construction of history in particular ways. Although important examples of state refusals to formalize processes of public accounting for past

atrocities—whether through truth and reconciliation commissions or otherwise—would include the glaring cases of postwar Germany and post–Soviet Russia,[6] anthropologists have also brought attention to the fraught search for justice in post-Soeharto Indonesia. Drawing on her long-term ethnographic fieldwork among survivors of state anticommunist purges, Leslie Dwyer explains that "July 2005 marked almost forty years since state-sponsored violence led to the deaths of some half to one million Indonesians—including 80,000–100,000 Balinese, or 5–8 percent of the island's population—and the imprisonment, surveillance, and curtailment of civil rights for hundreds of thousands of other alleged communists" (2011: 230; see also Dwyer 2017).

After Soeharto's New Order dictatorship ended in 1998, there were calls both within Indonesia and within what had become an increasingly professionalized nongovernmental transitional justice community for the nation to convene a truth and reconciliation commission. The hope was that an Indonesian TRC would examine more than three decades of the state's framing of history that subsumed the massacres of 1965–1966 and the repressive aftermath within an official narrative of national unity, anticommunism, and military heroism. This narrative was most starkly rendered in the "New Order's monumental Museum of the Indonesian Communist Party's Treachery in Jakarta, which concretized an official history of the military's triumph over leftist threat in celebratory statuary, gruesome dioramas, and . . . blood-red reconstruction[s]" (2011: 232).[7] But in December 2006, legislation authorizing a national truth and reconciliation commission was struck down by Indonesia's Constitutional Court, "earning Indonesia the dubious distinction of being the first country to authorize, and then cancel, such a body" (2011: 244).

Instead, as Dwyer demonstrates through her ethnographic research on the island of Bali, Indonesians were forced to develop grassroots, nonstate-sanctioned processes of truth and reconciliation to create public spaces where suffering could finally be acknowledged. But as her study reveals, even small-scale projects encountered resistance and created disruptures between deeply specific ways of referring to the violence and outside categories like "peace," "reconciliation," and "healing" drawn from transnational justice discourses, which functioned as "deflective terms" (2011: 228) in Dwyer's critical appraisal. The most serious conflict over a proposed "1965 Park" in Bali was between the younger generation and the generation that had lived through the violence. The youth viewed the debate over the park as a question of their individual agency—should they support it or not? The implication was that they could choose not to support it as one among a range of possible outcomes.

For the older generation, however, the park symbolized events of the past that were still all-too-present for them and which could not be ignored through a simple act of will. As Dwyer puts it, although those who experienced the violence of the New Order regime did so in a range of complex ways that could not be easily encompassed within the rhetorical categories of transitional justice, the memory of 1965–1966 "continued to channel and dam possibilities for speech, political action, and cultural meaning" (2011: 237). In the end, the presence of transnational justice discourses indelibly shaped these grassroots efforts at justice making outside the state, but not in ways that resolved local conflicts. Rather, the transnational demand that "Indonesians . . . decry state violations of human rights and . . . resolve legacies of conflict among neighbors . . . seemed to offer them little space for their own stories" (2011: 238).

## (In-)Justice and Citizen Security

Anthropologists of law have made further contributions to the study of justice by looking beyond both formal and informal legal processes to examine spaces of violence, insecurity, and citizen resistance in conditions of political and economic marginalization and rapid social change. In many ways, this line of research could be described as the anthropology of *injustice*, which has developed as a kind of disciplinary shadowy counterpart that examines the dark sides of state and transnational projects based in human rights, social equality, inclusion, and respect for diversity. Some anthropologists have theorized these dark spaces where the claims of justice meet the realities of chronic insecurity in (potentially) emancipatory terms, for example, as the grounds for new forms of "insurgent citizenship" (Holston 2007).

The more common approach, however, has been to examine these gaps and often violent responses as a critical window into the failings of state programs that promise legal and political transformation despite the lack of economic resources, political agreement, and—in conditions of ideological conflict—good faith (Arias and Goldstein 2010: Burrell 2010; Caldeira 2001). The anthropology of injustice and citizen security, as an emergent mode of critique within the broader anthropology of law, must be distinguished for obvious reasons from the work of the so-called security anthropologists like Montgomery McFate (e.g., Mc-Fate 2005), who collaborated with the U.S. military during the Iraq and Afghanistan conflicts in developing anthropological research as a tool of national security (see Selmeski 2007).[8]

Daniel M. Goldstein's long-term fieldwork in the periurban barrios of Cochabamba, Bolivia, has yielded perhaps the most well-developed anthropological analyses of the ways in which abstracted discourses of legal equality and human rights intertwine with various forms of insecurity to produce a context in which the performance of violence becomes a mode of both cultural expression and resistance to state incapacity (see, e.g., Goldstein 2003, 2004, 2012; see also Goldstein 2010). What is so valuable about this body of work within the anthropology of law is the fact that it spans a historical trajectory in which human rights discourse and international treaty ratification were adopted by a series of neoliberal regimes in Bolivia during the early and mid-1990s; these changes empowered social movements to fight against political corruption and historical marginalization based on ethnic identity; these conflicts led to the end of the *ancien régime* and the emergence of a "postneoliberal" revolutionary government (in 2006); and finally, the new regime continued to make human rights ideology—with cultural and mythological inflections—the basis for future national development. Goldstein's ethnographic research captures, not necessarily the rise and fall, but the rise and eventual *involution* of discourses of justice and human rights in the stark light of economic crisis, chronic poverty, the dislocations of rural to urban migration, and bureaucratic failure.

His first ethnographic study examined the troubling proliferation of lynching during the mid-1990s in Bolivia's cities. This was at the moment in the country's history when government policies that combined multiculturalism and human rights with the retreat of the state from traditional areas of responsibility had forced those living on the margins of urban areas to take justice into their own hands, as they described it themselves. The key tension for the anthropology of law, according to

Goldstein, was that the neoliberal state justified itself as the guarantor of international norms as a new solution to a wide range of local problems without being able to ensure that the new laws actually changed the structural conditions that affected people's daily lives. A kind of disenchantment set in once this basic gap became apparent to people; then disenchantment was transformed through expressions of communal rage that took place within a "carnival of violence" (2004: 182; quoting Comaroff 1994: xiii). As he provocatively argued:

> Lynchings in this context are not merely parallel justice systems intended to substitute for the inadequate enforcement of state law; nor can they be seen simply as "mob violence," the spasmodic reflex of enraged sociopaths bent on retribution. . . . Lynchings are also spectacles, intended to catch the eye of an inattentive state and to perform for it visually and unmistakably the consequences of its own inaction. . . . [V]iolence emerges as the socially subordinate and politically and economically powerless attempt to communicate—to themselves as well as to those powerholders whom they regard as having failed them—their grievances, their anger, and their political potential. (2004: 182)

But after 2005, the political context in Bolivia underwent profound changes. The old order of neocolonial and neoliberal regimes had been replaced by a revolutionary government led by the first self-identifying indigenous president in the country's troubled history. The new government promised to enact sweeping changes to the legal system, economy, political structure, and even to the framework of public moral discourse, by replacing an ideology of structural racism and capitalist individualism with an indigenous *cosmovisión* that privileged *vivir bien* ("living well") in harmony with Pachamama, or Mother Earth. And yet, despite the seismic shifts on Bolivia's symbolic landscape, as Goldstein discovered, residents of the country's poor urban neighborhoods were still caught up in spectacles of performative violence at the "nexus of rights and security" (2012: 203). To explain the nuances of this nexus, Goldstein develops a theory of legal pluralism called "outlawing," which is a way of describing the dark sides of legal multiplicity that function as a kind of dystopian analogue to the Portuguese sociologist Boaventura de Sousa Santos's theory of "interlegality" (Santos 1987, 1995).

Instead of the generative agency of "different legal spaces superimposed, interpenetrated and mixed in our minds, as much as in our actions, either on occasions of qualitative leaps . . . , sweeping crises in our life trajectories, or in the dull routine of eventless everyday life" (Santos 1995: 473), Goldstein's research in Bolivia reveals a legal wasteland in which people are "outlawed—they live outside the protections of state law, yet they are multiply subjected to its constraints; they must do without law's benefits, but they are criminalized as illegal occupants of urban space and perpetrators of mob justice" (2012: 3). This double-sided process of "negative inclusion and perilous exclusion . . . represent[s] different ways that the state produces [and] perpetuates insecurity . . . even as it establishes a certain kind of order" (2012: 29) in the spaces of contemporary life in which "human rights" and "justice" have become mere slogans of the "phantom state"—"incorporeal, sometimes terrifying, always flickering at the edges of perception" (2012: 83).

## Justice and the Politics of Representation

Finally, there is a much more diffuse line of contributions within the anthropology of law that examines the "multiplicity of justice" (Goodale and Clarke 2010) as a site of public representation that crystallizes conflict, grounds new forms of resistance, and often stands in for the assertion of power within a broader politics. These are the contexts in which anthropologists study "justice" in its most malleable forms—legal, moral, discursive. In his analysis of Islamic law courts in Morocco, Lawrence Rosen described the attempt to reduce emic categories of legal reasoning to forms that could be more easily compared with those from western jurisprudence as a futile effort to "determin[e] the indeterminable"(1989: 20 et seq.). The same could be said of anthropological approaches to justice and the politics of representation: instead of taking up justice as a substantive category itself, the best research in this area views it as a "template" (Niezen 2013b) that allows for inclusions and exclusions, transparency and deception, empowerment and denial.

In his opening statement to the 1945 International Military Tribunal at Nuremberg, Justice Robert H. Jackson, Chief of Counsel for the United States, made perhaps one of the clearest and most lasting arguments for an abstracted, nonpolitical understanding of legal justice: "That four great nations, flushed with victory and stung with injury stay[ed] the hand of vengeance and voluntarily submit[ed] their captive enemies to the judgment of the law is one of the most significant tributes that Power has ever paid to Reason" (quoted in Bass 2000: 147).

But almost immediately, legal critics from within the "four great nations" themselves spotted the shaping hand of political considerations in the way the charges were brought against the defendants, in the procedural rulings during the trials, and most importantly, in the legal reasoning underlying the eventual judgments. As the U.S. federal judge and legal scholar Charles E. Wyzanski argued as early as 1946, "[i]f in the end there is a generally accepted view that Nuremberg was an example of high politics masquerading as law, then the trial instead of promoting may retard the coming of the day of world law" (Wyzanski 1946).

This contested moment in the aftermath of world war, genocide, and moral crisis lent new urgency to enduring debates over the relationship between justice and politics, between national interest and the interests of humanity, and between power and reason. Yet even within the processes that gave rise to the most cosmopolitan and universalizing of postwar responses to the preceding calamity, the Universal Declaration of Human Rights (1948), it turned out that these processes masked as well a range of political and ideological conflicts, including the emerging Cold War divide, the stirrings of anticolonialism, and unacknowledged differences *among* the "four great nations," particularly between the United States and France (see Glendon 2001; Goodale 2018; Morsink 1999).

But as the later anthropology of justice would demonstrate, the debate over the relationship between justice and politics was often based on a set of assumptions that collapsed under the gaze of ethnographic studies that revealed a more nuanced set of interdependencies and points of contestation. Even more, the debate over justice and politics itself was folded back into the anthropology of justice as it played out in particular ethnographic contexts. This meant that struggles over an abstracted conception of fairness, the rule of law, and equity on the one hand, and, on the other, over interestedness, narrow-mindedness, and the imposition of will, were reframed as markers of a more fundamental struggle over categories and mechanisms of public representation in the movement from historical trauma to "affirmative repair" (Woolford 2011).[9]

In her multiple studies of the aftermath of the Sierra Leone Civil War (1991–2002), Rosalind Shaw has examined the ways in which debates about the meanings of justice produce "memory frictions" (2007)—that is, tensions that result when claims for justice intersect problematically with multiple and contrasting "memory projects," including those associated with international human rights organizations, those adopted by Sierra Leone's TRC, and those embraced by different local movements with often quite divergent goals and priorities. As she explains, post–Civil War Sierra Leone came to be seen as a "laboratory" by international legal experts in which a number of troubling postconflict binaries could be confronted and hopefully overcome—specifically, the apparent need to choose between a political process that focused on "truth" and a legal process that focused on "justice" (2010: 210–211). Shaw quotes from the former Chief Prosecutor of the Special Court for Sierra Leone, David Crane, who argued that "the Sierra Leone model is the right model. A plus B equals C. Truth plus justice equals sustainable peace" (2010: 211).

But as her ethnography of the postconflict process in Sierra Leone revealed, instead of resolving questions about the meaning of justice in favor of a higher synthesis (whether around "peace" or otherwise), it merely "reconfigured" them in terms of other contested categories that reflected struggles over representation, culture, and local moral values. She argues that an anthropology of justice must begin and end in the ethnographic specificity of "confusion, ignorance, irrationality, illiteracy, incomprehensibility, [and] noncompliance," difficulties which characterize the everyday lived experiences of people who must "live with the contradictions that already form part of justice interventions" (2010: 223). As she puts it, this is not simply what results when "universal justice meets local values" (223). Rather, it is what happens when people "have to rebuild their postconflict lives in conditions of state collapse, institutional failure, and chronic insecurity" (223) within the boundaries of normative categories like "justice" that reveal little about local realities.

Finally, in his ethnography of Canada's Truth and Reconciliation Commission on Indian residential schools, Ronald Niezen (2013b) shows how these tensions take place not only between the "universal" and the "local," but, we might say, within the local itself—in this case, within Canada's First Nations, whose members were forced to attend Indian residential schools as part of a long-term policy of forcibly assimilating Canada's aboriginal peoples into the majority language, religion, and canons of history. In addition, his study explores the idea that struggles over representation in the name of "justice" can also be generative for the victims, survivors, and advocates who have no choice but to "live with the contradictions," in this case those at the heart of the TRC.

As he argues, "Canada's TRC serves as an illustration of the way that public audiences are able to influence legal process, and of the way that legal process, in turn, can be a [new] source of social membership and identity" (2013b: xii). In this way, the ambiguous relationship between the normative claims of justice and the politics that grounds them creates spaces that can be both "socially formative" and "socially constructive" at the same time. What results from this dynamic interaction is not simply new "political and legal resources" that might or might not prove useful to survivors of historical traumas; rather, what results are "new ways of being and belonging in the world" (155) that, as Niezen argues, transcend their origins. He concludes his study by considering whether these new ways of being and belonging in the world can come to compensate for the manifest deficiencies and structural exclusions of the legal processes that gave rise to them. As he puts it, the performance of new identities through testimony in the TRC can come to "fill[ ] the space needed to understand the actual dynamics of residential institutions, the motives behind their establishment, the causes behind the corruption of their goals, and the qualities they might have in common with other, more contemporary forms of misguided power and opinion" (155).

## Conclusion: Justice in an Anthropological Key

Surveying the anthropology of justice in 2010, Sally Engle Merry explored the ways in which the concept of justice is open and aspirational yet also a powerful organizing device that remains "perennially appealing" (2010: 29). In this dynamic interaction between an "extremely vague and unspecified concept" and its enduring power to motivate action within some of recent history's most serious conflicts, justice differs qualitatively from human rights. As Merry argues:

> the idea of justice differs sharply from that of human rights, which has an elaborate set of legal texts and procedures such as conventions, treaty

bodies, compliance mechanisms, and civil society organizations that fer-
ret out abuses and translate them into human rights terms that are recognizable to these international institutions. (2010: 28)

Nevertheless, even though justice is a substantively open concept
with multiple referents within a long history of legal and political practice and interdisciplinary debate, recent anthropology does reveal broad
patterns within which particular ideas about justice emerge. Merry
identifies four discrete areas in which meanings of justice coalesce in
ways that can have transformative consequences. The first is the practice
of human rights. As a vague referent with the power to infuse conflicts
with a sense of moral purpose, justice is linked to human rights as an
ideological endpoint; the use of human rights documents, their ratification by nation-states, their invocation by social movements in the midst
of resistance, all are supposed to make the creation of a more just society more likely.[10] But as Merry emphasizes, the human rights-to-justice
nexus is itself ambiguous since it does not depend entirely on the "denotative power" (Goodale 2007) of human rights, that is, the capacity to
invoke human rights as a body of law (or, even more, *specific* laws) in the
course of ongoing struggles. As she explains, justice "has been picked up
in different ways in different places and made into something new, often
stretching beyond the documents themselves through processes such as
vernacularization" (2010: 29).

The second source of meanings of justice, according to Merry, is what
might be called the cultural: "local practices embedded in communities,
families, and neighborhoods" (29). This is obviously a grounding for
ideas of justice that is as substantively diverse as the distinct communities, families, and neighborhoods from which they are derived, although
as she explains, "[s]ome of these local justice ideologies have become
global" (29). In identifying the cultural as a distinct source of ideas about
justice within the anthropological literature, we must be careful to distinguish this key insight from something related to it, the "cultural turn,"
by which she means the often misguided efforts by international criminal tribunals to make essentialized understandings of local culture(s)
part of legal procedures (see Shaw 2010).

Third, anthropologists have shown the ways in which religion is an
important source for ideas about justice. As Merry argues, despite the

wide range of religious doctrine, from so-called world religions to local sects and "quasi-governmental religious organizations such as the Holy See," what they all have in common is a doctrine or concept that can be linked to "justice," no matter how substantively diverse. Even within the most violent conflicts, religion often serves as the basis for incipient conceptions of justice that are intertwined with cultural ideas about retribution, reconciliation, and recompense. For example, in his ethnography of Acholi rituals of justice making in war-torn Uganda, Sverker Finnström explains that such expressions of Acholi spiritual tradition reflect a sense of justice that is "not about remembering and assessing every detail of a long and violent conflict. Rather, it is about finding a consensual understanding about what the conflict was essentially about, and how to now coexist" (2010: 145).

And finally, Merry argues that anthropologists have identified various practices of cosmopolitanism as an important contemporary source of ideas about justice. The link between cosmopolitanism, law, and justice has its roots in earlier periods. Indeed, one would most likely begin, at least in the modern period, with Kant, who developed a "cluster of ideas revolving around perpetual peace, an international organisation, the reform of international law, and what Kant has termed cosmopolitan law or the law of world citizens (*Weltbürgerrecht*)" (Cavallar 2012: 95). Nevertheless, the idea of "thinking and feeling beyond the nation" (Cheah and Robbins 1998) as a form of transnational justice of a higher order of moral magnitude continues to motivate action, from important international agencies like the United Nations to indigenous movements that are based on ideologies of panregional ethnic identity and shared experiences of historical suffering. In contemporary Bolivia, for example, the ruling party has adopted the broadest possible conception of the "indigenous" to describe its affiliations and commitments, one that ties transnational (though not necessarily universal) belonging to an ideology of justice that emphasizes solidarity, equity, living in harmony with nature, and pluralism (see Goodale, n.d.).

Thus, to understand justice in an anthropological key is to be carefully attuned to the ways in which justice "operates at [both] symbolic and practical levels" and to the ways in which practices of justice play an important role in "legal consciousness, norm change, modes of appropriation and internalization of principle, and forms of resistance"

(Merry 2010: 31–32). And finally, an anthropological approach to justice is one that not only tracks its multiple instrumentalities; it is also one that examines what a 2016 volume has called the "sense of justice"—a type of phenomenological mapping that studies the ways in which the construction of justice takes place through dialogical negotiation, silence, and hope (Brunnegger and Faulk 2016). Here, well beyond the debate over the relationship between justice-as-power and justice-as-politics, anthropologists have come about as close as possible to the elusive "underneath of things" (Ferme 2001) where the endless search for justice signifies something more fundamental: the quixotic, but necessary, search for the forever "yet to come" (Brunnegger 2016: 142).

4

# Human Rights and the Politics of Aspiration

Anthropology's contributions to the study of the practice of human rights have become one of the discipline's most notable markers of influence on law within international and interdisciplinary spheres. This influence has been multifaceted. The anthropology of human rights has developed innovative approaches in methodology, epistemology, and ethics such that an anthropological perspective is now a common presence within academic debates over human rights, within international institutional policy making, and among human rights practitioners. That anthropology has become such a foundational part of the continuing evolution of human rights as theory, social practice, and ethics is itself a remarkable fact, particularly given the ways in which anthropology as a scientific discipline was held—and, to a certain extent, held itself—at a distance even before the Universal Declaration of Human Rights (UDHR) was adopted in December 1948. In many ways, the story of how anthropology went from being opposed to the postwar human rights project in the late 1940s to a discipline that has taken its place along with political philosophy, legal theory, and international relations, as an academic steward of human rights, mirrors key developments in the wider "sea-change in global politics" through which human rights became "the archetypical language of democratic transition" (Wilson 2001: 1).

This chapter examines this history in order to contextualize the areas in which anthropology has made its most significant contributions to human rights as a domain of law whose very boundaries are themselves contextual, spanning the range from a limited—if growing—body of international human rights instruments to those "protean forms of social action assembled, by convention, under a portal named 'human rights'" (Baxi 2002: v). Indeed, the very multiplicity of human rights in the contemporary world has itself been a topic for anthropological research and theorizing (see, e.g., Allen 2013; Goodale 2013b). In this way, the pervasive sense of epistemological openness that has characterized the development of the anthropology of law since the late 1980s put it in a unique position to respond to the "sea-change in global politics" that occurred over roughly the same time period.

It has also meant that perhaps more than other disciplines, anthropology has been the site of widely diverse forms of engagement with human rights, from full-throated human rights promotion as a mode of "engaged anthropology" (Low and Merry 2010) to the participation of biological anthropologists in mass atrocity investigations (Rosenblatt 2015) to the organization of transdisciplinary human rights symposia on key themes such as the ambiguous role of the state, the relationship between politics and human rights, human rights in the face of pathologies of power, and the problems of subjectivity in an age of human rights (see, e.g., Goodale 2013a).

Nevertheless, despite this diversity, the contributions of anthropology to the broader understanding of human rights can be articulated with some degree of precision. What is so revealing about these insights is that they are only in part about law—international, transnational, or otherwise. More broadly, as we will see below, the anthropology of human rights has become the critical ethnography of one of the key ideas of contemporary world-making, with lessons that go well beyond anthropology itself.

## From Cultural Difference to a Right to Culture

The history of anthropology's contributions to human rights is also inseparably a problem of historiography. Different scholars have approached this narrative with different objectives—analytical, methodological, and, perhaps not surprisingly, ideological. As a complicated social field that is bound up with profound questions of suffering, redemption, collective responsibility, social punishment, and justice, human rights demands introspection and even self-confrontation from the scholar or practitioner. This is particularly true for anthropologists, whose professional interest in the theory and practice of human rights is often motivated by personal experiences of activism, struggle on behalf of vulnerable populations (who might also happen to be longtime research interlocutors), and often a broader commitment to human rights as a powerful tool for opposing the pretentions of structural power.[1] But when scholars mischaracterize the early history of anthropology's relationship to human rights in order to promote contemporary anthropology as a discipline that can and indeed must support human rights advocacy, these efforts obscure what was in fact a surprisingly anthropological process to breathe multicultural life into what became the UDHR.[2]

In late 1946 and early 1947, the charismatic first Director-General of UNESCO, Julian Huxley, along with the first head of UNESCO's philosophy subsection, Jacques Havet, put into motion a process that was meant to establish the universal principles upon which a declaration of the "rights of man" could be legitimately established. The General Conference of UNESCO, meeting for the first time in November and December 1946, had charged the Director-General with this important task within the organization's first year of existence.[3]

Huxley and Havet first attempted to hold a small conference of scholars in the spring of 1947, a meeting that was intended to be private and composed mainly of leading French intellectuals and politicians. However, because they were closely and worriedly watching the developments in the UN Commission on Human Rights (chaired by Eleanor Roosevelt), which met for the first time formally in early February 1947, Huxley and Havet made the abrupt decision to abandon the idea of a small conference and undertake instead a rushed global survey that asked people to respond to a memorandum and questionnaire written by Havet. These documents discussed the history of human rights and then asked respondents to agree (or not) with a list of proposed rights and freedoms that might be included in what U.S. President Harry Truman had called an "international bill of rights" (quoted in Morsink 1999: 4).

Huxley and Havet were worried because it was not exactly clear in the spring of 1947 whether or not UNESCO would have the time to fulfill the role it envisioned for itself: that is, to "clarify the principles on which might be founded a modern declaration of the Rights of Man" (UNESCO 1947: 236). So beginning in late March, Huxley and Havet sent the memorandum and questionnaire to an intriguing range of people, academic institutions, nation-states, civil society organizations, political parties, trade unions, and religious officials, among others (see Goodale 2018).

Two anthropologists were among the list of approximately seventy people who eventually submitted responses to UNESCO throughout 1947: A. P. Elkin, professor of anthropology at the University of Sydney, and Melville Herskovits, professor of anthropology at Northwestern University. Elkin, who was a longtime advocate for Australian Aborigines, wrote an essay on the rights of "primitive peoples," an argument for the ways in which Aborigines ordered their social lives around conceptions of rights and responsibilities that might or might not be consistent with the legacy of the kinds of grand rights declarations that Havet invoked in his memorandum. Elkin's response to the question on behalf of "primitive peoples" was largely missed in the history of anthropology's relationship to human rights, even though it was published by UNESCO in a selection of responses in 1949.

It was Herskovits's response, rather, that became (depending on the ideological orientation) so (in-)famous for two reasons. First, because it made a principled set of arguments that, taken together, expressed deep reservations about the legitimacy of producing a universal declaration of human rights. But second, Herskovits's "Statement on Human Rights" took on a life of its own when it was published by the American Anthropological Association (AAA) in the December 1947 number of its flagship journal, *American Anthropologist*, with an added note that it had been "submitted to the Commission on Human Rights, United Nations by the Executive Board, American Anthropological Association." This note appended to Herskovits's response has led to historical misunderstanding and agonizing (see, e.g., Engle 2001; Messer 1993), since it was understandably construed by later scholars to indicate that the AAA had formulated a response on the question of human rights on behalf of the largest association of professional anthropologists in the world[4]—acting as its executive voice—and had transmitted this expression of collective skepticism to the commission working on what would soon become the UDHR.[5]

Nevertheless, Herskovits's principled opposition to the idea of a universal declaration of human rights would set the baseline starting position that for many anthropologists would later serve as a clear point of departure. Herskovits drew a careful distinction between the ideal of promoting peace and equality between peoples and the project to craft and promulgate a universal statement of rights that would carry the imprimatur of what he correctly imagined would develop into a powerful global institution. His cautionary reaction to the UDHR was based on epistemological, empirical, and ethical factors.

First, he argued that the "sciences that deal with human culture" had not developed a methodology for evaluating normative or philosophical principles in the abstract (AAA 1947: 539). Second, he drew a distinction between universal ends and universal means and argued that the record of anthropology could support claims regarding at least some universal ends ("resolv[ing] the problem of subsistence, of social living, [the] political regulation of group life, . . . reaching accord with the Universe and satisfying . . . aesthetic drives") but not universal means. "All peoples do achieve these ends," he argued, "[but] [n]o two of them . . . do so in exactly the same way, and some of them employ means that differ, often strikingly, from one another" (1947: 540). And finally, and most forcefully, Herskovits resisted the idea of a UN-sanctioned universal declaration of human rights because no matter how well-intentioned, it would eventually become a powerful doctrine "employed to implement economic exploitation and . . . deny the right to control their own affairs to millions of people over the world, where the expansion of Europe and America has not [already] meant the literal extermination of whole populations" (1947: 540).

Despite this early and dramatic reaction to the UDHR by at least one prominent American anthropologist, in the decades after 1948 anthropologists played almost no role in the development of human rights theory or practice, whether as critics, as scholars, or as activists. Yet this was not unique to anthropology. As Samuel Moyn (2010) has argued, apart from isolated groups of international lawyers and diplomats working to transform the UDHR into international law during the difficult years of the Cold War, a broad movement toward human rights did not occur until well into the 1970s. Thus, human rights was simply not available to anthropologists during this period as either a topic for research and analysis or as a mode for expressing solidarity with vulnerable populations. Even when the anthropologist David Marbury-Lewis and his wife Pia Marbury-Lewis cofounded Cultural Survival, Inc. as an NGO dedicated to the survival of indigenous cultures through political advocacy, education, and public awareness programs, they did so in order to bring attention to the "survival of specific tribal societies or ethnic minorities throughout the world" (Clay 1982: 1). "Human rights," or even "indigenous rights," were only later given a more significant role by Cultural Survival in the explanation of its raison d'être.

But by the mid-1980s, the incipient human rights movement was gaining momentum, with profound implications for anthropology. Scholars were becoming much more actively involved in the development and promotion of indigenous rights, a discourse whose rapid emergence at the time was best symbolized by the "Indigenous and Tribal Peoples Convention," established in 1989 by the UN International Labor Organization. At the same time, as the Cold War gave way to the period of the post–Cold War, the world experienced nothing less than a human rights revolution, albeit one that was confined to spheres such as the transformation of international development, the field of transitional justice, and the development of the normative blueprints that guided societies (like South Africa) in the midst of transition.

At least for some anthropologists, the newfound prominence of human rights provided the rationale for confronting the legacy of Herskovits's 1947 Statement. Within the AAA, this move culminated in the establishment of a permanent Committee for Human Rights (1995), which began work on a document that would definitively repudiate the Statement and firmly establish anthropology as a central academic and professional node for the promotion of human rights worldwide. The resulting "Declaration on Anthropology and Human Rights" (1999), which, unlike the 1947 Statement, was adopted by a majority vote of the general AAA membership, makes the argument that anthropologists have an obligation to promote human rights, particularly the putative "generic right to realize [a people's] capacity for culture" (AAA 1999). And in a series of high profile interventions, the AAA subsequently acted within this new mandate, writing letters on behalf of victims of human rights abuses, lobbying governments for better treatment of indigenous peoples, and sponsoring public education initiatives that were directed toward promoting an anthropological vision of human rights.[6]

At the same time that some anthropologists were working more actively to integrate human rights promotion into their research and writing, something else important was happening that would shape the extent to which anthropology would later contribute to the broader understanding of human rights as law, politics, and moral practice.

Throughout the 1990s and 2000s, anthropologists turned to human rights as a problem for ethnographic research and anthropological theory. Human rights had become a key "global assemblage" (Ong and Collier 2005) that demanded close anthropological scrutiny.

Anthropologists realized that the questions—ethnographic, ethical, political—raised by the "sea-change in global politics" had implications that went far beyond particular field sites or disciplinary trends. Scholars shifted, sometimes in the field itself, to document and then critically evaluate the various dimensions of this new global assemblage, including the pressure to ground state-making in the language of human rights (Wilson 2001); the capacity of local activists to theorize human rights in their own terms (Goodale 2008a; Speed 2008); the ways in which human rights ideology intersected with textual and bureaucratic practices (Riles 2000); the politics of human rights NGOs in the midst of national trauma (Tate 2007); the tensions between cosmopolitan aspirations and the protection of national cultures (Merry 2006a); the history of the international indigenous rights movement (Niezen 2003); the difficulties in translating human rights language into local categories of justice and national development (Englund 2006); and the aesthetic dimensions of human rights practice as a form of public history making (Slyomovics 2005), among others.

What this meant was that anthropologists now had a dual orientation to human rights. On the one hand, many anthropologists viewed their discipline as having a clear, and perhaps unique, role to play in the promotion of human rights and in the "expan[sion] [of] the definition of human rights within an anthropological perspective" (AAA 2001). But on the other hand, other anthropologists viewed their contributions to human rights from a critical distance; the orientation to the goals of the broader human rights movement was at most agnostic, and the immediate focus was on recasting the study of human rights as an emergent, and increasingly urgent, task for the anthropology of law.

The importance of this burgeoning area of ethnographic research was signaled by the publication of a trio of edited volumes of ethnographic essays that collectively marked a historic turning point in the anthropology of human rights. Wilson's *Human Rights, Culture and Context* (1997), Cowan, Dembour, and Wilson's *Culture and Rights* (2001), and Wilson and Mitchell's *Human Rights in Global Perspective* (2003), surveyed the results of anthropological research on the human rights revolution that began to unfold over the preceding decade based on case studies from a wide range of countries and ethnographic contexts.[7]

What these volumes did more than anything else was to set a research agenda for anthropologists for the next decade by emphasizing the role of ethnography in studying the emergence of human rights as both a category of law and mode of what might be described as the "politics of aspiration," that is, a form of political action that is grounded in the normative ethics of the "yet to come." Subsequent contributions of anthropology to the broader understanding of human rights were guided in part by this research agenda. As we will see below, these contributions can be grouped into four distinct areas.

## Human Rights and Its Networks

After the end of the Cold War, new networks appeared on the global landscape—financial, political, social, and legal (Castells 1996). Because of the rapid emergence of human rights promotion and its integration into preexisting channels of international and transnational development, it was not surprising that anthropologists found it necessary—yet again—to "study up" (Nader 1972). In addition, anthropologists of law had to learn how to study sideways in order to capture ethnographically the extent of the new human rights networks and what they revealed about the production of law both within and beyond the international system.[8]

An early and influential contribution to the study of human rights networks was Annelise Riles's *The Network Inside Out* (2000), her ethnography of the role of Fijian human rights technocrats and activists before and at the UN Fourth World Conference on Women in 1995 in Beijing. What she shows is that the idea of human rights—or, in this case, the idea of women's rights as human rights—is produced and promoted as much through the artefacts of institutional life as through the legal knowledge practices that are intended to implement human rights instruments like the Convention on the Elimination of All Forms of Discrimination Against Women (CEDAW) "by all appropriate means and without delay."

She also takes up the question of the human rights network as a sociolegal form that is imbued with a particular ontological ideology, one through which the network takes on a life of its own apart from the artefacts it produces. As she puts it, writing critically, human rights networks have come to be seen as "systems that create themselves," as socio-legal forms whose "existence is a good in itself" (2000: 173). Riles's study unpacks the pretensions and hidden agendas behind this human rights network ideology and in the process develops a model for how to study these networks from the "inside out," instead of taking their claims to promote and instantiate international law at face value.[9]

Other anthropologists have tracked the ways in which human rights networks became interpretative cultures through which orthodox accounts of human rights—for example, those expressed through declarations and covenants—were translated between, and in between, the global and the local. Sally Engle Merry (2006b), for example, developed the theoretical concept of human rights "vernacularization" to describe the intermediate discursive spaces in which legal "knowledge brokers" mediated human rights between and among different cultural and legal worlds. By "mapping the middle," Merry offered an ethnographic analysis that differed markedly from conventional accounts of how power and influence shape the development of new forms of international and transnational law. Moreover, as she also did in her book *Human Rights and Gender Violence* (2006a), she showed that the process of human rights vernacularization produced both new knowledge and new (and often contested) identities, as knowledge brokers from below confronted multiple and conflicting demands to interpret human rights in different ways to serve different interests.

Finally, anthropologists also documented the emergence of yet another kind of human rights network: the web of professional forensic scientists who developed the tools of mass atrocity investigation that could be used to reveal "buried secrets" (Sanford 2003). Nevertheless, the ethnography of these professional networks of human rights scientists—for example, the work of the Equipo Argentino de Antropología Forense (EAAF)—demonstrated that the intention to deploy the tools of science to uncover the truth, bring justice to victims, and create the conditions in which social reconciliation can take place, is problematic on a number of different levels.

For example, Adam Rosenblatt's (2015) ethnography of mass atrocity investigations in different parts of the world explores the way that alternative conceptions of death and the treatment of dead bodies come together to frustrate the abstracted mission of forensic human rights investigations since the manner in which people conceive of death has important implications for the ways in which the goal of justice can (and cannot) be pursued. In his ethnographic study of exhumations of two mass graves in a Spanish village, Francisco Ferrándiz (2013) takes up yet a different dimension to the rise of professional human rights investigation networks: the ways in which states, which often have an ambiguous relationship to past atrocities, turn to professional investigation teams as a form of "human rights outsourcing." In so doing, the state distances itself from the historical implications of crimes committed in its name and uses the rhetoric of international expertise to avoid the burden of accounting for these crimes and taking responsibility for the necessarily burdened process of public reckoning.

## Moral Creativity in the Practice of Human Rights

From the mid-2000s, anthropologists of human rights broadened the ethnographic scope from the earlier focus on "culture and rights" to encompass the entire sweep of human rights practices (see Goodale and Merry 2007). This work was notable both for the fact that ethnographic studies on human rights had been conducted by then across a wide range of regional, cultural, and transcultural contexts, and for the fact that the ethnography of human rights practices provided for the first time a fine-grained account of the paradoxical centrifugality at the heart of the post–Cold War human rights revolution. Human rights orthodoxy was structurally hostile to multiplicity—doctrinal, cultural, interpretive. The entire thrust of human rights activism was meant to shape social practices, state compliance, and moral ideology so that a global culture of human rights could take root. The "power of human rights," as the political scientists Risse, Ropp, and Sikkink (1999) described it, was the power to bring the full weight of international and transnational human rights advocacy to bear on states and societies so that domestic change could occur within a relatively narrow band of normative boundary markers.

At a conceptual level, Annelise Riles (1998) had already pointed to the tensions inherent in encapsulating the universal within well-defined limits—"infinity within the brackets" was her memorable way of capturing this dilemma. But it took a systematic ethnography of human rights practices to develop for the true scope of the paradox to become apparent. The more hegemonic human rights became at the level of everyday life, the greater was the diversity in human rights practices—the center did not, and could not, hold. Across this diversity, anthropologists showed that human rights practice could be fruitfully thought of a form of moral practice, one that was creative, potentially emancipatory, and more than anything else, marked by uncertainty.

For example, in his ethnography of the "moral landscapes" of villages in China's Sichuan province, John Flower (2009) describes the ways in which locals appropriated the language of human rights to negotiate the terms of development with the state. After the state had rezoned the region to allow for hydropower construction and the use of construction brokers who depended on the kind of structural corruption that has accompanied much of China's rise amidst its "age of ambition" (Osnos 2014), locals opposed to dam construction created a hybrid discourse that identified human rights with the morally righteous concept of "popular socialism." This proved to be a powerful weapon and one that could be joined with state policies that—at least formally—targeted corrupt business practices as obstacles to economic growth.

Similarly, Arzoo Osanloo demonstrated in a series of studies the ways in which both local activists *and* the state could creatively adapt the language of human rights to existing moral ideologies as a form of contentious politics. In an ethnography of women's rights activists in Iran (2006a), she documented how women used the mechanism of procedural reforms of the country's family law courts to expand the boundaries of rights subjectivity not against, but in relation to, the ideals of Islamic republicanism that had evolved since the 1979 revolution. But at the same time, the Iranian state was also finding creative ways to appropriate human rights imperatives to promote an image of itself as merciful, cosmopolitan, and an exemplar of Islamic justice (2006b). After the Iranian government announced a last-minute cancellation of a planned death sentence, it argued that the act was an expression of a uniquely Islamic conception of international law in which mercy should be seen as a fundamental human right.

And yet, moral creativity within the practice of human rights was not always or usually a form of strategic politics. More commonly, as anthropologists have shown, social actors in the midst of various kinds of struggles absorbed the logics of human rights deeply into existing moral imaginaries and what resulted could challenge the very idea of human rights itself. One of the clearest examples of how the creative encounter with human rights pushed it to its conceptual limits was recounted in Shannon Speed's (2008) ethnography of the production of human rights on the "local terrain." Her study of Zapatista activists and their Good Governance Councils in the decade immediately after the 1994 uprising against the Mexican state revealed the Councils to be laboratories in which indigenous articulations of human and indigenous rights were systematically developed over a number of years. In her description of what resulted, the Zapatista leaders took the profound step of reframing rights so that the "source of rights . . . lies in the actors themselves, who are collectively exercising them" (2008: 167). This organic theory of human rights had the effect of inverting the high-liberal orthodoxy that views each individual as a separate and complete rights-bearer, in which human rights are coextensive with an abstract notion of humanness. Instead, the Zapatista intellectuals and militants located the source of rights in the act of collective resistance against the Mexican state. What resulted was a theory of rights that was contingent, social, and performative.

Finally, the ethnography of the practice of human rights showed the ways in which international law and transnational legal discourse could be creatively deployed as a provocative expression of "war by other means" (Curtis 2014). In her study of contemporary "postconflict" Northern Ireland, Jennifer Curtis found that the different sides readily embraced human rights—both institutionally and discursively—as a way to gain ground on rivals and continue to prosecute the conflict through what might be called strategic moral positioning. In the process, even as the so-called postconflict years passed, ethnic and class divisions in certain cases actually deepened because of, not despite, the dominance of human rights as the pervasive rubric for peace building and community reconciliation.

## The Politics of Aspiration and the Limits of Human Rights

In her ethnographic analysis of the international Permanent Peoples' Tribunal (PPT), Sandra Brunnegger (2016) examines the ways in which legal knowledge and identity are produced through the stylized procedures of an indigenous rights forum that lacks international jurisdiction and powers of enforcement. The PPT is a nonstate forum founded in Italy in 1979 to conduct nonbinding inquiries into human rights violations committed against collectivities, especially those felt to be invisible to the international community. Because of its nature as an essentially symbolic legal institution, the PPT brings into sharp relief yet another general aspect of human rights promotion that anthropologists have carefully documented: the fact that the articulation of grievances in the language of human rights is deeply aspirational yet can be morally distant, even as it formally invokes past harms in the process of justice seeking. This tension between justice claim-making and a language of human rights that is "filled up with new social imaginaries [and] utopian visions" (2016: 142), as Brunnegger argues, is only partly resolved at the end of the PPT legal process: testimony is heard from many witnesses and victims; a distinguished jury (which in this case included a Nobel Prize laureate) considers the evidence; and, finally, an extensive judgment is rendered that finds fault and outlines a recommended course of corrective action.

But the judgment, which found more than thirty multinational corporations guilty of violating a swath of human rights standards in their operations in Colombia (with the collusion of both the Colombian and U.S. governments), had no effect whatsoever on corporate behavior in Colombia and the judgment itself received very little media notice outside Colombia. Yet as Brunnegger's study shows, the anthropology of human rights forces us to reconsider dominant notions of enforceability, social change, compliance, and even justice itself. This is because in the case of the PPT, subtle impacts were observed among the participants in the tribunal, if only because it provided a mechanism through which victims of corporate exploitation in Colombia could participate in the articulation of "new sources of legitimacy [and] accountability" (142).

But in other cases, the limits of human rights as a latter-day "weapon of the weak" (Scott 1985) have been exposed by anthropologists, with more troubling implications for the possibilities for social change and political restructuring. For example, in his ethnography among women in Karachi's ready-to-wear export garment industry, Kamran Asdar Ali (2010) examines what happened when grassroots activists within factories, inspired by transnational movements, introduced human rights language into their struggles for better working conditions. As Ali argues, although this transformation of the gender, social, and labor conflict raised the stakes and brought attention to the workers' claims, it also had the effect of suppressing the agency of women by reframing their individual experiences within an abstracted model of both exploitation and confrontation that could not capture the nuances of important cultural values like family honor and respect.

In another critical series of accounts (2009, 2013), Lori Allen confronts the impact on political agency and the experience of suffering that two decades of human rights activism has wrought within the occupied Palestinian territories. Allen points to the ways in which people under conditions of long-term physical and emotional duress are forced to turn to the language of human rights as a "politics of immediation" (2009), that is, the demand to call attention to particular kinds of suffering as an essential component of broader—and morally ambiguous— political projects. What she shows is that the ways in which human rights comes to circumscribe the terms within which a conflict can be mediated has implications not only for victims and their advocates but for all parties involved. Thus, through the emergence of a "shared charade" (2013), people and institutions in the midst of protracted social conflict learn over time to play parts in a series of moral, political, and legal performances that are expected of them. Eventually, as the roots of the conflict go even deeper, the performance of these roles within the drama of human rights becomes a kind of professionalized public spectacle that elides the lived trauma of occupation, pushing further into the distance any hope for a resolution of the conflict through structural transformation.[10]

And finally, another important anthropological critique of the limits of human rights is Harri Englund's (2006) study of how the structure of national development in Malawi was deeply altered by the ascendency of human rights as a new and dominant discourse for economic progress and social emancipation. Englund uses the problem of ethnolinguistic translation as a window into how concepts embedded in human rights orthodoxy can float problematically within a cultural and historical context—like postcolonial Africa—in which ideas about resistance, social justice, and collective action are central to national identity. For example, Malawian elites pushed for "human rights" to be translated in the Chichewa language as *ufulu wachibadwidwe*, which Englund renders as "the freedom one is born with" (2006: 51). The problem, according to Englund, is that putting the emphasis on "freedom" within national policies led to a series of unintentional cultural consequences and moral dead ends that did not add up to an effective response to the country's manifold economic and social needs.

Rather than suggesting a new compact between citizens and the state in which individual and collective action from below entails reciprocity and accountability from the state, *ufulu wachibadwidwe* was widely taken by people as a novel and ambiguous way to understand human nature, one that put a premium on individual choice that bordered on egoism. Englund examines some of the more publicly debated expressions of this new "freedom," including the fact that schoolteachers reported that children who had been taught the importance of *ufulu wachibadwidwe* refused to do homework and that women adopted new clothing styles that challenged traditional and conservative mores.

But regardless of where these manifestations of a newly free Malawi were ultimately headed, the real problem, according to Englund, was that they were clearly not pointing to a new form of collective, rights-claiming agency, one that could ground the kind of radical economic and social transformation that the country desperately needed. In what might be thought of as the dark side of vernacularization, Englund's ethnography of human rights reveals a process of "disempowerment through translation" (2006: 57): poor Malawians—newly self-constituted as vaguely and unpredictably "free"—were for that very reason not able to confront their conditions of vulnerability as citizens entitled to specific forms of redress and reallocation by the state.

## The Ethnographic Political Economy of International Law

The final area through which anthropologists have contributed to the wider understanding of human rights is the most incipient as a research domain but also arguably the most potentially far-reaching. As we have seen, the period of the post–Cold War was a time of liminal possibility in the longer history of human rights. If Moyn and other revisionist historians are correct and the 1970s was indeed the moment when the human rights movement first gained momentum as a form of utopian politics, then it wasn't until after the dissolution of the constraining logics of the Cold War that this momentum came to reshape the global landscape.

However, equally important to understanding the broader implications of the liminal period of the post–Cold War for the history of human rights is the fact that such periods are always by definition temporary; they mark the passage from one epoch to another. The emergence of the new epoch is signaled when the conditions of possibility lessen; hierarchy (of all kinds) reemerges; and vestiges of preexisting power structures reassert themselves anew, sometimes violently (see Goodale 2013b). For purposes of human rights, a growing body of literature has taken up this question and the evidence so far suggests that the liminal period of the post–Cold War has ended. The task, therefore, is to characterize the state of human rights now that the period that saw the emergent utopia of the 1970s later become a "sea-change in global politics" has given way to a new one.[11]

As they did in the 1990s, anthropologists have begun to examine this more recent shift. What is emerging are the outlines of what might be described as an ethnographic political economy of human rights, one that interrogates the broader—largely economic—forces that have prevented a globalizing "culture of rights" (Cowan, Dembour, and Wilson 2001: 13) from threatening the fundaments of the "neoliberal world order" (Ferguson 2006). Revealingly, many of these initial studies have focused on the trajectory of indigenous rights promotion in particular countries. As Maria Sapignoli has argued, the relationship between indigenous rights and economic sustainability can take a dark turn into "dispossession in the age of humanity" (2015; see also Sapignoli 2009). It is likely that the reason the ethnography of indigenous rights is proving so illuminating is that indigenous claims to resources, land, and political autonomy offer among the starkest contemporary challenges to the existing state-corporate assemblages that form the warp and woof of global power.[12]

Two thematics will suffice to demonstrate the ways in which anthropologists have begun to uncover the relationship between indigenous and human rights and structures of economic and political power: first, the ethnographic analysis of the role of international legal forums and actors, including the Special Rapporteur on the Rights of Indigenous Peoples; and second, the study of indigenous rights promotion in Southeast Asia, a region where the tensions, contradictions, and underlying vectors of economic power come together to shape the course of human rights promotion in ways that are both highly visible and troubling.

The mandate of the Special Rapporteur on the Rights of Indigenous Peoples was created by the United Nations Human Rights Council in 2001 in order to, among other things, "gather, request, receive and exchange information and communications from all relevant sources, including Governments, indigenous people themselves and their communities and organizations, on violations of their human rights and fundamental freedoms," and then to "formulate recommendations and proposals on appropriate measures and activities to prevent and remedy violations of the human rights and fundamental freedoms of indigenous people" (UN Human Rights Council Resolution 2001/57).

But as Fleur Adcock (2014) has shown, in a comparative ethnographic study of the impact of the Special Rapporteur in Guatemala and New Zealand, the so-called achievements of this new UN office were carefully managed by national leaders working under the close watch of the corporate interests that had the most to lose from the full implementation of binding instruments like International Labor Organization(ILO) Convention 169 (1989) and the promotion of the more recent Declaration on the Rights of Indigenous Peoples (2007). So when the intervention of the Special Rapporteur led to agreements with indigenous peoples in both countries, these were hailed by both sides as milestones in the protection of indigenous peoples through the rapidly emerging body of international jurisprudence.

And yet, Adcock's study demonstrates the importance of examining the gap between progress on "the international stage" and the failure—even, we might say, the impossibility—of countries to implement indigenous rights accords in ways that force structural changes to existing relations of economic power. This is why she draws a distinction between "soft" and "hard" markers of indigenous rights promotion. Soft markers, like support for cultural heritage or even state commitments to undertake bilingual education, allow governments to appear to meet the claims of indigenous rights activists, while at the same time drawing attention away from the fact that hard markers, like land redistribution and political self-determination, will be off the table.

In a study with similar implications, Laurie Medina (2014) analyzes the interplay between hemispheric human rights regimes, the role of the Special Rapporteur, and the persistent ability over time of economic interests, both within and across countries, to manage the "production of indigenous land rights." Her analysis begins with a 1998 petition to the Inter-American Commission for Human Rights on behalf of Mopan and Q'eqchi' Maya of southern Belize. The petition, written by the U.S. legal scholar and indigenous rights advocate S. James Anaya (who would become the second Special Rapporteur a decade later), asked the Commission to issue a ruling requiring the government of Belize to protect indigenous land rights. Its 2004 decision (that is, six years later) was filled with condemnation and the demand that Belize undertake hard markers of rights implementation. It found that Belize had "'fail[ed] to take effective measures to recognize [Mayan] communal property rights to the lands that they ha[d] traditionally occupied and used'" and it "directed Belize to demarcate and title 'the territory in which the Maya people have a communal property right, in accordance with their customary land use practices'" (Medina 2014: 12).

But despite the fact that the Commission's decision "circulated within the Inter-American system, shaping future petitions and decisions to elaborate a hemispheric jurisprudence on indigenous rights" (2014:13), and the fact that the judgment eventually "returned" to Belize and was reaffirmed by the Belize Supreme Court, its directives were never taken seriously by the state. Why not? Because the land in question had long been subject to large-scale logging and oil exploration concessions held by transnational corporations with open access to the Belize government. So seventeen years after the original petition was filed at the Inter-American Commission for Human Rights, and even though the extended legal process did much to "build [ ] a hemispheric jurisprudence on indigenous rights" (15), the fact remains that "the Belizean state has not implemented any of the decisions" (20).

The ethnographic political economy of human rights in Southeast Asia brings the shaping influence of global capital into even sharper relief. Despite having large indigenous populations, none of the countries of the region have ratified ILO 169. Instead, their histories reveal a pattern of state and commercial appropriation of indigenous land for resource exploration and extraction that dates in many cases to the colonial period (see Li 2007, 2010). However, the transnational indigenous rights movement eventually turned its attention to Southeast Asia, where conflicts over land involved logging, mining, rubber, and other transnational extractive industries. A series of studies demonstrates the fact that transnational capital in the region pursued two lines of defense and cooptation: first, by publicly withdrawing opposition to national reforms in favor of indigenous rights while pressuring governments behind the scenes to ensure that new legislation codified land-grabbing practices; and second, by exploiting the divisive potential in the legal concept of "indigenous" in order to create or deepen social conflicts among potential beneficiaries of the new legal protections.

For example, in her research on indigenous land titling in Mindanao, Philippines, Irina Wenk (2014) shows how the legalization of indigenous rights claims provided the means through which the granting of land concessions to extractive industries actually increased in the years after the country's historic Indigenous Peoples' Rights Act (IPRA) was passed in 1997. As Wenk explains, at the time, the transnational indigenous rights community celebrated IPRA as a major triumph for both the Philippines and Southeast Asia more generally. Nevertheless, the ethnography of IPRA almost twenty years later has shown it to be a Trojan horse that has allowed extractive industries to negotiate directly with local land owners, who are now free to transfer land rights as part of broader national policies of "sustainable development."

## Conclusion: The Anthropology of Contemporary World-Making

In their "revisiting" of the origins of human rights, the Finnish scholars Miia Halme-Tuomisaari and Pamela Slotte (2015) argue that the contemporary narrative of human rights is marked by a fundamental tension. In both academic studies and in international policy making, the ever-present push is to naturalize the ways in which the origins, legitimacy, and meaning of human rights are understood. Drawing on Bruno Latour's analysis of the history of scientific discoveries, Halme-Tuomisaari and Slotte explain (2015: 4) that the "textbook narrative" of human rights implies that its claims have become "cold," that is to say, taken off the table and tightly locked away in a "closed black box" (Latour 1987: 3). Yet in fact, as we have seen in this chapter, the ongoing practice of human rights in all its cultural, political, and epistemological diversity remains very much "hot"—and is getter hotter. Although some contend that the "intense passionate engagement" with the "open-ended and free-floating" (Halme-Tuomisaari and Slotte 2015: 3–4) debates over human rights is actually a sign of their "endtimes" (Hopgood 2013), the anthropology of human rights suggests a more nuanced appraisal.

In his often misunderstood "Statement on Human Rights," Melville Herskovits worried that a universal statement of human rights would become an instrument of moral imperialism, a normative straightjacket that would come to "deny the right to control their own affairs to millions of people over the world." At it turned out, Herskovits's troubled prophecy of a "world made new," as Eleanor Roosevelt put it (quoted in Glendon 2001: 201), through the moral clarity and institutional power of human rights, was flawed.

From the perspective of 1947, the emergent international governance regime of the United Nations certainly embodied a sweeping vision to remake a broken world through a radical assertion of the concept of human dignity enforced through new legal, political, and economic institutions. In the event, however, two dynamics worked against the global reshaping that Herskovits feared. First, the geopolitical logics of the Cold War suppressed the development of a full-blown international system structured by human rights norms. And second, abstract claims of universal human dignity became difficult to reconcile in practice with the reality of subsequent decades in which colonial violence and political persecution continued to haunt the global landscape.

Nevertheless, as we have seen, the end of colonialism and the eventual end of the Cold War marked a turning point after which both international and transnational human rights would transform development, international politics, and the moral grammar of social conflict. But the force of these changes was ultimately tempered by countercurrents of culture, capitalism, nationalism, and the more mesmerizing expressions of religious extremism. As anthropologists have shown, the idea of human rights remains a potent symbol of contemporary world-making. But if it is true, as Victor Hugo once wrote, that "on résiste à l'invasion des armées, on ne résiste pas à l'invasion des idées," recent anthropology suggests that the idea of human rights has been, if not exactly defeated, then at least checked in its advance.

5

# Shaping Inclusion and Exclusion through Law

[A]nalysis of the eighteenth century . . . calls into question
the validity of separating off the law as a whole and placing
it in some typological superstructure. The law when considered as institution . . . or as personnel . . . may very easily be
assimilated to those of the ruling class. But all that is entailed
in "the law" is not subsumed in these institutions. The law
may also be seen as ideology, or as particular rules and sanctions which stand in a definite and active relationship (often
a field of conflict) to social norms; and, finally, it may be seen
simply in terms of its own logic, rules and procedures—that
is, simply *as law*.
—E. P. Thompson, *Whigs and Hunters: The Origin of the
Black Act*

The first two chapters in Part II surveyed the ways in which anthropologists have examined the emancipatory, generative, and empowering
dimensions of law. From justice to human rights, from international
criminal tribunals to grassroots social movements, law has been an
important mechanism through which new categories of political action,
new discourses of resistance, and new modes of institutional development have been forged. At the same time, anthropologists have studied
a series of countervailing currents of law, those that enact power, restrict
or channel action in particular ways, and set limits on the extent to
which real innovation is possible within movements for social, economic, and political change. The question of how these two aspects of
law—the generative and the limiting—relate to each other remains an
open and contested one. At a more basic level of social theory, we know
that periods of social creativity and change are closely related to periods of hierarchy and social structure, that the often violent pressure of
social norms can only be applied for purposes of social control over

the long term if they are interrupted regularly by temporary moments of challenge, social liberation, even chaos. Thus, it might be said that law-as-agency and law-as-regulation are similarly interdependent, that they express a deeper dialectical logic of social control and resistance through which societies accommodate their own ongoing internal contradictions—at least for a time.

This chapter explores the anthropology of one side of this dialectic: law in its register as a mode of regulation. One could argue that regulation, broadly defined, is simply one among several characteristics of law, that "regulation" is just another way of describing the force of the "logic, rules and procedures" that E. P. Thompson believed marked out law in its purest form—law *as law*. But this chapter will consider the relationship between law and regulation somewhat differently. As we will see, the contemporary anthropology of law has revealed the extent to which the boundaries of law have come to intersect with the logics of broader political economic systems. This is a coalescence of governance, subjectivity, financial circulation, and migration that depends upon the legal protection of certain social categories and the suppression of others, the legal construction of nature in ways that facilitate its commodification, and the legal management of risk as a form of capital accumulation. In this sense, law enables a range of practices and structures by defining the limits of what is possible within a "generalized capitalist system" (Li 2010: 400)—and, therefore, what is not possible. Thus, law as a logic of regulation should be understood as a way of shaping the inclusions and exclusions that have come to define much of what we experience in contemporary life.

As we will see, anthropologists have tracked these inclusions and exclusions across an extensive empirical range. This chapter focuses on four key developments in the literature. First, it surveys studies of the way the law has been used to define nature, to delineate its value for the market, and to create new property regimes that can be used to enforce rights to nature, ideas, even the human body itself. The problem of the relationship between law and "things" (Pottage and Mundy 2004) is only partly a question of "legal fabrication"—how legal categories both construct things and regulate them at the same time. Rather, there is also a more ominous side to the process through which "legal chains of reference" (Latour 2004; 96; see also Latour 1999) divide up the "natural world" (a concept that is itself partly a legal fabrication) into that which deserves to be reduced to "institutional artefacts" (Pottage 2004: 11) and that which does not. As we will see more fully below, this working of law upon the very substance of life can under certain conditions lead to the emergence of what the Norwegian anthropologist Marit Melhuus (2012) has described as the "sorting society" (*sorteringssamfunnet* in Norwegian): the use of the law to sort people into categories that correspond to notions of a human ideal that carries echoes of past practices of eugenics and legalized racial discrimination.

Next, the chapter explores the ways in which anthropologists have studied the relationship between law, value, and values. Much of this work has intersected with some of the leading edges of the broader discipline of anthropology, including the anthropology of global finance, transnational and international networks, and international institutions. Increasingly, the law is being used to regulate financial markets that are also spaces through which cultural and religious values are promoted and protected. New financial instruments, new theories of economic relations, and new "spatialities of debt" (Peebles 2012) all depend on the creative use of law as a tool of regulation. At the same time, law is deeply involved in regulating value in other ways. As we will see, within some of the world's most influential international institutions, struggles have taken place over which values should be promoted through institutional policy—for example, economic independence or respect for human rights—and how these choices will be implemented through legal regulations.

The chapter will then reverse the focus of the lens, to consider how the mechanisms of law regulate the subject. Here, the process of inclusion and exclusion is critical. This is particularly clear in cases of cultural conflict, for example, within the conflict over the Islamic headscarf in France and in cases in which what might be called "emergent subjectivities" meet up against legal limits that are meant to enforce dominant cultural boundaries. Anthropological studies of the rapidly evolving LGBT movement, the regulation of migration, and the role of law in defining and parsing subjects of historical oppression, highlight these tensions.

From this subject's eye view, the chapter then moves back out to examine the ways in which the law regulates collective belonging: Which groups are legitimate? Which collectives deserve legal protection? Who deserves to belong to a nation and who doesn't? Which categories of labor should receive legal protection and which should be suppressed? Which groups of displaced people should be forced to live in "zones of non-law" (Makaremi 2008) and which groups should be re-placed within zones of legal inclusion? And which groups should be considered by the law as "dangerous others" in a historical conjuncture in which citizenship, and perhaps collective belonging more generally, has been "re-culturalized" (Eckert 2008b: 7)?

The chapter concludes by returning to the broader question of how legal regulation is related to mutually constitutive processes of inclusion and exclusion. This provides an opportunity to take up from a different angle the concluding remarks on the exercise and rule of law from E. P. Thompson's study of the Black Act of 1723. Thompson's reflections on the relationship between law's logics, power, and violence provide unlikely building blocks for a theoretical framework that organizes recent anthropological studies of regulatory assemblages and the role of law in the "constitution of the social" (Pottage and Mundy 2004).

## Regulating Nature, Property, and "Life Itself"

In her ethnography of "bioprospecting" in Mexico, Cori Hayden (2003) examines the development of novel regimes of legal regulation that give multinational pharmaceutical companies access to potentially lucrative new drugs in exchange for royalties that are meant to preserve biodiversity by commoditizing it. At the same time, these new forms of legal regulation are meant to empower indigenous peoples by making them economic managers of their lands' potentially valuable resources. The complex assemblage she studied was comprised of large multinational corporations, plant biologists and other academic researchers from Mexico's elite National Autonomous University, a diverse group of plant collectors and merchants, government officials who often had conflicting interests in promoting the initiative, and an equally diverse group of indigenous leaders and institutions that had been created to participate in the bioprospecting project.

Hayden argues that bioprospecting in Mexico took place against a backdrop of developments in international and national law that set the stage for new forms of legal regulation. These regulations sought to alter the traditional boundaries between what could and could not be converted into forms of intellectual property. The central tension in Hayden's analysis is between those who argue that the use of law to commodify nature threatens the "capitalization of life" itself (2003: 37; citing to Aoki 1998 and Shiva 1993) and those, many from within Mexico's indigenous communities, who argue that the "*idiom* of intellectual property ... [can be] used in many different ways ... to imagine how native and indigenous resource holders might become new kinds of participants or rights-holders in a so-called global knowledge economy" (2003: 37; emphasis in original).

The "capitalization of life" is conceptualized as a sinister new expression of a broader pattern of neoliberal governance through which biopolitical control through law is asserted even over the building blocks of life itself—DNA (see Rabinow 1999). At the same time, as Hayden explains, the use of intellectual property law to empower indigenous people in the Global South can be seen to have innovative and counter-hegemonic potential. As she puts it, "[w]hy, the question goes, should corporate innovation be the only form recognized and granted protection under intellectual property law? Should not traditional knowledge, folklore, artisan works, and medicinal plants (among other things) be worthy of protection for its 'original' holders" (2003: 37)?

Despite these theoretical possibilities, Hayden's ethnographic study demonstrates the limits of a model through which local empowerment is achieved in the long term through the commodification of indigenous knowledge practices. As she argues, the "Lockean calculus" at the heart of contemporary intellectual property law—"nature + intellectual labor = value" (2003: 40)—promises to indigenous peoples a new strategy of inclusion at the same time as it ushers in new forms of legal, political, and economic *exclusion*. As Hayden puts it, the ethnographic story of what happens when nature has "gone public" is still unfolding. One thing is clear, however—the economic interests of the large pharmaceutical companies who hold out promises of economic and social inclusion as a reward for access to a commodified nature. As one Mexican biotechnologist explained to Hayden, "[w]hat companies want is a genomic database or databank ... they want material at their fingertips, just in case, a build-up of natural capital" (2003: 236).

In her wide-ranging ethnographic and critical study of intellectual property, Rosemary Coombe (1998) focuses on the commodification of "culture" itself—how culture gets made in "commercial landscapes" (23) in ways that challenge conceptions of personhood, agency, difference, and marginalization. What her research reveals is the polyvalence of "culture" within a broader historical context in which legal regulation marks sites of colonial domination, resistance, and appropriation. As she argues in a key section, the struggle over culture and Aboriginal Title in Canada is a struggle about inclusion and exclusion. Particular legal definitions of culture—those that fit within dominant modes of appropriation—bring native peoples in Canada within the protections of the state; other definitions, especially those articulated and developed by native peoples themselves, challenge existing cultural and intellectual property laws and are therefore ignored or denied. As Coombe puts it, "[f]or Native peoples in Canada, culture is not a fixed and frozen entity that can be objectified in reified forms that express its identity, but an ongoing living process that cannot be severed from the ecological relationships in which it lives and grows" (1998: 246).

But there is also an important strategic dimension to this struggle over how the law regulates culture. The willingness, even necessity, of native peoples in Canada to fight for Aboriginal Title is a recognition that the law shapes conflict in terms that are in large part defined by "the colonizers" (1998: 246; quoting from Todd 1990: 148). This means that the struggle over different understandings of culture through law is already, in a sense, prefigured. Nevertheless, despite the fact that legal categories are capable of accommodating certain conceptions of culture and not others, the encounter carries the potential to reverberate beyond native communities themselves. As Coombe argues, there is also an important lesson for majority Canadians in the struggle over Aboriginal Title. As she puts it, the "abstraction, commodification, and separation of land from people's social lives and from the cultural forms in which we express meaning and value as human beings living in communities represent only a peculiar, partial, and limited way of dividing up the world" (1998: 246–247).

As Marit Melhuus shows, in her ethnography of the implementation of Norway's 2003 Biotechnology Act, other ways of "dividing up the world" through legal regulation reflect a problematic understanding of the world by judges and policy makers "that is both real and imagined" (2012: 112). Norway's law takes a strict position on the relationship between biotechnology and the reproduction of family—egg donation and surrogate motherhood are prohibited by the law and anonymity is not allowed for the procedures of artificial insemination that are permitted. Melhuus argues that these fine distinctions in legal regulation are an attempt to "project[ ] socio-cultural values deemed central to Norwegian society" through the body of law on reproductive technologies. These values "revolve fundamentally around kinship and the relationship between individual and society . . . [and] concern notions of personhood, parenthood and family formation as well as equality and choice" (2012: 113).

However, the implementation of the Biotechnology Act in Norway also revealed something else: a troubling convergence through which the "growing capacit[y] to control, manage, engineer, reshape, and modulate the very vital capacities of human beings as living creatures" (91; citing Rose 2006: 3) was used as the basis to sort potential life into categories of desirable and undesirable. What resulted, according to Melhuus, was a society in which selection based on a set of "socio-cultural values deemed central to Norwegian society" could be justified on ethical and medical grounds. Melhuus's ethnography shows that the debates over the emergence of a "sorting society" in Norway evoked memories of eugenics projects from the past and the more ominous associations with racial selection and genocide. Melhuus quotes a young politician from a religious party who argued that the "biopolitics of the Socialist Left Party can create a sorting society that is reminiscent of Hitler's Germany" (2012: 89).

As the debate evolved into a more charged set of encounters, it became detached from its origins in the legal regulation of biotechnology to intertwine with deeper conflicts in Norwegian society over the relationship between the individual and a particular vision of the collective. The role of the law in shaping the fundamental paradox of Norway's social democracy, in which the abstract subject of "human rights" can be used as the basis for denying agency to *specific* humans, was reinforced through the "persuasive power of the sorting society" (104). As she explains, the use of biotechnology for ethical purposes is based on "an idea of society to which Norwegians do adhere, while simultaneously glossing over some of the major controversies and inconsistencies that these technologies entail. . . . The sorting society is used to summon universal values that are deemed central to Norwegian society" (104) by encouraging selection of human life based on choices deemed ethically warranted rather than a "systematic selection" based on group characteristics. Nevertheless, as Melhuus's study reveals, such nuanced sociolegal distinctions can become confused when legal regulation becomes the basis of the "politics of life itself" (Rose 2006).

## Regulating Value(s)

Anthropologists have also examined the ways in which law has been used to define and regulate value and to develop particular values while suppressing or excluding others. Much of this work has intersected with some of the major contemporary currents in the broader discipline of anthropology, including the anthropology of global finance, transnational and international networks, and international institutions. As David Graeber (2001) demonstrated, in his study of the ideology of value both within and beyond anthropology, *how* value itself comes to be defined and deployed reflects underlying political and moral imperatives. These imperatives often take the form of legal regulations that combine the social and discursive power to include and exclude with the political and economic power of sanction, economic redistribution, and governmental surveillance. More broadly, the anthropological study of the intersections between legal regulation, value, and values lends support to Graeber's efforts to articulate a culturally synthetic theory of value that reconceptualizes it as a basic model through which humans construct and contest meaning.[1]

In his study of Islamic banking practices and the creation of alternative modes of exchange, Bill Maurer shows how legal regulations and new financial instruments depend on a value described as "laterality": that is, a form of moral practical reason that "exploit[s] the gap between representation and reality" that is present in understandings of money and financial transactions (2005: xiv). He argues that the study of Islamic banking practices and alternative local currencies reveals the ways in which different conceptions of value can oscillate between and among different logics of legal regulation as a function of "to-one-sideness" reasoning—the capacity, even the necessity, for financial practices to be justified by thinking that amounts to a "species of casuistry" about the relationship between representation and reality.

For example, his ethnography examines the case of the Ithaca HOUR, a local alternative currency that began circulating in the upstate New York university town in 1991. As Maurer explains, "HOURS are notes printed on natural fiber paper (originally made from cat-tail pulp) and come in six denominations. . . . Since 1991 over ten thousand HOURS have been issued, and the total value of all transactions conducted in HOURS since that time is estimated to be around $2 million" (2005: 43). The story of the origins of the Ithaca HOUR alternative currency exchange are bound up with negotiations with the U.S. Internal Revenue Service (IRS) over legal regulations, an underlying local culture of progressive politics, and the relatively comfortable socioeconomic status of many participants in the exchange, who inhabit a world in which "Ithaca is ten square miles surrounded by reality" (2005: 42).

As he does with Islamic banking, Maurer examines debates over the Ithaca HOURS that use examples of legal regulation, among others, to make neat and tidy divisions between real and artificial transactions and between currency supposedly backed by something solid (like gold) and alternatives that are backed by "gimmicks" (2005: 55). He argues that the relationship between legal regulation and systems of parallel reasoning cannot be reduced to a distinction between values that can be fixed in time and space and those that cannot. As he puts it, the anthropology of alternative forms of exchange demonstrates the necessity of understanding them—as well as those that they are framed against—through their movement "*between* the various worlds they inhabit and construct" (57; emphasis added).

In his analysis of the legal regulation of debt and debtors, Gustav Peebles (2012) similarly explores the ways in which people move within and between categories of value that determine who will be allowed to access the law in order to be eventually reintegrated into social and economic life and who will be forever excluded. As Peebles puts it, the comparative anthropological study of debt and bankruptcy regimes leads to the question "Who is . . . permitted, and indeed encouraged, to disappear into social death, while others are ritually cleansed and returned to the social?" (2012: 429). He compares the rise and fall of debtors' prisons in the nineteenth century with the dynamic contemporary spatialities of debt that reflect values of community belonging, moral forgiveness, and economic necessity. At the outer limits, the boundaries of legal debt regulation define the "very bounds of community itself," since laws that provide for rehabilitation only "extend[ ] as far as social power holds sway" (2012: 440).

Peebles shows that the values constructed by the various debt-forgiveness regimes operate at two critical levels. On the first, legal regulations allow wealthier debtors to exercise a relatively radical "freedom from credit and debt relations" altogether by moving wealth into inaccessible offshore accounts or, in the more extreme circumstances, going into exile by passing into a "ritual sanctuary," a "high-priced zone of debt-evasion" that is only open to the few who can afford it (2012: 440). But these outliers are kept few in number by legal regulations so that the "credit/debt system as we know it [does not] break down" (440).

At the second level, the extension of regulations that create a system of debt forgiveness also come with an "accompanying surveillance regime" (444). In this way, the vast majority of debtors are kept closely bound to the community whose survival is equally closely linked to the perpetuation of a credit-debt system that must be kept intact at any cost. As Peebles argues, the construction of values like forgiveness, thrift, and social responsibility through the differential application of legal regulations is ultimately linked to the survival of global capitalism itself.

If Maurer's research examines the way legal regulations shape oscillations between competing systems of values, while Peebles's study explores why legal regulations maintain multiple competing systems of values at the same time, Galit Sarfaty's (2012) ethnographic analysis of the World Bank pursues yet a third problem: the ways in which values are, or are not, translated and contested within international institutions whose legal and political influence shapes global policy and economic development. Where Maurer uses the concept of "lateral reason" to capture the movements and relationships between legal regulation and value systems, Sarfaty accounts for a similar ethnographic phenomenon within the World Bank through the lens of "competing rationalities" (2012: 8).

The specific boundaries across which values are translated within the World Bank are those defined in terms of economic rationality on the one side, and on the other, those defined in terms of human rights. As she explains, these boundaries are not equally thick, or equally high:

Economic knowledge has become dominant within the world of bureaucracies as well as in domestic and international policy making. The Bank is both a producer and an effect of this phenomenon. It has facilitated the global expansion of capital through the mission of poverty reduction but has also mirrored the effects of economic globalization in its bureaucratic practices, for instance through the quantification of many issues that are value-laden and politically contested. (2012: 8–9)

Her study tracked conflicts within the World Bank between policy makers and technocrats who promoted the dominant economic rationality and a much smaller group of primarily lawyers who agitated to have a human rights rationality made part of Bank aid programs and country evaluations and then translated into legal regulations that would oversee the Bank's relationships with donor countries. As Sarfaty observed, human rights advocates within the Bank had to decide whether translation across the boundaries of value systems would lead to qualitative changes. Because of the overwhelming influence of economic rationality at the core of the Bank itself, there was no question but that human rights values would have to be "economized" (2012: 127). But the fear among the translators was that, as a senior Bank official put it, "[human rights] language [could not be] made into economic language without compromising the substance" (127).

In the end, the small group of lawyers did not develop a comprehensive strategy of value translation that could be put into practice through the legal regulations that structure the Bank's programs. Sarfaty's ethnographic narrative provides additional support to findings on the limitations of value translation between regimes of law and culture. As Sarfaty's research shows, when a value system like human rights, which is aligned on the side of change and resistance, is translated "too far into the existing power structure," as Sarfaty puts it (2012: 131), something fundamental is lost.

## Regulating the Subject

From the more abstract spaces of value translation within broader political and institutional economies, anthropologists have also studied the ways in which legal categories regulate at the most intimate of levels—that of the subject. How does law function as a logic of regulation to shape identity? As Eve Darian-Smith has argued, the relationship between legal categories and identity is partly one of marking social boundaries: "how [is] legal distinctiveness . . . drawn, argued, and justified through interpreted histories . . . and mythologized genealogies of certain peoples living in specific terrains[?]" (1999: 20). But law also works at deeper layers of personal meaning to intersect with and bracket basic conceptions of self and other, individual and society. This inside/outside dynamic is one that is often unresolved and closely connected with broader social conflicts that it only partly reflects.

Across a range of interventions, John Bowen has studied and analyzed the inside/outside nature of law through one of the most important of contemporary conflicts: the struggle at the heart of Europe over strands of cultural diversity that appear to challenge well-developed national ideologies of secularism, equality, citizen participation, and liberal individualism (e.g., Bowen 2007, 2010, 2016). The case that symbolized this conflict more than any others was the law of March 15, 2004 in France, which banned the wearing of articles of clothing or other signs that "clearly showed" affiliation with an organized religion. Although the law was content-neutral as to which articles of clothing or religious symbols were banned, the post–September 11, 2001 context in France—and not just in France—had become one in which Muslims faced pressure from both state institutions and "popular" opinion. At issue, according to Bowen (2010), was a fundamental question: Can Islam be French? That is to say, are Islamic forms of subjectivity, moral reasoning, and public debate in France consistent with the French republican ideology of *laïcité*, a term that represents a "philosophy about religion's place in politics and society" (2007: 2).[2]

In Bowen's analysis, the conflict over religious signs in public schools—and in public spaces more generally—involved a complex interrelationship between subject formation and the possibilities of personal expression, debates over how to reconcile integration with cultural autonomy, and perhaps most important, the place of difference within a democratic republic that promotes and regulates what Bowen translates as "the life together" (*la vie commune*) (2007: 249). Yet as Bowen points out, this conflict was not in fact content-neutral. The 2004 law was not a generalized regulation in response to a generalized threat to the tradition of *laïcité*; rather, it was a legal regulation directed against one particular religious sign, the veil, which in French public opinion of the time "had become a symbol of mounting Islamism and decaying social life" (2007: 242). And although prominent supporters of the law argued that it was necessary in order to protect Muslim girls who did not want to wear the veil, it was also true that the law was seen by its critics to violate the personal autonomy of the many schoolgirls who demanded the right to wear it.

Bowen identifies a paradox at the heart of the French veil controversy that has significance for other efforts to use legal regulations to shape identity in terms of national cultural and political ideologies like *laïcité*. The law was ostensibly passed to regulate and enforce a particular form of public identity, one in which individual autonomy and freedom of expression were the bases for full participation in civic life. But to accomplish this, it was necessary to prohibit and suppress the expression of forms of identity that did not fit with the image of secular citizens living together in conditions of republican integration. As he puts it, supporters of the law

> [c]ome[ ] close to saying that an entire class of Islamic forms of reasoning are by their very nature beyond the pale of a common life in France, and that the choices made by women to wear such garments are inadmissible, presumed to reflect unacceptable coercion or a "defect of assimilation." This form of "block thinking" substitutes generalizations across a category of people for an inquiry into the motives of particular individuals. (2010: 196)

Thus, the legal regulation against the veil excluded the expression of some forms of subjectivity in order to permit or include others that were seen to fit within a broader narrative of republican values and a history of disagreement over the role of religion in public life. Bowen concludes his ethnographic analysis of the conflict by arguing that an alternative framework of value pluralism, one more tolerant of expressions of difference in the public sphere, can be found within the traditions of French law itself. This framework would permit a "pragmatics of convergence" (2010: 196) that is actually more consistent with *laïcité* than the more rigid interpretations underpinning the March 2004 law.

But how does legal regulation relate to processes of subject formation and the expression of identity in cases in which the bedrock of supposedly solid national or cultural ideology is being undermined by seismic shifts in public opinion? Or relatedly, how do laws regulate identities that are shaped by transnational cultures that in part transcend more local value systems and in part come into tension with them? As Ryan Thoreson's ethnography of the global LGBT movement reveals (2014), an understanding of the relationship between legal regulation and identity depends upon *both* transnational currents of activism and political pressure and much more localized dynamics of culture, religion, and gender relations.

For example, although the transnational LGBT rights movement he studied has had tremendous success in advancing the cause of sexual rights from the UN to the national legislatures of many countries, the transnational sphere has also been the site of activism—often promoted through religious doctrine—pushing in the opposite direction.[3] The result is that legal regulation has become a key tool for forming sexual identity in ways that both celebrate LGBT rights and empowerment and demonize them at the same time depending on time, place, and circumstances. Thoreson gives a sense of this phenomenon as it occurs on a global scale:

> Homosexuality has been rejected outright by Iranian president Mahmoud Ahmadinejad; labeled "un-African" by presidents Robert Mugabe of Zimbabwe, Sam Nujoma of Namibia, Yoweri Museveni of Uganda, Daniel arap Moi of Kenya, and Julius Nyerere of Tanzania; and deemed contrary to "Asian Values" by the government of Singapore. In the Americas, Australia, and parts of Europe, political leaders similarly invoke national and religious traditions in their opposition to homosexuality and LGBT marriage and adoption. In the North and South alike, governments regularly use debates about sexuality to define national identity, whether

through their insistence on the preservation of a heterosexual order or assertions of tolerance and diversity. (2014: 5)

What is critical to underscore about the case of LGBT rights and identity is the fact that in situations in which the supposedly settled value system is itself undergoing rapid change, the effects for both legal regulation and subjectivity will be equally unsettled. This point is perhaps no better illustrated than by the June 2015 U.S. Supreme Court decision of *Obergefell v. Hodges*, in which a bitterly divided court ruled in a 5–4 decision that same-sex couples in the United States have a fundamental right to marry in all fifty states. As late as 2004, less than a third of Americans supported marriage equality, but by February 2015, a few months before the court decision, 63 percent believed that same-sex marriage should be a constitutional right.

In her ethnography of legal regulations against human trafficking in Italy, Cristiana Giordano argues that the law can be used to shape "both the willed and imposed multiplicity of subject positions" (2008: 588) depending on how those who fall within the scope of the law are characterized. She studied the implementation of a law (Article 18) that gave victims of human trafficking residence permits, but only if they agreed to two conditions: one, to bring a legal action against their perpetrators; and two, that they participate in a government-sponsored program run by religious organizations that promised "rehabilitation" from prostitution.

The content of the rehabilitation programs under Article 18 was diverse, but it focused on re-forming victim subject positions in ways that were consistent with narratives of "redemption and expiation" (2008: 589) derived from Catholic conceptions of the "Italian way of being" female (2008: 589). Through "living in a shelter (usu. run by nuns); professional training in Italian language, cooking, and housekeeping 'Italian style'; [and] elderly care" (2008: 588–589), women who "willed" themselves into the protections of Article 18 were gradually refashioned into "confessional citizens[ ]" capable of performing their new identities despite their "ambivalent inclusion" (2008: 593) into Italian society.

Finally, anthropologists have examined the ways in which legal regulations shape subjectivity instrumentally, as part of deeper histories of colonialism and the projection of racial power. In his study of the legal regulation of Indian-White relations on the Rosebud Reservation in South Dakota, Thomas Biolsi (1995) argues that the role of law has not been sufficiently appreciated for what it can become: a central mode through which structures of power can reach down to the level of the individual and define the terms through which people see themselves and their life possibilities. Among these key structures of power, the state is foremost. As he puts it, "[i]t is not possible to think of subjectivity . . . without seeing law . . . as one of the basic, constitutive axes of social self and other, and it should not be possible to . . . write about any kind of power . . . without bringing in law, and thus the state" (1995: 543–544).

The "power of the state in the medium of the law" (544) expresses itself on the Rosebud Reservation through a pervasive condition of what might be called unstable legal identity. On the one hand, members of the Lakota tribe define themselves through two categories of rights: the right to be exempt from South Dakota state law and the right to exercise jurisdiction over non-Indians on reservation territory. But on the other hand, these categories of rights are viewed with fundamental suspicion by both federal courts and legal scholars, who consider them as "having fundamental contradictions and [of] being incoherent" (545).

As Biolsi explains, the unsettled status of Indian legal identity is the product of its incompatibility with an "industrial capitalist society legally constituted on the basis of formal equality" (545). The result is that federal and state governments (mis-)shape Indian legal identity by preserving Indian rights as an exceptional category of law at the same time as they challenge these rights in court and criticize their application in particular conflicts. This dual working of power through and against categories of Indian legal identity is not an unintended by-product of jurisdictional complexity; rather, it is built into the very fabric of state control. To the extent to which Indian law carves out spaces of action for Native Americans, it provides a means through which they can participate in "larger social formation[ ]" (1995: 558), despite the ongoing realities of grinding poverty and social hopelessness on and beyond the reservation. But to the extent to which Indian law faces continual downward pressure from the very institutions of state power that must ratify it, it represents a "coded denial of experience" (558) that forecloses the possibility of more autonomous alternatives.

## Regulating Collective Identity

To conclude this survey of the ways in which anthropologists have studied and theorized law as a logic of regulation, we move out from the individual to consider the problem of law and collective identity. If the relationship between law and subjectivity is one that involves questions of individual autonomy, agency, and tensions between self and community, the relationship between law and collective identity, by contrast, is one that involves—among others—questions of cultural rights, legitimacy, citizenship, and national security.

As political theorists like Will Kymlicka (1995, 1996) and Duncan Ivison (2002) have shown, the normative move from the individual to the collective is not simply a quantitative one—the legal regulation of the individual writ large. Rather, the normative shift from the individual to the group is a qualitative one in which many of the underlying assumptions, particularly those derived in one way or another from the history of liberalism, are called into question. For purposes of legal regulation, in which the law functions as a logic of inclusion and exclusion, the collective embodies characteristics that challenge many contemporary legal doctrines, from criminal law to human rights.

To take one example within international criminal law, it is the individual that can be found guilty or not guilty of crimes, not the nation, the ethnic group, the political party, the tribe, or the trade. As Gerry Simpson (2007) has argued, the opposing position, that a collective should be liable for crimes within international criminal law, carries strong overtones of the Romantic conception of the *Volk*, collective will, and in its darkest expressions, collective punishment. And for Kymlicka, the predicament of indigenous and minority groups, particularly within liberal democracies, creates basic challenges for the promotion of human rights, the doctrine of equality before the law, and the promotion of antidiscrimination regulations.

In perhaps his most well-known—and controversial—formulation of this dilemma, Kymlicka (1996: 29) argued that apart from "cases of gross and systematic violation of human rights, such as slavery, genocide, torture, or mass expulsions," indigenous and minority groups should be free to engage in "rights violations within the community" without the interference of the state or majority population, if indigenous leaders have a "broad base of support and . . . dissidents are free to leave" (1996: 29). The justification for permitting low-grade violations within collectivities, according to Kymlicka, is the fact that the rights of a fragile and historically oppressed collective take precedence over the rights of particular individuals within these groups.

But just because the law has a difficult time encompassing collectivities within the boundaries of its doctrines does not mean that its regulations do not influence collective identity in powerful ways. Indeed, as we will see in the next chapter, some contemporary collectivities have been created by legal regulations; to paraphrase Malagón Barceló (1961: 4), they were "born beneath the juridical sign." Yet more broadly, the forces of legal regulation, of inclusion and exclusion, often form the grounds on which collective identity must be forged, particularly in cases in which groups struggle for recognition, greater political power, protection from violence, or social legitimacy. Two ethnographies of different conflicts in France illustrate the ambiguous status of law in cases in which collectivities suffer from political persecution, the mistrust of state officials, and cultural isolation.

In her study of *zones d'attente*, or "waiting zones," near France's international borders, including those at the country's international airports, Chowra Makaremi (2008) argues that asylum seekers as a group are constructed by the law as much through emotion as through the analysis of whether or not claimants meet legal criteria in particular cases. The overriding public emotion, according to Makaremi, is one that allows France to open its borders to those who seek the embrace of liberty, equality, and fraternity, but only up to a point. She quotes the former prime minister, Michel Rocard, who memorably said (in 1990) that "France cannot welcome all the world's misery" ("La France ne peut pas accueillir toute la misère du monde") (2008: 81).

As Makaremi's ethnography reveals, once legal and political officials in the *zones d'attente* decided, or rather felt, that the invisible limit to their republican generosity had been reached, those who remained were treated very differently. For them, the waiting areas became, as Makaremi argues, zones of "non-law," spaces in which legal regulations were enforced irregularly and often unjustly, and where legions of humanitarian workers did their best to ameliorate conditions among people whose collective identity had become defined by the fact of their imminent expulsion from French territory.

In her ethnography of the multiplicity of prostitution in Paris, Gwénaëlle Mainsant (2013) shows how agents of legal regulation—in this case, the police—collaborate with subjects of law to produce collective identities that partly reflect social prejudices but also partly create spaces in which legally vulnerable actors can maneuver. As she found, police officers in Paris enforce laws against various activities that are associated with prostitution (which is not illegal *per se*) such as soliciting (*racolage*), human trafficking, and pimping (*proxénétisme*), in terms of a simplistic understanding based on a single image of the "street prostitute" (2013: 485).[4]

But as Mainsant's research shows, there are many categories of workers, brokers, and customers who form discrete underground networks that can diverge quite far from the model assumed by legal regulations and the agents who enforce them. What results is a productive tension between the divergent collective identities from below among sex workers in Paris and the legal and social efforts to maintain a single collective identity from above. As Mainsant argues, identities and categories from below are closely connected with the nature of the work itself in all its diversity. The simplistic category of "prostitute" constructed from above by the police, however, is an "instrumental category" (2013: 489) that can be explained by the exigencies of police procedure filtered through the lenses of prevailing cultural, gender, and even racial stereotypes.

And finally, anthropologists have examined the ways in which the relationship between legal regulations and collective identity is affected by broader histories of armed conflict, the mobilization of propaganda, and the rise of states of exception as a form of governance. In her analysis of the role of legal regulation in the "restructuring of political space" after the September 11, 2001, attacks on the World Trade Center in New York City, Carol Greenhouse (2005) argues that collective identities were altered through the use of legal regulations that embodied discursive shifts intended to justify the expansion of state power well beyond the boundaries of any one threat. For example, the idea that "everything had changed" encouraged people to see themselves as living in unprecedented times in which they confronted unprecedented dangers, when in fact, "the war on terror did not introduce new conditions or consequences *sui generis*, but new political opportunities" (Greenhouse 2005: 197). The remaking of both political and discursive spaces in this way through law eventually led to "[p]rocesses of . . . compression and decompression" that came to "dictate the contours and content of . . . identities . . . including cultural identities" (2005: 203; quoting in part from Cowan, Dembour, and Wilson 2001: 11).

But as Julie Eckert (2008b) argues, in another anthropological study of the relationship between law and collective identity after September 11, 2001, the role of culture itself within these "processes of compression and decompression" has been problematic. In her analysis, the nature of collective belonging underwent a key shift during this period. The role of politics as a mode of agency was replaced by the "re-culturalization of membership" (2008: 7). The legal regulations that comprised the "new security regime" (7) depended upon constructions of the "dangerous other" that measured threat levels by the presence or absence of assumed cultural traits. What resulted was an imprecise instrument that eventually gave way to something much more general—the war on "terror" (not necessarily terrorists), involving "spectral" (Makdisi 2002) antagonists who could, by definition, be anywhere or nowhere. Of course, as Eckert argues, the reculturalization of collective identity into a culture of ghosts had very real consequences. Very quickly, this war on specters became the "foundation for a [global] campaign of investigation, interrogation, confiscation, detention, surveillance, torture, and punishment" (quoting Makdisi 2002: 267).

## Conclusion: The Return of E. P. Thompson

The anthropology of law reveals the consequential ways in which law regulates many aspects of contemporary life. As we have seen, as a key logic of regulation, law shapes understandings of nature (including the nature of life itself); it embodies, and often constructs, the values that society wants to promote (and those that it believes it must suppress); it establishes categories within which individuals imagine empowerment, conceive of resistance, and seek protection; and it often sets the terms within which group identity is legitimated (or marginalized) within broader movements of history, political economy, and social change.

But if anthropologists have demonstrated the diverse ways in which law can—and indeed must—be seen as one of the most important regulatory categories of social life, then it would be useful to conclude this chapter by pushing the matter a bit further to ask how and why law functions in this way. To suggest an answer to these questions, I return briefly to E. P. Thompson's analysis of the Black Act of 1723. At one level, Thompson's study is a social and political history of one of the most notorious laws ever passed. The law, which was pushed through the British parliament without any comment or debate, "creat[ed] at a blow some fifty new capital offences" (1977: 21) for a wide range of violations against property, including poaching animals, cutting down trees, and "sending anonymous letters demanding 'money, venison, or other valuable thing'" (22). The "black" in the Black Act referred to the fact that some poachers in early eighteenth-century Britain took to "blacking" their faces before entering the massive estates of the landed gentry. Indeed, very quickly the scope of the Act was enlarged so that "Blacking might constitute in [itself a] capital offence[ ]" (22).

The standard interpretation of the Black Act had been that it was a simple case of the moneyed and propertied classes using the law as an instrument of class domination; that judges, lawyers, and other legal officials shared the same class affiliation with property owners and so formed a kind of juridical crime syndicate; and that the rural and peasant defendants in the cases brought under the Act suffered yet another historical instance of class oppression legitimated through the mechanisms of governance. And indeed, Thompson's study does support the historical view of the Black Act—it was a nasty piece of legal history, a statute written "in blood" (24), and a turning point in British social and political life in which the class power of the bourgeoisie was reinforced through the "ascendency of the gallows" (23). But at the end of his research, surprising even himself, Thompson was forced to admit something else: on certain occasions, despite all the forces pushing in the other direction, a defendant here and there was found not guilty, or the government withdrew from a case because it could not prove it according to the rules of evidence.

Thompson's explanation of this unexpected finding was that the law contained logics that were independent of any uses to which it was put—

whether on the side of the powerful or on that of the powerless. As he explained:

> On the one hand, it is true that the law did mediate existent class relations to the advantage of the rulers. . . . On the other hand, the law mediated these class relations through legal forms, which imposed, again and again, inhibitions upon the actions of rulers. For there is a very large difference, which twentieth-century experience ought to have made clear even to the most exalted thinker, between arbitrary extra-legal power and the rule of law. . . . The forms and rhetoric of law acquire a distinct identity which may, on occasion, inhibit power and afford some protection to the powerless. . . . [T]he rules and categories of law penetrate every level of society, effect vertical as well as horizontal definitions of men's rights and status, and contribute to men's self-definition or sense of identity. (1977: 264–265; 266–267)

Thus, if the law can and should be understood as a logic of regulation, as this chapter argues, then it is a logic that works to regulate in ways that can only partly be explained through the various intentions and ideologies that are used to justify it. As an ethnographic question, we need not agree with Thompson's normative conclusion that the emergence of law's logics is a "cultural achievement of universal significance" (265) to appreciate the importance of his findings for the anthropology of law. As the studies surveyed in this chapter demonstrate, the law regulates identity, value, and belief in often contradictory ways. But to the extent to which the logics of law constrain power as much as they enable its projection, we must view this paradox (as Thompson did for the eighteenth century) as one that sets the outer limits to exclusion (but also to inclusion), inequality (but also to equality), and injustice (but also to justice).

## PART III

# Law and Identity

# 6

## Law and the Fourth World

Contemporary anthropologists of law have made important contributions to the study of the relationship between indigeneity, international law, and political mobilization. This is partly a legacy of a broader history in which anthropologists took a systematic, often politically engaged, interest in collectivities that would come to be defined as "indigenous" within international legal categories that anthropologists themselves played a role in developing through expert testimony, research, and participation in treaty bodies and international legal commissions. Indeed, as we saw in chapter 4, the study and promotion of indigenous peoples through law was—and to a certain extent continues to be—a major mode through which anthropologists have explored the increasingly important role of international law in defining the terms of political struggle, social change, and collective recognition.

At the same time, anthropologists have also explored the problematic theoretical, historical, and cultural linkages between indigeneity as a concept and social category and the law (see, e.g., French 2004). These linkages have been both a source of empowerment for collectivities that have suffered under the weight of centuries of discrimination and at times a discursive yoke (see Povinelli 2002) that impresses itself unevenly in the zones of "friction" (Tsing 2005) in which conflicts unfold in the contemporary world. After comparing the histories of "ethnicity" and "ethnic group" to "indigenous," Ronald Niezen argues that the latter is unique in important respects:

> A proud Serbian might refer to him- or herself as a Serb, not as an "ethnic Serb" or an "ethnic person." The term "indigenous," however, has been taken a step further. It is not only a legal category and an analytical concept but also an expression of identity, a badge worn with pride, revealing something significant and personal about its wearer's collective attachments. (2003: 3)

And yet the assertion of this category of identity through law has the effect of shaping and defining the very terms of the category itself, so that, as Niezen has shown, indigeneity can become a self-referential form of legal and political expression that can trap those who embrace it within its boundaries. The result is that indigeneity emerged as a powerful organizing principle at a global level at the same time that its legal grounding remained fraught with jurisdictional, institutional, and even philosophical weaknesses.[1] As Niezen explains, "indigenous" is "both a fragile legal concept and the indefinite, unachievable sum of the historical and personal experiences of those . . . who share . . . the notion that they have all been oppressed in similar ways for similar motives by similar state and corporate entities" (2003: 4).

But as Niezen has also cautioned, this tension is not the only one that has shaped the relationship between indigeneity and law. Even if the development of an "international underclass" around a shared imagined history has proven to be a potent tool for mobilization and the creation of transnational solidarity, it has also had to contend with the dilemmas of "third-party representation" (2003: 11). This is yet another example of how dominant populations construct the exotic Other as a form of cultural projection, self-critique, and repressed longing (Said 1978). As Niezen puts it:

> There is, in popular imaginings of the inherently ecological Indian or egalitarian hunter, an element of fertile nostalgia, a longing for things that cannot be found in conditions of modernity. Indigenous leaders must struggle against a temptation to take both libels and outrageous flattery as the truth about themselves and their peoples. (2003: 11)

The origins of indigeneity as a legal and political category have their roots in the development of the International Labour Organization (ILO), which was founded in 1919. This is a significant and often overlooked fact and one with implications for how indigenous rights law fits within the wider political economy of international law and institutional relations. While the architects of the ILO were influenced by the emergent international labor movement, which promoted workers' rights and the regulation of working conditions, the organization was conceived from the outset as a tool to reinforce the global capitalist system. The

Russian Revolution of 1917 was a stark and recent reminder of how extremes of economic inequality and social exploitation could, under certain circumstances, lead to violent upheaval and social implosion. As
Steiner and Alston explain, although the ILO was established "to guarantee 'fair and humane conditions of labour,' it was [also] conceived as
the response of the Western countries to the ideologies of Bolshevism
and Socialism arising out of the Russian Revolution" (2000: 242; see also
Shotwell 1933).

The role of the ILO within the history of twentieth-century global
capitalism has been explored at length by historians of the institution.
Throughout its development, the ILO has worked to regulate labor relations in ways that reinforce a global division of economic labor that
has reproduced lines of inequality and the selective allocation of capital.
As the economist Guy Standing has put it, the programs and legal conventions of the ILO are intended to function as a "means of locking in
the international division of labor . . . to the advantage of the affluent
capitalist countries" (Standing 2008: 357).[2] In developing a framework
of workers' legal protections that ameliorate the worst working conditions, particularly those that affect health, the ILO has contributed to
the reinforcement of what another scholar of the ILO, in a discussion
of the Agreement on Trade-Related Aspects of Intellectual Property
Rights (TRIPS), has called the "global capitalist state" (Richards 2004:
105).

It was against this political and ideological backdrop, therefore, that
the ILO crafted a scheme for protecting "indigenous and other tribal
and semi-tribal populations" by preparing them to be assimilated into
national capitalist labor markets, both existing and, even more important, those that would be developed after the end of colonialism and the
creation of dozens of new nation-states. Thus, although ILO Convention
107 (1957) was later criticized for its assimilationism and lack of respect
for indigenous self-determination and autonomy,[3] what was perhaps not
as well recognized was the fact that the convention was first and foremost—in keeping with the ILO's broader mandate—a mechanism for
dramatically enlarging the pool of potential workers "to the advantage
of the affluent capitalist countries."

Twenty-seven countries eventually ratified ILO 107 and it remained
the legal foundation for indigenous rights within international law until

1989, when it was revised through a new convention, ILO 169. Although some countries with large indigenous populations, particularly India,[4] remain states parties to the "assimilationist" ILO 107, ILO 169 quickly became the standard for indigenous rights protections and a source of inspiration for new political and social movements organized around the push to change existing laws within nation-states. As of 2015, only twenty-two countries had ratified ILO 169, fifteen of them in Latin America or the Caribbean.[5] Nevertheless, indigenous groups and organizations participated in several years of lobbying and consultations during the drafting of ILO 169. These efforts, which involved extensive debate over whether the new convention would refer to "indigenous peoples" or "indigenous populations" (as did ILO 107), produced mixed results.[6]

On the one hand, despite its history of spotty ratifications and association with an international organization committed to the regulation of labor within an exploitative global economic system, ILO 169 did become a symbolic lodestar for both indigenous people and the many transnational NGOs that were founded after 1989 to promote the cause of indigenous rights around the word. But on the other hand, concrete enforcement of ILO 169 within both national and international law has more often than not encountered intractable resistance from state–capital resource assemblages, particularly when "hard" (Adcock 2014) rights like extensive land redistribution or territorial self-determination are asserted. The result is that ILO 169 "has generally not met the expectations of indigenous peoples or organizations," whose leaders considered it a "missed . . . opportunity to do much more" (Niezen 2003: 39–40).

Despite the fact that the twin ILO conventions of 107 and 169 remain the basis for indigenous rights within international law, the United Nations General Assembly adopted a Declaration of the Rights of Indigenous Peoples (UN-DRIP) in September 2007. Perhaps not surprisingly, given that the Declaration was not meant to be a legally binding instrument, support for it was much greater than for the earlier ILO conventions: 143 countries voted in favor, 11 abstained, 34 countries were "absent" from the vote, and 4 countries voted against it (Australia, Canada, New Zealand, and the United States). As an example of how support for the Declaration seemed to correlate with its merely "aspirational" status,[7] China voted in favor despite the fact that its government does not officially recognize the category of "indigenous people" (IWGIA 2015).

Finally, in 2001 the UN Commission on Human Rights (now the Human Rights Council) created a Special Rapporteur on the rights of indigenous people as part of the historical process through which the Commission took an active role in developing indigenous rights protections apart from the parallel, and much longer, developments of the ILO. To date, there have been three Special Rapporteurs: Rodolfo Stavenhagen (2001–2008), a Mexican sociologist born in Germany and one of the leading Mexican academics and intellectuals of his time (Camp 1985); James Anaya (2008–2014), a Harvard-educated American Indian law professor; and Victoria Tauli Corpuz (2014–present), an indigenous Kankanaey Igorot activist from the Philippines who was the chair of the UN Permanent Forum on Indigenous Issues (2005–2010) while the UN-DRIP was being drafted and eventually adopted by the UN General Assembly.

As between the first two Special Rapporteurs, James Anaya had arguably the most significant impact, in large part because of the way he used the office of Special Rapporteur to intervene in legal and political conflicts in which indigenous people were involved, and more broadly because of the way he promoted the cause of indigenous rights despite tremendous institutional, economic, and jurisdictional difficulties. However, as Laurie Medina (2014) has shown, through an analysis of the contemporary impact of Inter-American indigenous rights jurisprudence on specific conflicts over land and resources, even when the Special Rapporteur makes a concerted effort to leverage the power and attention of the mandate, the capacity and willingness of states to enforce legal judgments is severely limited when they cannot be reconciled to the more important demand to "govern through the market" (Medina 2015).

This chapter examines the ways in which anthropologists have studied, critiqued, and, on occasion, promoted the development of indigenous rights across the trajectory of these historical developments. If it is true, as the American Anthropological Association's Committee for Human Rights argues (2001), that anthropologists have a professional obligation "to expand the definition of human rights within an anthropological perspective," it is also true that the domains of indigenous rights and law have received particular attention from scholars—both historically and in the present. In the next section, the chapter surveys the ways in which anthropologists have explored the political dimensions of indigenous rights practices in the contemporary world. For many indigenous organizations and social movements, legal maneuvering takes place as a strategy of highly contested cultural politics framed as a response to various forms of resistance and violence from the state, corporations, and majority populations.

Following this, the chapter takes up the question of authenticity as it has influenced the anthropological study of indigenous rights and political organizing. Beginning with Jean Jackson's (1995) seminal study of the legalization of "Indianness" in Colombia in the early years of indigenous rights mobilization, this section considers how the legal concepts embedded in indigenous rights processes are constructed within broader histories of colonial violence and postcolonial resistance. Next, the chapter turns to the ways in which anthropologists have revealed surprising interconnections, even interdependencies, between indigenous legal activism and juridical versions of "accumulation by dispossession" (Harvey 2003).

Within the broader consolidation of a neoliberal world order in which transnational corporations form deep alliances with national actors ranging from government officials and military elites to rural "micro-capitalists" (Davis 2006, quoted in Li 2010), perhaps it should not be surprising that the promotion of indigenous rights through law has accompanied the absorption of vast tracts of land into "global land investment assemblage[s]" (Li 2014a: 10). Nevertheless, anthropologists have discovered close historical and epistemological links between the juridification of indigeneity and capitalist expansion that are obscured within apparently neutral legal categories like "delineation" (Jefremovas and Perez 2011) and "ancestral domains" (Leeman 2014). Finally, the chapter concludes with a discussion of the limits of defining and promoting cultural identity through legal institutions that are both abstracted from the realities of life for most people and dependent on the state for bureaucratic management, resources, and legitimacy.

## Cultural Politics and Legal Maneuvers

In her ethnography of the "cultural politics and structural predicaments" of the indigenous rights movement in Tanzania, Dorothy Hodgson (2002) provides a critical account of the ways in which legal categories of indigeneity can distort already contentious political processes because of the impact of outside pressure from transnational organizations on a mission to establish a new discourse of empowerment (see also Hodgson 2011). As she explains, the historical trajectory of indigenous rights in Africa is deeply bound up with the cultural politics of postcolonialsm. Within postcolonial sub-Saharan Africa, the category of the "indigenous" has been deployed by cultural minorities within states whose majority populations of "Black Africans" had been previously oppressed under colonial regimes. But these distinct groups of cultural minorities like the Maasai are themselves numerous and highly differentiated within particular nation-states, which complicates the attempt to bring them together within a single legal and political category. As she describes it:

> Since 1990, over one hundred INGOs [international nongovernmental organizations] have emerged in . . . northern Tanzania, attempting to organize people around diverse claims of a common "indigenous" identity based on ethnicity, mode of production (being a pastoralist or hunter-gatherer), and a long history of political and economic disenfranchisement by first the colonial and now the postcolonial nation-state. (2002: 1086–1087)

This new and powerful process of cultural reorganization in Tanzania took place against a backdrop of existing conflicts over resources and identity. From the perspective of the INGOs and their local partners, indigenous rights mobilization was imagined as a new mechanism for both recognizing and legitimating existing grievances and establishing the basis for a new national multicultural political synthesis. Nevertheless, as Hodgson's ethnography demonstrates, the political aspirations of the indigenous rights movement can struggle to take root in the face of structural barriers (e.g., chronic resource scarcity) and the more general problems that come with rendering transnational and international legal categories like "indigenous" into the cultural and political vernacular. The result, as Hodgson's study suggests, is that the overlay of indigenous rights can actually deepen and enlarge existing conflicts. As she explains:

> Despite attempts to foster unity, promote common political agendas (such as the protection of land rights), and coordinate their activities through innumerable meetings and workshops and the creation of at least two "umbrella" coordinating groups, the indigenous rights movement in Maasai areas has continued to splinter into even more groups and to become fractured by sometimes quite hostile disagreements over priorities, competition over resources, and tensions over membership and representation. (2002: 1087)

Other anthropologists have demonstrated the ways in which indigenous rights mobilization can not only destabilize long-standing relations of power, but also lead to reconfigurations of basic categories like citizenship and sovereignty. In a series of ethnographic studies of treaty negotiations between the Nisga'a First Nation, the provincial government of British Columbia, and the Canadian federal government, Carole Blackburn (e.g., 2007, 2009) has examined the broader implications of the Nisga'a's long struggle to have their rights recognized through a treaty. As Blackburn shows, as with all of Canada's aboriginal peoples, the Nisga'a's relationship with various levels of state government was one historically characterized by exclusion and the denial of cultural and political alterity within a unifying ideology of the liberal polity.

Although the Nisga'a's eventual legal and political victory carried significant implications for both their local economy and land ownership,[8] what was most far-reaching, according to Blackburn, was the fact that the treaty—known as the Nisga'a Final Agreement—codified a "form of legally and conceptually differentiated citizenship" (2009: 66) that challenges dominant norms and offers an alternative account of Canadian history, one that recognizes the Nisga'a as a "preexisting political community" (67). As a comparative question, this represents an important exception to the more general finding of anthropology that the legal recognition of indigenous rights is often followed by a process of "being disciplined by [the] normative criteria of belonging" that were so hard-won in the first place (67; citing to Ong 1996).

But even though the Nisga'a have managed to introduce an alternative category of citizenship into Canadian political discourse, one based on differentiation and a theory of rights that "flow[s] from their relationship to their lands" (2009: 67), their achievement must nevertheless be qualified. This is because their rights under the treaty are not exercised in a legal or cultural vacuum. Even an "indigenous differentiated" theory of citizenship is still a theory of citizenship, that is, a category of belonging that is intimately bound up with "hegemonic ideals of equality linked with universal rights and modernist subjectivities" (67). As she argues, this broader context in which indigenous rights must necessarily be promoted and protected imposes ultimate limits on indigenous political aspirations that seek to contest dominant legal categories of the state at their foundations.

At the same time, other anthropologists have explored the ways in which the "juridification of indigenous politics" (Kirsch 2012) can lead to paradoxical outcomes in which traditional relationships with land and cultural identity are preserved despite the desire by indigenous people to more fully integrate, even with a measure of ambivalence, into a wider polity. In her ethnographic study of these tensions within France's Polynesian *Territoires d'outre-mer*, or Overseas Territories, Sophie Chave-Dartoen (2002) examines the "Wallisian paradox"—the fact that the legal recognition of Wallis Island required the French state to craft a law that perpetuated a kingship even though the Constitution of the Fifth Republic (1958) (re-)established France as a democratic republic in which sovereignty is derived from its citizens. The law incorporating Wallis Island (and the Island of Futuna) into the French Republic "guarantees to the population . . . the free exercise of their religion as well as the respect for their beliefs and their customs as long as they are not contrary to the general principles of law" (2002: 637). As Chave-Dartoen explains:

The Wallisians are thus French citizens but governed by a unique law that falls under the responsibility of a chiefdom that is organized around a "king" (*hau*), six "counselors" (*'aliki fa'u*), a war chief (*Pulu'i uvea*) and twenty village chiefs (*pule kolo*). A representative of the "king" (*fai pule*) within each of the three districts and four "maîtres d'œuvre"[9] (lagi aki) per village relay information and decisions and also take charge of organizing ceremonies and the distribution of social goods at the community level. (2002: 637)

But over the decades in which the 1961 law formed the basis for Wallisian social and political organization, it had the effect, according to Chave-Dartoen, of reinforcing, not diminishing, the principle of divine kingship. This was despite the fact that metropolitan lawmakers at the time saw the incorporation of Wallis Island into the French Republic—perhaps recalling the assimilationism of the 1957 ILO 107—as a legal mechanism for the eventual transformation of Wallisian society in terms of the categories of republican citizenship. And yet the perpetuation of the Wallisian paradox took place at the same time that Wallis Island continued to experience cultural changes due to the influences of Catholicism, which was first introduced on the island in the nineteenth century.

As Chave-Dartoen's ethnography shows, these changes revolved primarily around the key legal and cultural category of "'aliki," which she translates as "what is of higher value." Whereas historically 'aliki was embodied by the Wallisian king, it had over time gradually been transferred to the Christian God. Nevertheless, this fundamental shift did not result in the loss of Wallisian cultural identity and their assimilation to an ideology of French citizenship. Instead, as Chave-Dartoen argues, the legal incorporation of Wallis Island into the French Republic created a space in which important cultural categories could shift in meaning while others were reinforced or hardened. In this way, her study complicates notions of "tradition," "change," and "integration" and problematizes dualistic assumptions about the relationship between indigenous peoples and the modern (often liberal) state.

## Indigenous Legal Identity, Genuine and Spurious

Anthropologists have also tracked the ways in which the juridification of indigenous politics and identity raises questions of authenticity: Who can, should, and does speak for indigenous people? Does the representation of indigenous identity differ depending on whether it is directed toward outside actors like the state or NGOs or internally, as part of community struggles over political power and economic resources? Do legal categories shape indigenous identity in ways that change it fundamentally, making it less authentic? Is the old Sapirian distinction between "genuine" and "spurious" expressions of culture sustainable when the concept of culture itself has "become part of the very social reality" (Jackson 1995: 16) that we might hope to bracket analytically?

In an important early study of the relationship between indigenous rights mobilization and problems of cultural authenticity, Jean Jackson (1995) showed that the pressure to conform to legally embodied notions of Indianness created a discursive "race to the bottom" through which indigenous populations competed amongst themselves to present the most authentic image to state officials, NGOs, and other outside actors whose distribution of resources depended on the acceptance of such images. The end result of this process of forced self-presentation was the emergence of the "hyperreal Indian" (Ramos 1994), that is, the "fabrication of the perfect Indian whose virtues, sufferings, and untiring stoicism have won for him the right to be defended by the professionals of indigenous rights. That Indian is more real than the real Indian. He is the hyperreal Indian" (1994: 161).

But as Jackson argues, the forces that compel the creation of an orientalized conception of indigeneity through law are diverse and "evolve constantly" (1995: 4). For the Tukanoans of the northwest Colombian Amazon, these included a wide and chaotic array: "missionaries, government and NGO personnel, colonists, coca paste traffickers, guerrillas, and the military" (4). But these multiple, and often contradictory, influences can exacerbate conflicts *between* indigenous populations because the stakes have become so high. For example, the Tukanoans found themselves competing for the "right to be defended" with the neighboring Makú people, who are hunter-gatherers (the Tukanoans live along rivers, where they fish for their livelihood). As Jackson explains, "Tukanoan classifications of themselves . . . are being contested in a context where hunter-gatherer Indians are increasingly seen as purer, almost hyper-Indians, giving Makú a symbolic superiority greatly resented by Tukanoans, who have traditionally considered themselves superior to Makú in almost every respect" (1995: 20, fn. 1).[10] Jackson concludes that traditional concerns with cultural authenticity through indigenous rights must give way to a "multivocal" account of identity that does not draw analytical distinctions between real and false, genuine and spurious. And as later research on indigenous communities in legal conflict with the state and transnational corporations revealed (see, e.g., Golub 2014; Kirsch 2014), indigenous actors themselves are sophisticated advocates for multivocal and nonreductionist approaches to identity that reflect an awareness of the "intersectional" (Radcliffe 2015) reality of historical marginalization and cultural and economic occlusion.

If anthropologists have shown how the promise of resources derived from the legal recognition of indigeneity can at times heighten existing tensions and even create new modes of conflict, other anthropologists have found that something like an opposite dynamic can develop. As Shaylih Muehlmann (2009) argues, in her ethnographic study of fishing rights conflicts between the Cucapá of northern Mexico and the neoliberal Mexican state, the process of cultural differentiation compelled by indigenous rights can be used strategically by the state and local NGOs to *deny* the allocation of resources to populations that attempt to maneuver within the fraught boundaries of juridification. In a sense, Muehlmann's research reveals the dark side of the "hyperreal Indian," the ways in which the reification of indigenous identity through law excludes as much as—or perhaps more than—it includes.

Muehlmann's research tracked the ways in which the Cucapá people have increasingly turned to modes of struggle sanctioned by indigenous rights legislation in Mexican national law as a response to the "devastating effects of reduced flows from the [Colorado] river as a result of the construction of the major dams upstream in the United States" (2009: 468). As the river flow diminished over time on the Mexican side of the international border, the Mexican government created a biosphere reserve in the region that had the effect of criminalizing the Cucapá's traditional livelihood. Although the legislation granted legal permits to fish outside the biosphere's boundaries, these concessions did not address the Cucapá's concerns that they confronted a policy of "cultural genocide" by the government (2009: 468).

But as Muehlmann explains, as a response to the Cucapá's frustration with their inability to use indigenous rights to reverse governmental policy, their own lawyer turned on them for their failure to be sufficiently Indian as contemplated by national law. Muehlmann's account of the lawyer's diatribe is memorable: "[the lawyer] told the group that they had to speak their indigenous language if they wanted their government to take them seriously 'as Indians.' 'How is the government even supposed to know you're Indians?' he concluded, pointing to one of the women. 'You dress and speak like Mexicans!'" (2009: 468).

Muehlmann argues that these processes of exclusion are the result of a discontinuity between the normative and cultural imperatives of indigenous rights mobilization at the national level and the pressures of neoliberal reforms that "drive[ ] a wedge between claiming cultural rights and claiming control over the resources necessary for those rights to be realized" (2009: 476). Ethnographic studies like Muehlmann's underscore the analytical value of scrutinizing what might be called the negative spaces of indigenous rights mobilization—those instances of failure, denial, and exclusion that are not an unimagined effect of legal struggle but an integral aspect of it.

Another key finding from the anthropology of indigenous rights is the fact that strategic maneuvering, which can include the creative articulation of what one of Kimberly Christen's interlocutors in Australia described as "culture work" (2006: 416), can become a tool of empowerment associated with economic independence, the assertion of cultural pride, and the possibility of "remapp[ing] commercial spaces" (2006: 416) in a global market in which indigeneity has value.

Christen conducted research among the Warumungu people of Tennant Creek north of Alice Springs in Australia's Northern Territory at a time when the full implications of the 1993 Native Title Act were still rippling through Australia's aboriginal communities.[11] Christen followed a group of women who had decided to make and market a compact disc of female ancestor songs in collaboration with an ethnomusicologist from the University of Sydney. As one of the Warumungu singers explained to Christen, the songs were in part an effort to aesthetically codify key markers of Warumungu "law," which is the English term used:

> To designate a wide range of cultural and ritual activities, practices, and institutions that inform, define, and sustain their community's boundaries. Many use the term as a substitute for *dreaming*, a term that has a long history of mistranslation across the continent . . . No doubt the term is also meant to register the relative weight of their cultural and religious practices in relation to national laws. (2006: 438, fn. 8; emphasis in original)

But in addition to using the production of the compact discs as a new way to express Warumungu legal and cultural identity in the aftermath of the 1993 Native Title Act, it also gave the singers an opportunity to destabilize existing assumptions within broader Australian society about Aboriginal spirituality that supposedly distinguished "material gain from sacred use, [thereby] shoring up the romantic notion of 'traditional' aboriginality as an inherently anticapitalist, nonmaterial form of being in the world" (2006: 419). In part because of the national and eventual global circulation of the compact discs, their production challenged at least some of the stereotypes about Aboriginal "law."

Yet as Christen argues, their circulation did not take place in a historical void. Instead, they were produced during a period in Australian history in which the commercialization of Aboriginal culture was part of a boom in cultural tourism, a mode of exchange given prominence during the 2000 Summer Olympic Games in Sydney. And even more broadly, the Warumungu recording was produced and marketed "at the intersection . . . where social and legal value regimes compete. They [were] inserted into a market what wants them to be traditional and authentic. Their aboriginality must be recognizable for their consumption to be palatable by sometimes suspicious consumers" (2006: 422).

Finally, as Renée Sylvain's (e.g., 2002, 2005) research demonstrates, the kinds of circulations that are important for understanding the multivalent relationships between law and indigenous identity are not only those that involve the commodification of culture; they are also those that involve indigenous people themselves. Sylvain conducted research in postapartheid Namibia in the period after Namibia gained independence from South Africa in 1990. The San people of Namibia—and across southern Africa—have become increasingly visible advocates for their rights as indigenous people with the collaboration of organizations like the Working Group of Indigenous Minorities in Southern Africa (Sylvain 2005: 354). This activism has taken San leaders outside Namibia to participate in international rights forums, workshops, and planning meetings. The result, as Sylvain explains, is that the San have become increasingly integrated into "the new global order" in which they are able—after suffering under centuries of different forms of oppression and political violence—to participate as "vocal and sophisticated" members of a broader pan-indigenous legal and political community. Nevertheless, the circulation of San within the professional networks of global indigenous rights mobilization is "fraught with contradictions and challenges." This is because

[a]t the very moment they are beginning to travel the world, speak at international conferences, and keep in regular email communication with interested parties overseas, primordialized and essentialized representations of primitive "Bushmen" are being vigorously reasserted in mainstream media and NGO rhetoric. These representations are often difficult to distinguish from colonial stereotypes. (2005: 354)

As Sylvain shows, these contradictions and challenges can undermine locally what the San have been able to accomplish on the global stage. She focuses in particular on the economic implications of these disjunctures, including the ways in which the emergence of different socioeconomic classes within San society can be attributed to the exploitation of the disorder that has marked postcolonial Namibia, where there has been a "general deterioration of human-rights standards and an alarming increase in corruption" (2005: 360–361). She observed stark differences in the way San represented themselves between the mid-1990s and the early 2000s. For example, during the first period, San would pose for photographs in the "best clothes they could borrow and . . . with their most prized possession—usually with radios or, if one was available, with a bicycle" (2005: 366).

But during the later period, after indigenous rights discourse had fully absorbed the San both abroad and nationally, "an opportunity to be photographed sen[t] the San . . . to dress up in beadwork and animal skins," despite the fact that the people she worked with were farmers who did not dress in that "traditional" manner. Thus, even though the "displays of the San in beadwork and animal skins were genuine expressions of cultural pride" (2005: 366) in the moment, they reflected deeper divisions within San society and the emergence of socioeconomic lines between the indigenous haves and the indigenous have-nots. As Sylvain argues, the case of the San illustrates what can happen when legal categories require hard and fast cultural distinctions to be drawn and attaches resources to these distinctions. As she puts it:

In situations of extreme marginalization and class inequality, [the idea of culture] easily becomes another instrument for continued exploitation. And, as the idea of culture becomes essentialized, the San's own distinctive but class-shaped culture—the lived patterns of practices and beliefs that make up their moral identity—goes unnoticed. (366)

## Indigenous Rights and/as Capitalist Accumulation

As the foregoing suggests, the relationship between law and indigenous rights mobilization is one that can in certain cases create a paradoxical situation in which legal recognition deepens, rather than ameliorates, patterns of social and economic inequality. But as the ethnographic research of other anthropologists has demonstrated, these effects might be more closely connected to the very structure of international indigenous rights law than was previously assumed. In a series of studies of the implementation of indigenous rights legislation across a range of different national and cultural contexts, scholars have documented the extent to which the promotion of indigenous political aspirations through law must be seen in part as a reflection of broader political economies in which "land-grabbing" and the creation of new labor markets function as forms of risk management and late-capitalist resilience. As the Introduction to a special forum of the *Journal of Peasant Studies* explained:

> The convergence of global crises in food, energy, finance, and the environment has driven a dramatic reevaluation in landownership. Powerful transnational and national economic actors from corporations to national governments and private equity funds have searched for "empty" land often in distant countries that can serve as sites for fuel and food production in the event of future price spikes. This is occurring globally, but there is a clear North-South dynamic that echoes the land grabs that underwrote both colonialism and imperialism. (Borras et al. 2011: 209)

As anthropologists have revealed, the response to these converging crises has been the emergence of multilayered state-capital assemblages that both feed on the "fuzziness" (Li 2014a: 10) of the legal regulation of land markets within domestic law and take advantage of reforms that establish new processes through which indigenous peoples can seek collective titles for ancestral lands. Rather than sealing off indigenous lands from the downward pressures of capitalist encroachment and environmental degradation, the implementation of indigenous rights legislation has often made vast tracts of territory more widely available, legally, to be commoditized as part of national development programs, eco-tourism initiatives, and the global management by resource industries of the "risky business" (Li 2015) of land investment.

Even more, the "bureaucratic Orientalis[t]" (Jefremovas and Perez 2011: 84) processes through which collectivities must pass in order to receive legal recognition of collective land rights require the production of immense cultural, geographical, economic, and historical justifications that, taken together, have proven to be a bonanza for investors. In the most extreme cases, the process of collective titling has become what the critical development scholars Saturnino Borras and Jennifer Franco have called a "one-stop shop" (2010: 8). Requirements within many indigenous rights bureaucracies include the state-monitored resolution of local conflicts over land; the creation of often new authority positions with the right to make decisions over large territories; the mapping of "ancestral domains" using both geospatial and cultural technologies like oral history; and the presentation to the state of "development plans" that contain detailed analyses of available resources and potential markets. The result is that the complicated realities of land tenure and social relations among indigenous peoples are materialized and rationalized through the mechanisms of national rights legislation in ways that have proven extremely attractive to investors, who have been more than willing to play along with the "cultural politics of difference" (Fraser 1995: 69).

In a particularly stark ethnographic case of how the "one-stop shop" has become in certain regions a new form of capitalist accumulation, Esther Leeman (2014) has conducted research on the implementation of the 2001 Land Law of Cambodia among the Bunong people. Although no Southeast Asian country is a party to either ILO 107 or ILO 169, different countries enacted indigenous rights legislation beginning in the late 1990s as a response to the same currents of transnational indigenous rights activism that were shaping policy elsewhere around the world. For example, the Philippines passed the "Indigenous Peoples' Rights Act" in 1997, which established a process through which "Indigenous

Cultural Communities/Indigenous Peoples" could apply for collective rights after submitting themselves to a carefully calculated regime of governmentality called "delineation" that culminates in the production of an "Ancestral Domain Sustainable Development and Protection Plan" (see Jefremovas and Perez 2011).

Through her ethnographic research in Cambodia, Leeman was able to track the implementation of the 2001 land law over separate periods. When she first began her research in 2011, the Bunong villagers had formed an alliance with transnational indigenous rights activists in order to guide their application under the 2001 law. At the time, Bunong land was threatened with encroachment by expanding private rubber plantations. As Leeman discovered, the political discourse around the land law and its supposed benefits had created a spirit of optimism among her interlocutors and their allies. Yet when Leeman returned for follow-up ethnographic research in 2013 in order to evaluate the course of the Bunong land claim, she found that the situation in the region had changed dramatically.

As she explains, the 2001 law creates a complicated framework that is similar to the requirements of "delineation" under IPRA in the Philippines. As with IPRA, applicants in Cambodia must self-constitute as a cultural collectivity with claims to a defined "ancestral domain" described in topographical, economic, and political terms. At the end of the process, claimants who manage to wend their way through a "tedious, costly, red tape nightmare" (2014: 2) must register the new collective land titles under a provision of the law that establishes apparently "absurd and arbitrary limit[s]" (2014: 4), such as the fact that under a 2009 revision to the 2001 law, only seven hectares of "spirit forests and burial grounds per community can legally be protected" (4).

However, seen in light of the broader political economy of indigenous rights legislation in the region, this qualification is neither arbitrary nor absurd. Spirit forests and burial grounds represent precisely the kind of forms of land that are most difficult to materialize, commodify, and add to the shelves of the "one-stop shop." As a question of risk management, it is not surprising that the Cambodian law puts strict limits on these problematic categories, despite—or perhaps because of—the fact that the "spirit places (mountains, ponds, streams, rivers, waterfalls, forest areas, etc.) are inextricably intertwined with Bunong's ancestors" (2014: 4).

As of 2014, only *eight* indigenous communities in Cambodia had received collective land titles in the thirteen years since the land law's passage. Yet during this same period, more than 2 million hectares of Cambodian territory were transferred to a group of 227 agro-industrial companies under a separate section of the 2001 law that gives the Ministry of Agriculture, Forestry and Fisheries the ability to grant long-term Economic Land Concessions (ELCs). As the office of the UN Special Representative of the Secretary General for human rights in Cambodia reported in 2007, the effects of ELCs on indigenous people have been significant. As a summary of the Special Representative's report put it:

> Communities living on land granted in concessions are often subjected to forced eviction, involuntary resettlement or poorly designed relocation. This can often increase poverty by limiting access to income generation, water and sanitation, electricity, health services, and education. Currently, there is no legal framework to regulate evictions by private entities. Further, ELCs . . . have led to deforestation as large tracts of forestland are cleared for plantations. (Open Development Cambodia 2015)

To conclude this section, it is important to acknowledge the extent to which anthropologists have revealed different strategies of resistance and adaptation by indigenous peoples to the cooptation of the "politics of recognition" (Fraser 1995) by state–capital resource assemblages.[12] This is not to say that these moments of creative slippage, or ethnographic examples of "commonplace forms of resistance" (Scott 1985: xvi), have worked to undermine the broader global systems within which indigenous rights must be understood as *both* a language of cultural empowerment *and* a relatively new mechanism of capitalist accumulation. Rather, it is that the "dynamic specificity" (Li 2010: 400) to be found at every link in the chain that connects the struggle for indigenous rights in rural villages to the boardrooms of (for example) palm oil conglomerates in places like Kuala Lumpur and Singapore[13] creates openings for what might be called destabilization in a minor key.

For example, in his ethnography of the politics around the ongoing implementation of the Alaska Native Claims Settlement Act of 1971 (ANCSA) and its later revisions, Kirk Dombrowski argues that one response among indigenous people to the "manipulation of Native claims and identity" (2002: 1062) by industrial timber and pulp producers was to simply "opt out" of "state-sponsored indigenism" (2002: 1068) by rejecting the economic and political categories that this dominant mode of appropriation requires. His study focused on indigenous villages at the margins of the mainstream Alaskan native rights movement, which had fully participated in the payments scheme authorized under the ANCSA. For these marginal regions, "ongoing issues of environmental destruction, economic marginality, alcohol and personal abuse, substandard housing, and general economic and social insecurity" were more pressing concerns than whether or not their villages could present the "clear picture of ethnic, racial, and tribal 'differences' . . . [demanded by] cruise ship tourists and local consumption" (1068). Although the specific expression of opting out in his study—the emergence of radical Pentecostal churches that aggressively reject the politics of indigeneity— "played a minor role in the political life of the region" (2002: 1069), it did represent an unusual, if problematic, response to the extension of "state power under industrial capitalist development" (1062).

Finally, Rudi Colloredo-Mansfeld's research underscores the extent to which the manipulations of indigenous rights by state–capital resource assemblages that occur from Southeast Alaska to Southeast Asia must be understood on a broader political economic landscape in which indigenous people, like other vulnerable populations, confront "failing subsistence production, growing consumerism, and expanding transnational migration" (2002: 637). Based on a study of an "emerging indigenous economic elite" (638) in Otavalo, Ecuador, which forms part of a "native leisure class" (1999), Colloredo-Mansfeld argues that the growth of indigenous activism has been accompanied by greater socioeconomic inequality within indigenous populations.

The native merchants of Otavalo, who have created a transnational market in Andean material culture, have "one of the most successful and enduring commercial histories of all native Andean people" (2002: 641). In this case, the revitalization and juridification of indigeneity in Ecuador in the late 1980s and early 1990s clearly worked in favor of an indigenous population whose economic self-reliance and transnational scope of vision had already been long established (see Salomon 1981).[14] And yet the very success of this native leisure class only served to reinforce the effects of the "invidious segmentation" (Colloredo-Mansfeld 2002: 640) of indigenous society more generally. As he puts it, the lucrative transnational market savvy of the Otavalo merchants in an era of indigenous rights mobilization revealed the "moral dissonance of professing communitarian values while allowing the neglect of poorer segments within native society" (640).

## Conclusion: At the Crossroads of Law and Sky

In his landmark ethnoastronomical study of the "dark cloud" (*pusuqu* in Peruvian Quechua) constellations of the Milky Way in Andean cosmology, Gary Urton explains the importance of these celestial bodies to his indigenous interlocutors:

> An informant in Misminay described the Milky Way as composed of two rivers which originate in the north, arch through the sky in opposite directions, and collide in the south near α Crucis; the "foam" of their collision is called *pusuqu*. Thus, the foam which results from the union of celestial rivers is referred to in Misminay by the same term that is used in Tomanga [a nearby village] for the arch and the oval as symbols of the unification of terrestrial rivers; therefore, the *union* and the *foam* can be symbolized by the arch, the oval, or . . . the ellipse. Note at this point that foam, and moving water in general, are equated in Andean symbolism with semen, the masculine force of fertilization. (1981: 202)

To get to this point, the conclusion of his study, Urton had to draw out the ethnographic nuances of an ontologically rich cultural world in which indigenous cosmology, meteorology, topography, and local sociopolitical organizations are part of an integrated system that is partly bound by place and time but also in part connected to longer pre-Columbian and colonial histories. Urton's research took place well before the "politics of recognition" and indigenous rights mobilization had affected village life in Peru (indeed, his research was conducted even before the Maoist Shining Path movement had begun its violent campaign). It was a time before indigenous knowledge had become Indigenous Knowledge, a reductive epistemological category recognized and celebrated in international law.

The subtleties and importance of the "crossroads of the Earth and the Sky" for villagers in Misminay in 1976 were simply present as the practice of everyday life itself. After discussing the reason why everyone in the village was keeping a close eye on a group of stars called *Collca* (or "storehouse") during a tense part of the rainy season in which a drought threatened the season's potato crop, Urton realized that "the stars are discussed so seldom not because they are unimportant or uninteresting, but because their role in the life of the community is a matter of such great seriousness" (1981: 3).

This account of the "particularity of indigenous life projects" (Blaser 2004) could be repeated, in its own irreducible complexity, for as many life projects or indigenous "cosmovisions" as there are anthropologists— native or nonnative, professional or amateur—to reveal them.[15] But as we have seen, the anthropological study of the juridification of indigenous politics has demonstrated how the ways and means of legal recognition can unfold far from these deep particularities. The meaning and "great seriousness" of spirit forests and ancestral burial grounds are often suppressed and go legally unrecognized precisely because of what they are—and even more troubling, what they are not. Some indigenous populations have thrived, in concrete and sustainable ways, through the development of legal regimes inspired by the broader "human rights revolution" (Iriye, Goedde, Hitchcock 2012) that was shaping the postwar world. Yet on balance, the anthropological record suggests that the relationship between indigeneity, international law, and political mobilization is riddled with contradictions, overshadowed by the potential for economic exploitation, and perhaps most important, long overdue for critical reassessment.

7

# Law and the Moral Economy of Gender

The historical relationship between the anthropological study of law and "gender" is as old as the anthropology of law itself. In the historic year of 1861, two foundational works were published by the proto-anthropologists of law Henry Maine and Johann Jakob Bachofen that were fundamentally concerned with the ways in which legal categories shaped what later would be called gender relations—and how this relationship influenced cultural evolution (as it was understood at the time) more generally. In *Ancient Law*, Maine used Roman codes to demonstrate the ways in which the early Roman law regulated women's lives within a broader system of kin-based property ownership. In his arresting phrase, Roman law required the "perpetual tutelage of women" within a society marked by deep patriarchy organized around the control and management of inherited property.[1]

In his *Das Mutterrecht*, by contrast, Bachofen argued that early societies were essentially matriarchal, a period in history characterized by peace, social equality, a reverence for the land (including the emergence of chthonic mystery cults), and sexual freedom. However, because of the difficulty in establishing paternity in the period of "mother-right" (what Bachofen described as "gynaecocracy"), the law evolved to limit sexual freedom, enforce monogamy, and consequently replace the rule of women with the rule of men. Bachofen called this final period in sociolegal evolution the "Apollonian" phase. It is marked by the development of private property regimes, social inequality, and the institutionalization of violence as a mechanism of control (see Gossman 2000).

The Scottish proto-anthropologist of law John McLennan's 1865 *Primitive Marriage* likewise can be seen as an early analysis of themes that—in different theoretical terms, within different social and political milieux—would later reappear as central concerns for the anthropological study of law and gender. His argument for the primacy of law in the regulation of marriage was one that emphasized the interplay between power, competition for resources in conditions of economic scarcity, the ritualization of violence (in the form of so-called collusive abductions), the control of female bodies, and the links between sexuality and warfare.[2]

Even in his short chapter on the "law of marriage" in his 1926 *Crime and Custom*, Malinowski took up the question of law's regulation of gender roles, in this case the way in which "primitive law" in the Trobriand Islands required a wife's brother to assume a position of perpetual guardianship over her and her children. The wife's brother had to provide lavish amounts of yams for his married sister and her children in the course of elaborate public displays that diffused and regulated social and economic power within a "chain of mutualities" (1926: 37). In return, the sociolegal relationship between a wife and her brother imposed duties on her and her sons, who will "[l]ater on . . . come directly under the authority of their maternal uncle; the boys will have to help him, to assist him in everything, to contribute a definite quota to all the payments he has to make" (1926: 37). As for a man's sister's daughters, they "do but little for him directly, but indirectly, in a matrilineal society, they provide him with his heirs and descendants of two generations below" (37).

And yet despite this early intellectual history, a distinct anthropological study of law and gender took decades to emerge from within the more established themes of marriage, kinship, and social control. An important transitional work is Elizabeth Colson's *Marriage and the Family among the Plateau Tonga of Northern Rhodesia* (1958), based on fieldwork between 1946 and 1950, in which Colson studied the impact of major social and economic changes on gender relations based in part on an analysis of local court cases.[3] By the early 1960s, Laura Nader was also turning to questions of law and gender, albeit within a broader theoretical framework in which such relations functioned as forms of social control (e.g., Nader and Metzger 1963), although even at this time there were initial gestures toward questions that would emerge in her later research. In her study of Zapotec legal processes, for example, she observed that there were certain circumstances that "forced women to take recourse to formal law agencies as plaintiffs" and that gender relations influenced the use of types of law among the Zapotec—"women are rarely defendants in dispute cases involving assault and battery, while men on the other hand are rarely defendants in slander cases" (1965: 23).

Nevertheless, major programmatic syntheses of the anthropology of law over the next decade did not identify the relationship between law and "gender" as a likely topic for future research. In her 1969 *Biennial Review of Anthropology* article on "law and anthropology" (the "first article on law to appear in the *Biennial Review*"), Sally Falk Moore identified history, the relationship between legal rules and "practices in ordinary life" (1969: 293), the relationship between formal disputes and social conflict, and the study of "legal concepts as . . . manipulable, value-laden language" (1969: 294), as the most promising ways to fulfill the "classic task of legal anthropology," which was to "understand the relationship between law and society" (294). Even with transformative developments that included the rise of the women's liberation movement in international politics, the creation of women's and gender studies within the academy, and the adoption of major international women's rights treaties, most notably the 1979 Convention on the Elimination of All Forms of Discrimination Against Women (CEDAW), anthropologists of law still had not fully problematized gender as a central topic for research by the mid-1980s.[4]

For example, at the important 1985 meeting in Bellagio, Italy, that was conceived to "develop[ ] new ideas and methods for studying the anthropology of law," a distinguished group of international scholars brought contemporary theoretical currents together in order to "expand the concerns that characterized the decades of anthropology of law since the 1960s" (Starr and Collier 1989: 23). As part of the exploration of new common themes such as the relationship between "asymmetrical power relationships and legal change," the collective settled on a broad framework that reflected the influence of various strands of anthropological theory that had sought to break down epistemological barriers by revealing the "totality of interconnected processes" (Wolf 1982: 3).[5] As the editors of the resulting volume put it, "[w]orld history emerged as the relevant integrative framework" (1989: 23). Among the fourteen published essays from the meeting, only one, June Starr's rereading of Henry Maine's *Ancient Law*, touched on questions of law and gender, and in this case only obliquely.[6]

But within ten years, the study of law and gender in anthropology had moved to the center among a number of key problems that reflected the tensions between what a 1994 volume (based on meetings in 1991) described as "law, hegemony, and resistance" (Lazarus-Black and Hirsch 1994a). In a striking contrast with Starr and Collier's programmatic intervention from 1985, by the early 1990s, a concern with what Hirsch (1998) would later call the relationship between "legal processes and the discursive construction of gender" had become a significant presence in the field. Of the eleven essays published in the 1994 work, six focus directly on the relationship between law and gender, including studies of domestic violence hearings (Merry), "Muslim women's multiple subordination" through legal categories (Moore), and battles over motherhood in antebellum Philadelphia (Grossberg).

Indeed, in her ethnography of "legal consciousness among working-class Americans," Sally Engle Merry (1990) had already fully problematized the relationship between law and gender as a key device for understanding the ways in which power infuses, and is infused by, the law. As she explained in introducing her study:

> [T]he population of people who bring personal problems to court is largely women. Women are more likely to take their neighbors, husbands, lovers, and children to court than are men because they are relatively powerless in these relationships. In this social world, relative power depends to a large extent on strength, willingness to use violence, and economic resources. Women are usually less well endowed with these qualities than are men. They turn to court because they feel vulnerable and because they hope it will provide an ally. (1990: 4)

Here we have, in condensed form, all the elements that explain how and why an anthropological focus on the relationship between law and gender emerged from the margins of more well-established—indeed, as we have seen, formative—intellectual histories in which questions of gender and power were present but latent, within studies of law and kinship, marriage, family structure, and property. Gender had become a central social theoretical and political economic category through which struggles over power, identity, and legal rights took place.

This transformation in anthropology, which followed major developments in international law like the adoption of CEDAW in 1979, rather than preceding it, took place during a time when political theorists like Nancy Fraser were already beginning to worry that the "politics of rec-

ognition," of which gender was a key symbol, was beginning to over-
shadow the equally important "politics of redistribution." As she put it:

> Insofar as women suffer at least two analytically distinct kinds of injustice
> [one political-economic, the other cultural-valuational], they necessarily
> require at least two analytically distinct kinds of remedy—both redistri-
> bution and recognition. The two remedies pull in opposite directions,
> however. They are not easily pursued simultaneously. Whereas the logic
> of redistribution is to put gender out of business as such, the logic of rec-
> ognition is to valorize gender specificity. (1995: 79–80)

Despite the worry of social critics like Fraser, the constitutive relationship between law and gender identity continued to strengthen over the
next two decades, a process that anthropologists tracked with insight
and analytical creativity. Nevertheless, as this chapter demonstrates, the
anthropological study of law and gender has encompassed much more
than simply questions of rights protection and legal enforcement.

For example, the next section surveys the ways in which anthropologists have studied the specific relationship between law and gender violence. The struggle against gender violence took on heightened
importance, especially as the CEDAW enforcement regime crystallized
and began to exert a significant influence on national politics and debates over the meaning of culture. As we will see, ethnographies of these
politics and debates revealed, among other things, their irreducibility to
a "simple jural formulation" (Comaroff and Roberts 1981: 167).

Following this, the chapter explores the way anthropologists have
conducted studies among populations that inhabit the "invisible visible"
(Baer 2010)—spaces of gender identity that fit uneasily, or not at all,
within clear-cut categories that have been legitimated within international law. Next, the chapter considers how anthropologists have problematized the relationship between law and the body. Here, scholars have
studied processes like sex trafficking, prostitution, debates over fertility,
and struggles over cultural practices like Female Genital Circumcision/
Mutilation to understand how the body itself becomes a site on which
the "politics of intervention" (Shell-Duncan 2008) plays out. Finally, the
chapter concludes with a discussion of how what might be called the
juridification of gender comes into tension with other, broader, concep-

tions in which gender identities circulate within moral economies of cultural creativity, resistance, and transgression.

## Gender Violence and Legal Discipline

In her cultural study of gender violence, Sally Engle Merry (2009) emphasizes the importance of approaching the problem from a historical perspective. As she explains:

> Gender violence is not a new problem. It takes place in virtually all societies around the world, but only in the last thirty years has it become visible as a major social issue. Historically, forms of violence taking place within the family were treated as less serious than those occurring in the public sphere. . . . In the 1990s, gender violence was defined as an important human rights violation for the first time. Now it is considered the centerpiece of women's human rights. (2009: 1)

Anthropologists—including, of course, Merry herself—have explored the ethnographic nuances of a central insight here: the fact that gender violence both is, and is not, a socially constructed phenomenon. That is, the point in time in which violence against women—as women, because they are women—was recognized as a "major social issue" deserving of close and sustained legal, political, and economic scrutiny was not just the next point on a historical timeline. It was a qualitative turning point, a moment when the meaning and significance of patterns of behavior shifted—often with new and destabilizing consequences.

This moment in time was not a date in history, for example, December 18, 1979, when CEDAW was adopted by the UN General Assembly, or September 3, 1981, when the treaty entered into force after the twentieth country had ratified it. Indeed, the history of CEDAW demonstrates that the turning point through which gender violence went from being an unacknowledged daily tragedy for many women around the world to the "centerpiece of women's human rights" was drawn-out and contested. Violence—against women, or otherwise[7]—is not mentioned at all in CEDAW. Instead, the focus is on eliminating "discrimination," which the treaty defines as any "distinction, exclusion or restriction made on the basis of sex which has the effect or purpose of impairing or nullifying the recognition, enjoyment or exercise by women, irrespective of their marital status, on a basis of equality of men and women, of human rights and fundamental freedoms in the political, economic, social, cultural, civil or any other field" (CEDAW 1979).

In the years after the adoption of CEDAW, however, the absence of any mention of violence against women in the treaty became a point of increasing contention. In 1992, the Committee on the Elimination of All Forms of Discrimination Against Women, the group of international human rights experts charged with monitoring implementation of CEDAW, announced General Recommendation 19 to the treaty, which defines "gender-based violence" and specifies that it "is discrimination within the meaning . . . of the Convention." The following year, at the UN Conference on Human Rights in Vienna, the problem of gender violence was at the top of the agenda. As Merry explains, a "worldwide petition campaign gathered over 300,000 signatures from 123 countries, putting the issue of violence against women at the center of the conference" (2006a: 22). Other developments of the mid-1990s completed the turning point, including the adoption in 1993 by the UN General Assembly of the Declaration on the Elimination of Violence Against Women and the 1995 Fourth World Conference on Women in Beijing, during which the problem of gender violence as a human rights violation received wide-ranging visibility.[8]

But even if gender violence had been transformed into a major social issue through international law by the mid-1990s, it was what followed—local legal implementation, cultural resistance, the expansion and contraction of social categories—that became the subject of close ethnographic attention. In her study of the implementation of a 2006 law against sexual violence in the Democratic Republic of Congo (DRC), for example, Gaëlle Breton-Le Goff (2013) argues that the use of law to prevent violence against women exposes in practice the law's "outer limits." As Breton-Le Goff explains, the 2006 law was passed by the Congolese parliament through an unusual process of international and national nongovernmental advocacy in which the American human rights NGO Global Rights supported local social activists and human rights lawyers in drafting the law and introducing it into the legislature (2013: 75).

As she puts it, "the adoption of the 2006 law by the Congolese parliament was considered to be an important mark of progress that gave rise to hope among women's rights activists that the law would lead to a better chance of diminishing the violence committed against women" (2013: 75).[9] And yet, "six years after the promulgation of the law, these hopes were dashed" (75). At a general level, Breton-Le Goff points to the small number of prosecutions "in relation to the magnitude of the crimes committed," and the fact that the law has been "only partially or badly applied," as the main reasons for the failure of the 2006 law in the DRC (75–76).

But more importantly for our purposes here, she shows how the intention to apply the law in situations of sexual violence confronted resistance from local village chiefs, who preferred to use customary law to manage an extraordinary situation in which the social status of large numbers of young women had been transformed through sexual violation. She concludes that in the implementation of women's rights legislation, a fundamental, structural tension exists in many parts of the world between customary law, national law, and international law, despite the efforts to harmonize these distinct categories.

But as Mindie Lazarus-Black's (2001; see also 2007) research demonstrates, these tensions can also create spaces in which compromise, negotiation, and the "pragmatics of inclusion" can take place. Lazarus-Black's ethnography tracked the long-term consequences that followed the turning point in the legal regulation of gender violence in Trinidad and Tobago, beginning with the passage of a domestic violence act in 1991. Her description of this moment captures the nature of the qualitative shift. The passage of the act was

> [a] radical legal development, a coup of social engineering sparked in large part by the efforts of a progressive women's movement in Trinidad that mobilized government attention and nongovernmental groups' intervention. For the first time, violent words and acts that formerly remained unspoken, invisible, and irrelevant to the project of the state became highly conspicuous and subject to immediate legal sanction. And for the first time, people—mostly women—some who had been terrorized and nearly all of whom are counted among the most socially, economically, and politically subordinated people of the country, gained access to and attention from the courts. (2001: 388)

Yet as Lazarus-Black discovered, an uneven implementation of the domestic violence act in Trinidad and Tobago evolved over time and was shaped by preexisting structures of poverty, cultural beliefs about the moral standing of victims, and degrees of separation from the power of the state. As a question of domestic violence and legal agency, she observed that there were four specific categories of women who found formal protection under the law: "wives with alcoholic husbands, mothers with addicted [and abusive older] children, women who [were] beaten in the homes they . . . helped to pay for, and the former partners of obsessed men" (2001: 399).

However, by looking beyond the simple number of cases of domestic violence brought under the law, Lazarus-Black was able to show how "success" could also be measured in different ways. Even for the many other victims who were not able to receive state protection in the form of a temporary restraining order, the process of making an (ultimately unsuccessful) application under the law marked their first empowering engagement with the state. The not-so-simple act by (mostly) women of attempting to use the law reflected "a new way to think about themselves and their relationships," one that encouraged them to "adopt[ ] the language of the law" on their own behalf (2001: 400). As she argues, the consequences of connecting new cultural understandings of gender violence with the law could be gauged through these pragmatic and informal effects, which—as much as with formal uses of law—represented a "critical index of social, cultural, and political transformation" in Trinidad and Tobago (400).

In his ethnography of gender violence and law in post-Soviet Kazakhstan, Edward Snajdr (2007) shows how processes of implementation and advocacy are often filtered through a politics of ethnicity that reflects changing histories of power and multicultural relations. As he explains, the "collapse of the Soviet Union left all of the Central Asian republics the dual challenges of creating independent states and dealing with the post-colonial legacy of multicultural populations" (606). Kazakhstan was unique among the Central Asian states because it had the "distinction of becoming a new republic whose titular ethnic group [the Kazakhs] was a minority in its own state" (606). As a response, the Kazakh president undertook a long-term policy that aggressively promoted and revitalized Kazakh ethnic identity in areas of "language policy, formal education, the arts, and . . . religion" (606).

It was within this general context in which the state actively sought to "ethnicize the subject" that governmental policies around domestic violence encountered points of resistance. When Snajdr began his research in Kazakhstan in 1999, the country had recently acceded to CEDAW as an independent country.[10] As we have seen elsewhere, the accession to CEDAW by Kazakhstan was likewise promoted by an active network of international, transnational, and local activists. Indeed, Snajdr himself participated in this activism as the codirector of a development project funded by the U.S. State Department that used capacity-building workshops to train local police officers about the problem of domestic violence and the use of strategies for enforcement and protection. Drawing on this dual capacity as an engaged anthropologist with project management responsibilities, Snajdr found that the state's promotion of ethnic pride and ethnic nationalism brought it into conflict with its obligations to "pursue by all appropriate means and without delay a policy of eliminating discrimination against women" (CEDAW 1979, Art. 2), which, as we have seen, had been interpreted by 1992 to include domestic violence.

A complex web of cultural beliefs about kinship, female sexuality, and religion made the enforcement of the anti–domestic violence programs difficult because, as Snajdr's research showed, these beliefs were deeply rooted. Even if the promotion of Kazakh culture had been manipulated by the government in order to justify its hold on power, this influence took place against the backdrop of preexisting gender expectations in which physical violence against women—particularly wives—was expected and even encouraged by a wide range of family members.

In one telling encounter, the head of a major state domestic violence unit, an army colonel who was also a woman, explained that "from early childhood, Kazakh males are the bosses. It is normal for a husband to beat his wife" (2007: 607). Snajdr explains how wife beating plays an important role within the *kalym*, or bride-price, system in Kazakhstan, in which the disciplining function of domestic violence is believed to be necessary to protect the financial security that bride-price can bring a woman's extended family. Thus, a "man is expected to control his wife, who is considered to be essentially his family's property. . . . Divorce would entail her parents' returning bride-price to her husband's family and would damage the finances and reputation of the bride's kin group" (607).[11]

And yet, the relationship between culture and domestic violence in Kazakhstan was not a dialectical one; rather, other stakeholders drew from cultural tropes depending on their interests and goals. For example, Muslim women's groups "play[ed] up the legacy of Russian domination and downplay[ed] Kazakh linkages to violence in an effort to promote their political agenda of ethnic revitalization through religion" (616); "Kazakh police use[d] ethnicity . . . to explain the problem [of domestic violence] . . . and to excuse their own ineffectiveness as state actors" (616); and "[w]omen's NGOs play[ed] along with cultural themes as a strategy to open up dialogues with the state about other important factors such as gender inequality and patriarchal power" (616). Snajdr argues that rather than setting up a false opposition between culture and the universality of gender rights protections, it would be better to understand how different groups "ethnicize the problem in different ways" (617), even within the same society.[12]

Finally, as Sally Engle Merry's (2006a) research on the development and implementation of the CEDAW monitoring system demonstrates, the kind of anthropological nuance that Snajdr urges must also encompass the multiple stakeholders, political interests, and processes of cultural vernacularization that shape dynamics in the ambiguous spaces *between* the global and the local (see Goodale and Merry 2007). Merry's innovative multisited and multiscalar ethnography—a process described as "deterritorialized" (2006a: 28) anthropological research—led her to follow the circulations of international women's rights law across both time and space. Her research developed at the "interface between global and local activism" (2006: 3) and followed the movement of ideas about gender violence and law as they were debated, contested, and produced from major international meetings in places like New York and Geneva to "local community centers in Hawai'i, Delhi, Fiji, and Hong Kong" (3).

In perhaps the most emblematic finding from her study, Merry followed the various controversies surrounding Fiji's first ever country report to the CEDAW Committee. During Fiji's 2002 presentation at the UN in New York City,[13] country representatives acknowledged that a customary practice called *bulubulu* was being used to influence rape cases in court and that this created a conflict with the country's obligations under CEDAW (which it had ratified in 1995). But as Merry explains, the CEDAW experts used this revelation to attack the practice of bulubulu itself, which is a custom in which "a person apologizes for an offence and offers a whale's tooth (*tabua*) and a gift and asks forgiveness. The offended person is [then] under some pressure to accept the apology and make peace" (2006a: 113–114). Committee members chastised Fiji's representatives for not taking stronger steps to outlaw bulubulu in the country. As the role of bulubulu was understood by the CEDAW Committee, it allowed fathers of victims to accept gifts from their daughters' rapists and therefore absolve them, without their daughters' consent.

Yet when Merry pursued the controversy back to Fiji itself, she discovered key points of slippage and nuance that had been overlooked by the formal mechanisms of treaty implementation and monitoring. The country officials who had made the report in New York City felt overwhelmed by the legal and bureaucratic process and objected to the full-blown critique of bulubulu during and after the hearings. As Merry found, from the vantage point of the national and local level the complexities of bulubulu as a dynamic and contextual cultural practice could not be either easily translated into the terms of a women's rights report or accurately represented to a body of experts who were conditioned to view cultural practices with suspicion.

At the same time, while the resistance to UN criticism of bulubulu was in part the result of the "disjunctures between global law and local justice" (103), it also took place during a period in Fijian history in which a "nationalist ethnic . . . movement [was] asserting the centrality of Fijian village life to the nation" (117). Thus, the Fijian reaction to the CEDAW Committee's criticism was also a consequence of internally directed national politics. As she dug further into the ethnographic subtleties of these disjunctures, she concluded that the culture versus women's rights dialectic was both analytically and practically flawed. Instead, as she argues, to understand the controversy over bulubulu, it was necessary to examine broader processes of "economics, politics, and social class" as these reflected the "effects of globalization[,] . . . the spread of capitalism and the shrinking of state services" (133).[14]

## Law and the "Invisible Visible"

If the role of law in regulating—and ideally preventing—violence against women as a category of illegal gender discrimination has become well established at an international level and within many countries in the world across a range of cultural traditions, the same cannot be said of the relationship between law and transgressive or minority gender and sexual identities. Even if it is now widely accepted that "women's rights are human rights," the same cannot be said worldwide of people who identify as lesbian, gay, bisexual, or transgender (LGBT). Although in historical retrospect, it is likely that the current moment will appear as a drawn out turning point in the struggle to have LGBT rights recognized under international law, equivalent to the process through which discrimination against women became a human rights violation, there is no indication (as of 2016) that a "CEDALGBT" is on the horizon. Indeed, the world is starkly divided over how the law should apply to people who identify as LGBT. Whereas the law offers broad protections of equality and recourse in cases of discrimination in some countries, in others the law denies LGBT equality, criminalizes LGBT relationships, and, in some extreme cases, mandates the death penalty for these relationships.

Thus, anthropologists study the relationship between law and LGBT issues (rights movements, criminalization, identity construction, political resistance) on a troubled ethnographic landscape on which the "fusing [of] human rights and sexual politics" (Thoreson 2014) confronts discrimination, violence, and various forms of forced invisibility. Indeed, in her ethnography of LGBT mobilization in Poland, Monika Baer (2010) uses the concept of the "invisible visible" to explore the interconnections between civil society, sexuality, and political action. What she means is that the law mediates a complex social context in Poland in which the law pretends to neutrality in relation to the LGBT population yet without specifying any positive sanctions or remedies in cases of discrimination.

As she explains, although homosexuality was decriminalized in Poland as early as 1932, and homosexual prostitution decriminalized in 1969, contemporary Polish law "makes no direct mention of homosexuality" (2010: 250). Thus, despite the fact that Polish law does not criminalize transgressive sexual minorities, it also does not offer an obvious mechanism for defending them or advancing their political interests through rights protections. In this way, as Baer argues, "social and legal practice in Poland situates the country in the stage of pre-emancipation" (250) for people who identify as LGBT.

Nevertheless, Baer's research among LGBT activists at a university demonstrates that for this "invisible visible" population, the law is not the only outlet for building support through the creation of new public spaces in which the fact of transgressive sexuality can be discussed. Paradoxically "visible" because of the law's supposed neutrality but at the same time "invisible" precisely because of this supposed neutrality before the law, Polish LGBT activists turn to more informal, interpersonal forms of resistance and advocacy. These informal practices have themselves changed over time and reflect broader developments in Polish politics and economic life.

Within this trajectory, the fall of the communist regime in 1989 figures prominently. As one of her interlocutors explained, in the early years of postcommunist Poland, "to organize a club party or to publish an erotic magazine was a political act. Then, the club parties and pornography became businesses and then they didn't have anything more to do with militancy" (2010: 251). Yet as Baer concludes, new spaces for informal militancy arose to take the place of clubs and publications, for example, student organizations based on "gender" and "queer studies" (concepts that Baer argues were imported from outside the country after 1989). The result shows that the concept of "civil society" itself must be expanded beyond formal institutions or organizations with a clear political purpose.

Likewise, in her study of the relationship between homosexuality and international development in Central Asia, Laëtitia Atlani-Duault (2007) examines the ways in which the legal status of LGBT communities has been fundamentally shaped by wider historical and political-economic forces. She describes the profound implications of these broader changes:

In 1991, the disappearance of the Soviet Union resulted in the political independence of the former Central Asian Soviet republics. For nearly 55 million people in Central Asia, all of whom had been born citizens of the

Soviet Union, their nationality suddenly changed. Even though they had identified as members of a great world power and had lived a relatively comfortable economic life, the vast majority now lost their purchasing power and experienced the dismantling of an economic system put in place during the Soviet period. (2007: 97)

Thus, the early post-Soviet period in Central Asia was marked by both the search for new political and cultural identities to replace those that had disappeared with the fall of the Soviet Union and a rapidly worsening economic situation that saw many people's earning power and quality of life collapse.

It was against this backdrop that the legal and political situation of Central Asia's LGBT population took on heightened importance. The success of the American gay rights movement in the fight against the HIV epidemic inspired the strategies and rhetoric of new Central Asian gay rights networks, which were formed in the early 1990s in countries in which homosexuality was both legally criminalized and culturally stigmatized. Beyond the creation of novel and precarious social networks that spanned "heterogeneous nationalities, professional positions, institutional memberships, and . . . geography" (2007: 93), the dynamic interaction between local actors and the transnational gay rights movement also required the appropriation of "universalist norms like *advocacy* and *lobbying*" as "principal weapons" in the emergent struggle (93; emphases in original).

However, as the post-Soviet period approached the end of its second decade, other identities mobilized around citizenship and religion were promoted by the state in ways that had serious consequences for the development of a viable pan-regional LGBT movement in Central Asia. On the one hand, Central Asian states developed increasingly elaborate security programs to monitor the work of political and social organizations with links to transnational (particularly Western) institutions. As Atlani-Duault argues, this was in part a legacy of Soviet governance, since many of the elites in the new Central Asian countries had played important roles during the Soviet regime.

But on the other hand, the promotion of "virulent" forms of nationalism in the Central Asian republics, organized around ideal conceptions of Kazakh, or Uzbek, or Tajik personhood, led to a countermovement against all minorities, "ethnic or sexual" (2007: 107). In this context, the idea of using the law as a progressive tool to protect the LGBT community was inconceivable. Indeed, as she argues, the situation for activists in the late 2000s was worse than ever, since those who had participated in the creation of gay rights networks in the early 1990s found themselves especially vulnerable.

Finally, John Borneman's (2012) research on incest prosecutions in Berlin reveals the ways in which legal categories shape the very understanding of sexuality itself beyond political and social identities. His study is grounded in a longer intellectual history within anthropology in which scholars have used the cultural forms of prohibition to incest—taboos—to examine how these structure the terms of human sociality more generally. As he puts it, for many anthropologists who have studied incest taboos, they are "said to regulate the entire symbolic order, marking the transition from nature to culture and orienting relations between generations and males and females. It is the one human universal on which most anthropologists would concur" (2012: 182).[15]

Borneman used both archival and ethnographic methods to examine the way that the legal and psychological treatment of incest reflected a broader shift in German society through which the category of the "despotic father of a paternal order" (2012: 193; quoting from Perner 2006) had disappeared from the German cultural landscape. Borneman argues that the incest taboo has its origins in modes of kinship and the social regulation of sexual life that no longer exist. As he puts it, in the absence of the "despotic father," which "figure or institution will serve as the modality of law to regulate questions of physical intimacy that constitute the relations between generations and genders?" (2012: 193). And with the advent of "new reproductive technologies [and] invasive surgical procedures to create transgendered beings" (193), the original purposes of the incest taboo become even more delinked, since the prohibition was fundamentally a basis for the reproduction of a heterosexual sociolegal order. Borneman concludes that these gaps between legal prohibition and changing practices of intimacy shine a light on the way sexuality more generally comes to be regulated by the state through the legal categories that define the terms of the "lived experience of transgression and illegality" (2012: 199).

## Law and the Contested Body

A final sphere of anthropological research on the relationship between law and the moral economies of gender revolves around the body as a site of legal and political contestation. These dynamics play out in revealing ways in a number of areas of focus, including the regulation of sex work/prostitution within transnational trafficking networks; in debates over fertility and reproductive rights; and in the charged settings in which cultural practices like female genital cutting (FGC) become the locus of struggles over autonomy, national identity, and the place of legal rights in regulating the (typically female) body.

In a series of ethnographic studies, Sophie Day has examined the ways in which contemporary debates over how the law should regulate sex work reflect longer processes of cultural change through which the body must carry a "weight of meaning" (2010: 816) for questions of freedom, sexual autonomy, moral corruption, and the value of labor. Day's research involved an innovative longitudinal study of sex workers in London through the Praed Street Project, a "a sexual health and support service for women from all over the world who work, have worked or are associated with any part of the sex industry within London" (National Health Service 2015). Day found that historical images of slavery, prostitution, and female subordination shaped both the daily lives of sex workers in Britain and the development of international norms meant to control migration in which sex work was implicated.[16] The ethnography of these intersections also revealed something surprising about the relationship between sexuality, labor, and beliefs about moral worth.

Within the antitrafficking movement, as she argues, discourses of exchange are used to structure legal regulation and moral condemnation. The focus on the "initial separation of women from their previous lives" (2010: 829) is grounded in an ideology of exchange in which people ideally exercise their rights and obligations on an equal footing and without coercion. But in conducting ethnographic research over the long term among sex workers in London, Day found that many of them had constructed "counter-publics" that offered new forms of freedom even if they were structurally fragile, since they were not based on "the usual solidity of social processes reproduced over time, transmitted to the next generation and built into the material landscape" (830).

The women were "free" of many of the burdensome and even abusive demands of socially sanctioned relationships—both in the countries from which they migrated and in Britain. In perhaps the most provocative finding from her research, Day (and colleagues in the Praed Street Project) found that although sex workers experienced a rupture between past and present that amounted to a form of "social death," the passage to the other side of this process offered the women a kind of protection "from the weight of the past (and future) with its lasting, legible, and visible social practices, where they could enjoy intense and possibly transient associations within the horizon of the present" (830).

Legal and political contestation around the female body is also a key concern for anthropologists who study cultures of fertility. In her ethnography of the combustible crossroads at which fertility intersects with nationalism and moral panic in postsocialist Russia, Michele Rivkin-Fish (2003) argues that the legacy of Russia's Soviet past created an ideological context in which contemporary political parties ignored socioeconomic analysis in favor of culturalist positions to explain the rise of inequality under Russian capitalism. Despite the rapidly widening economic gaps within Russian society, class analysis of inequality was viewed with suspicion because of its ideological links to the Soviet past. Instead, scholars and politicians alike responded to a series of very real health crises that followed in the wake of the collapse of the Soviet Union—"[f]ertility decreased, morbidity and male mortality skyrocketed, and rates of infectious diseases including syphilis and tuberculosis grew exponentially . . . result[ing] in a net population decline" (2003: 293)—by pushing for a series of legal and political measures that were "pronatalist."

Women's fertility became a central arena of struggle and a means through which supposedly traditional Russian family values were offered as a solution to the dislocations caused by the new market economy. The argument went something like this: women were not fulfilling their historical role of reproducing the Russian nation with energy and purpose because the imploding economy meant that there was not enough to eat, not enough work, and not enough state support to sustain normal fertility rates. As a response, legal regulations were proposed during the 1990s that would have forced higher fertility rates by banning abortion and even legalizing polygamy in Russia, a move that was intended to "ensure that no woman remains without a husband and children" (293).

Although these legal initiatives were ultimately not adopted, they reflected a wider pattern in Russian society in which women's fertility became a primary means through which Russians grappled with transition and uncertainty. And even if the most extreme expressions of this politicization of fertility were blocked, others were not. As Rivkin-Fish explains, through other legal reforms, "nationalists . . . succeeded in hindering family planning and sex education programs in the name of national survival" (293). She concludes that anthropologists must examine how these struggles over the female body and its forms of social reproduction reflect broader anxieties about the absence of "paternalistic state assurances" in the face of "wage-labor bereft of workers' rights, . . . wages often below subsistence levels . . . and blatant gender discrimination" (297).

The relationship between law and the contested body is perhaps no better illustrated than in the legal, political, and cultural debates around female genital cutting (FGC).[17] Bettina Shell-Duncan's (2008) ethnographic research examines the trajectory of legal struggles over FGC at both the international and local levels. As she explains, anti-FGC activists had originally not used the law as a way to fight against the practices. During the 1970s and 1980s, anti-FGC campaigns were grounded in health initiatives "centered on a community-based education approach of delivering a message on the adverse health effects" of FGC (2008: 226). However, the health approach was largely ineffective as a strategy for a number of reasons, including the fact that community propaganda materials tended to focus on cases of extreme outcomes that appeared to exaggerate the health dangers for women who felt "the risk . . . worth taking in light of the social and cultural importance of the practice" (226). At the same time, the emphasis on the health risks and medical treatment of FGC was believed by some activists, particularly in Africa, to carry the risk of medicalizing the practice by offering safer options that would weaken the preferred "zero tolerance" strategies (226–227).

But beginning in the early 1990s, as the end of the Cold War created a normative vacuum that was quickly filled by human rights discourse, institutions and activists within what had become a global anti-FGC movement dropped health as an organizing principle in favor of rights. As Shell-Duncan's research reveals, this move was in part an effect of the rise of the women's rights movement more generally, which, as we have already seen, gathered momentum during the early 1990s around key international conferences and the development of the CEDAW enforcement regime.

During multisited ethnographic research "at the WHO in Geneva and UNICEF in New York, Kenya, and Ethiopia" (227), as well as during international meetings in other sites of international legal and political regulation, Shell-Duncan was able to document how the full spectrum of emerging rights frameworks was appropriated to transform the way FGC practices were reframed through law. Despite concerns from legal scholars about "potential problems or weaknesses," several different legal arguments were brought to bear against FGC, including the "rights of the child, the rights of women, the right to freedom from torture, and the right to health and bodily integrity" (227).[18]

And yet, as Shell-Duncan argues, the move from a medical approach to a legal one "create[d] as many problems as it [sought] to resolve" (229). Invoking David Kennedy's (2004) critique of human rights and the "dark sides of virtue," Shell-Duncan argues that anti-FGC activists have had a difficult time in realizing their objectives because an orthodox human rights approach "articulates problems in political terms and solutions in legal terms." Instead, her research points to alternative strategies, anchored in ethnography, that "investigate the social meanings and purposes of [FGC] and . . . develop an understanding of varied positions concerning the practice within the society" (233). In this way, an anthropological perspective on FGC focuses on "both protection and respect for the autonomy of those women and families concerned" (233).

## Conclusion: Gender, Moral Practice, Transgression

In his ethnography of practices of "defiant desire" among Namibia's working-class lesbian community, Robert Lorway (2008) examines the ways in which gender identities, political expression, and sexual transgression become sources of creative resistance for marginal populations marked by intersectional vulnerabilities. His study is a powerful example of the fact that the relationship between law and moral economies of gender unfolds in equal measure beyond courts and through the production of international norms. Although his interlocutors drew deeply from international human rights discourse in order to legitimate bodily desire as an expression of a transgressive self, the specific practices of lesbian sexuality he examined—which included women dressing as men—also had political economic implications.

As he argues, the importance of cross-dressing among Namibia's working-class lesbians is that it is also a way for them to "share solidarity with [straight] working-class Namibian women's everyday struggles with men" (2008: 31). Lorway's study of transgressive sexuality in a broader context of state persecution and (in this case) heterosexual subjugation is thus a useful anthropological reminder that the "universal frame of sexual minority-rights discourse," which is so closely connected with the law, can obscure other, less conventional, practices that nevertheless work to empower and forge subversive categories of belonging.

More broadly, as the various surveys of anthropological research in this chapter demonstrate, law occupies an ambiguous position as a framework for both regulating and defining gender and sexuality. On the one hand, as we have seen with the anthropological study of the women's rights movement and the emergence of international enforcement regimes, the law can underpin cultural change in ways that promote individual autonomy, call attention to patterns of patriarchal violence, and draw normative bright lines that link the struggles of local women to a global activist community. Yet on the other hand, these same legal capabilities create difficulties, some anticipated, others unintended. Because the relationship between law and gender often develops within nation-states in the midst of cultural and socioeconomic transition, the progressive impulses of law can confront strong countercurrents of nationalism, religious mobilization, and anticolonialism.

And finally, as Saba Mahmood's (2012) ethnography of sectarian conflict and family law in Egypt demonstrates, gender identity is often not the most important category through which struggles over political power, personal autonomy, and equality take place. Instead, questions of gender equality and sexual rights can become suppressed during periods of historical violence and radical social change, as the basic social contract is renegotiated in the light of long-term grievances felt by cultural and religious collectivities. Yet as Mahmood also argues, questions of gender and sexual difference must eventually be confronted within these new settlements. The hope is that what results progressively reorients gender relations rather than simply reestablishing patterns of inequality in "unique and contradictory ways" (2012: 60).

8

# Ethnonationalism and Conflict Transformation

As we have seen throughout this book, the ways and means of law underwent profound shifts in the decades after the end of the Cold War. From the creation of new tribunals of international criminal law to the establishment of global treaty enforcement regimes, and from the use of law within political and social conflicts like the headscarf debate in France to the development of indigenous rights as a new form of social identity, in each case, the law was mobilized in order to promote universal (or at least transnational) values as against those that represented the opposite: sectarianism, nationalism, ethnic difference, and state exceptionalism. And as we have also seen, the attempt to forge various forms of cosmopolitan legality in the post–Cold War confronted a range of obstacles. From the conflicted orientation of women's rights activists from the Global South, who were forced to advocate for universal rights at the same time as they defended against attacks on their countries' cultural traditions, to the indigenous rights activists who triumphed in the courts only to watch as new laws opened the door for massive accumulation of indigenous lands by multinational corporations, the emergence of the post–Cold War's cosmopolitan juristocracy was marked by contradiction, compromise, and vulnerability.

Despite these tensions, perhaps there was no better evidence of the powerful currents of universal legal values during this period than the effort by the U.S. government to reframe its rationale for invading Iraq in 2003 once it was clear that so-called weapons of mass destruction had not been found. Even though the Bush Administration was intent on invading Iraq and replacing Saddam Hussein after the September 11, 2001 attacks on the United States, it nevertheless went through the diplomatic motions of arguing that Iraq was in possession of weapons that were a threat to regional and eventually international security. When it became clear in the first months of the war that the justification based on the presence of WMD had been wrong (either intentionally or through mistaken information), the Bush Administration turned to human rights, arguing that even if Iraq had not possessed WMD, the invasion was justified in order to allow the country to take its place among the community of nations governed by national versions of universal legal standards.[1]

But within this generalized post–Cold War era of cosmopolitan and transnational restructuring, the law was also being used to ground quite different normative visions, sometimes in opposition to the currents of human rights and global activism, sometimes as the expression of ethnonationalist mobilization in the aftermath of political and social transition. For example, in the early 1990s, a range of "state agencies and political figures from Singapore, the People's Republic of China, and Malaysia" launched a "counter-hegemonic" legal defense against the "already-powerful and prominent Western discourse on universal human rights" based on the principle that "culture is destiny" and the idea that the "East Asian Confucian past" offered a regional, but clearly nonuniversal, source of norms inspired by "[f]amily, filial piety, commitment to education, hard work, and thrift" (Bell 2001: 23, 24). As a high-ranking Singaporean diplomat of the time put it, "many East and southeast Asians tend to look askance at the starkly individualist ethos of the West in which authority tends to be seen as oppressive and rights are an individual's 'trump' over the state" (quoted in Bell 2001: 25).[2]

And as Robert Hayden (1992) discovered, through long-term ethnographic fieldwork both during and after the critical years in which the former Yugoslavia disintegrated, the pull toward universal norms was so strong in the early post–Cold War that it was necessary to create entirely new legal forms that were both "clear to the faithful" and yet "in some way masked" (1992: 655), so that the intention to use law to privilege certain ethnic groups over others was obscured. As we will see more fully below, the emergence of "constitutional nationalism" was only one among several examples in which legacies of ethnic discrimination, and the social impact of "chosen traumas" (Volkan 1997) formed the background against which legal doctrine and identity were developed that promoted mechanisms of collective exclusion, expulsion, and (in certain cases) ethnic cleansing (see Hayden 1996).

As anthropologists have shown, these conflicts went far beyond simple struggles between those who advocated for universal normative principles and those who promoted varieties of "ethnic pride" that carried within them the seeds of "ethnic terrorism" (Volkan 1997). But there can be no doubt, as the research surveyed in this chapter reveals, that the law became the grounds during the years after the end of the Cold War on which a much older fracture was reopened between what Isaiah Berlin characterized as the "pursuit of the ideal" on one side, and on the other, the "revolt against the myth of an ideal world" (Berlin 1991). Yet as we will see, the relationship between law and ethnonationalism during periods of transition cannot be explained simply as the result of the "disordered imagination" (Berlin 1991: 220) working on behalf of the "consciousness of nationality" (Berlin 1996: 247), even if the legalization of nationalism is often accompanied by images of prophecy, apotheosis, and a kind of fevered anticosmopolitanism. Rather, as Cowan, Dembour, and Wilson (2001) have argued, the invocation of collective difference and its codification in law can also be read as a political tactic; that is, the mechanisms of *Realpolitik* working in terms of and through categories of legal identity.

But as will become clear, certain key themes reoccur in the anthropological study of law, ethnonationalism, and conflict transformation that involve problems of more general concern, such as the role of culture within international law; the relationship between nation and state, particularly in regions in which these emerge from distinct ideological histories; and the unstable position of nonstate legal orders that come to "emulate" (Timmer 2010) state legal models at the same time as they exist in structural opposition to them. And as will also become clear, there is a defined trajectory in the development of these key themes in the anthropology of law over the almost thirty years since the end of the Cold War system. For example, ethnographic research on law, the state, and nationalism from the early to late 1990s took place during a period of cultural, technological, and normative liminality. This was a time in which social and political structures were being reconceived in ways that could be both creative and violent at the same time; the old hierarchies of economy and communication were apparently giving way with the emergence of a global "network society" (Castells 1996); and the "curious grapevine" of transnational rights activism that Eleanor Roosevelt had imagined in 1948 was finally making it possible for the transformative commandment of human dignity to "seep in even where governments are not so anxious for it."[3]

Yet by the end of the first decade of the new century at the latest, some twenty years after the end of the Cold War, this critical period of liminality had ended, giving way, as all periods of liminality must, to the reemergence of hierarchies, the formation of new forms of structural violence, and, perhaps most critical for our purposes here, the realization that history had not in fact ended, but that it continued with uncertain prospects for the old dreams of the Kantian *Weltbürgerrecht*.[4] Thus, at the same time in which a culture of cosmopolitan norms was becoming a "core aspect of a new global, transnational culture, a *sui generis* phenomenon of modernity" (Cowan, Dembour, Wilson 2001: 12), global economic inequality was widening (Piketty 2014), the mechanisms of development and aspirational politics were being co-opted by multinational corporations (Goodale 2017b; Li 2014b), and even the processes of climate change were being commoditized in ways that made anti–climate change actions unprofitable and therefore extremely unlikely to be undertaken (Keucheyan 2014).[5] By 2016, the only "multitude" that appeared capable of "constructing a new ontological reality" based on "geographical mythologies that mark . . . new paths of destiny" (Hardt and Negri 2000: 395, 397) was one committed not to global citizenship and emancipation from capitalism, but to moral and religious purity, the decimation of unbelievers, and the glory of a martyr's death.

Although it is not possible to trace the full implications of these historical developments on the anthropology of law over the same period, it is important that they be kept in the background for reference and also in order to understand why discussions of, for example, the relationship between culture and law, took different forms at different moments. In the next section, the chapter examines the ways in which the law—particularly national constitutions—has been used to create categories of collective exclusion that in some cases became the basis for what the Slovenian anthropologist Uršula Lipovec Čebron (2012) has called legal "erasure." The chapter then takes up the contested place of "culture" within international law. As scholars have shown, the legal engagement with the multiple senses of culture reinforces Raymond Williams's argument (1976) that culture is among the most complicated and elusive of contemporary concepts, one that is capable of being mobilized, for example, both for and against human rights (see Cowan, Dembour, Wilson 2001).

After that, the chapter surveys the ways in which anthropologists have studied the relationship between law, legal orders, and the state. As Jaap Timmer (2010) has argued, ethnic and labor collectivities that organize around distinct and local legal traditions seek at a certain level to be "seen like the state," yet this form of recognition can lead to conflicts over the rule of law and state sovereignty. Finally, the chapter concludes with a reflection on how anthropologists of law are likely to respond to the fact that cosmopolitan legal forms are giving way in the face of strengthened nation-states, the weakening of supranational regional bodies like the European Union, and the rise of transnational normative orders grounded in exclusionary and even violent ideologies.

## Legal Exclusion and the Imagined Community

Much like in the years after the collapse of the Austro-Hungarian and Ottoman empires at the end of World War I, the collapse of the Soviet Bloc system likewise unleashed a range of political and social movements in Central and Eastern Europe organized around the associated but ideologically and analytically distinct concepts of "nation" and "nationalism." As Raymond Williams has argued, the English word "nation" has its origins in French and Latin words that meant "breed" or "race" and this usage has been common (in English) since the late thirteenth century, "originally with a primary sense of a racial group rather than a politically organized grouping. Since there is obvious overlap between these senses, it is not easy to date the emergence of the predominant modern sense of a political formation" (Williams 1976: 213). Although it is not possible to review here the many and sharp contemporary debates around nation, nationalism, and nation-state, for our purposes it is enough to note that a major line of analysis divides approaches that emphasize the essentially modern, political, and functionalist nature of nations and nationalism (e.g., Gellner 1983), from those that emphasize their cultural, ideological, and nonrational dimensions (e.g., Connor 1994).[6]

A similar set of issues with which anthropologists have been centrally concerned revolves around the extent to which the "nation" should be seen as a particularly unstable cultural construction whose contextuality offers the possibility that it can be destabilized, undermined, and eventually replaced, especially when the "nation" becomes the basis for various forms of systematic violence. Some anthropologists have argued that scholars have an obligation to emphasize the "imagined" nature of nations and thus of nationalism, even when such a contingent and constructivist account would not be recognizable to many nationalists themselves. At the same time, other anthropologists have countered that this type of analytical imposition is itself a form of violence, even if it is driven by moral commitment and a desire to use anthropological knowledge on behalf of victims of ethnic persecution.[7] Despite these disciplinary divisions, there is consensus on the fact that in periods of nationalist ascendance the instruments of state governance, including the law, often become the mechanisms through which discriminatory policies are justified and implemented.

In a series of anthropological studies in the years leading up to and soon after the collapse of Yugoslavia, Robert Hayden documented the ways in which the law became a central instrument of exclusion under the guise of accepted norms of European liberal democracy. Hayden (1992) described these new applications of law as an expression of "constitutional nationalism," which he defines as "a constitutional and legal structure that privileges the members of one ethnically defined nation over other residents in a particular state. . . . [C]onstitutional nationalism envisions a state in which sovereignty resides with a particular nation (*narod*), the members of which are the only ones who can decide fundamental questions of state form and identity" (1992: 655–656).

Based on both ethnographic and comparative methodologies, Hayden's research shows that at the same time in which the discourse of universal human rights and individual equality was being diffused around the world, in the former Yugoslavia a radically different theory of rights was taking root, one in which an allegedly ancient collectivity— the nation—was the bearer of a set of rights that it alone possessed. For example, Hayden analyzes the preambles and introductory sections of the various constitutions of the Yugoslav republics as a rich source of symbolic rhetoric that most clearly crystalized the aspirations of constitutional nationalism. The 1990 Croatian Constitution begins by invoking the "thousand year national independence and state continuity of the Croatian nation"; asserts the "inalienable . . . right of the Croatian nation to self-determination and state sovereignty"; and establishes the "national state of the Croatian nation" accompanied by the "republic's ethnically Croat coat of arms and flag," which, as Hayden points out, "were very similar to those used by the fascist 'Independent State of Croatia' during World War II, under which hundreds of thousands of Serbs were killed" (1992: 657). The 1991 Slovene Constitution asserts "the basic and permanent right of the Slovene nation . . . to self-determination" and legalizes "the historical fact that the Slovenes have formed . . . their own national identity and established their own statehood" (1992: 659). Finally, the Macedonian Constitution of 1991 is grounded in the "historical, cultural, spiritual and statehood heritage of the Macedonian people" and establishes the republic as a "national state of the Macedonian people," albeit a people with an obligation to "permanent[ly] cohabitat[e] . . . with . . . [the other] nationalities living in the Republic of Macedonia (1992: 659–660).

As Hayden argues, states that use law to legitimate and promote an exclusionary collectivity "defined in terms of race, language, and culture . . . seem likely to alienate minority populations and to produce not democracy or freedom but civil war and its consequent authoritarian policies—the tragic fate of post-socialist Yugoslavia" (1992: 670, 673; see also Hayden 1999).

Jean-François Gossiaux's (2002) ethnographic research on the ethnic wars in the former Yugoslav republics examines another aspect of law, in this case the legal bureaucracies of census taking and demographic reckoning through which both the ethnic nation and national minorities were established as legal subjects entitled to different types of rights and public goods. Gossiaux also emphasizes the fact that the principle of legalized ethnonationalism was not something created within the Yugoslav conflict but was rather a basic approach to state building from the late nineteenth century to the end of World War I, when it became part of Woodrow Wilson's platform for national self-determination (Gossiaux 2002: 53).

In Gossiaux's analysis of the relationship between the differential codification of ethnic power and violence in the former Yugoslav republics, he argues that the most critical problem was the fact that the legal categories implied a theoretical fixity that was belied by the lived realities of actors on all sides of the conflicts. His research demonstrates that the gap between the legalization of ethnonationalism and the "never ending process of ethnicity building" (2002: 53) creates both the potential for violent conflict and also the potential for new forms of negotiation that might constrain this violence.

Finally, Uršula Lipovec Čebron's (2012) ethnography provides an insider scholar's perspective on how these multiple potentialities unfolded in practice. She both conducted research and was herself a social actor in Slovenia during the tumultuous period immediately after independence in 1991. As she explains, the first action the authorities in the new republic took was to "redefine the rules of citizenship" (2012: 241). The large majority of people who were found to possess "Slovenian nationality" anywhere in the former Yugoslavia were automatically granted citizenship in the new Slovenian republic. Everyone else who was a citizen of another ex-Yugoslav republic was required to apply for citizenship within six months. All those who failed to apply within six months, or whose applications were rejected, were automatically converted to the status of undocumented migrants (*migrants sans papiers*). As Lipovec Čebron puts it, "in effect, the new Interior Ministry deleted them from the population registry of the Slovenian republic. Thus was born a group of 25,671 people who called themselves the 'erased ones.' Fully legal citizens before the independence of Slovenia, they lost all their political, economic, and social rights in just a few months" (241).

The new citizenship regulations, the manner through which they were applied, and their consequences of erasure for those who did not fit into standard definitions of Slovene nationality, were all part of a program of state governance to ethnically "homogenize the national territory as much as possible" (241). Through a "xenophobic and racist" discourse promoted by Slovene political parties, particularly those on the right, the goal was to make it impossible for non-Slovenes to "attach themselves to the new country" (241). As Lipovec Čebron's study reveals, this program of legal erasure was largely effective over the next decade of ethnic conflict and hypernationalist political posturing. Even if Slovenia was never ethnically "homogenized" in the way imagined by nationalist politicians during the birth of the new republic, the use of law to create stark categories of inclusion and exclusion resulted in the suppression of groups that were physically present yet legally marginalized.

## Epistemologies of Culture in International Law

As anthropologists of law have shown, "culture" occupies an ambiguous place conceptually, ideologically, and institutionally within international law. This is also true of the role of culture in the domestic legal regimes of countries around the world, in which an "accurate cross-cultural jurisprudence" (Renteln 2005) has not yet gained wide acceptance.[8] Yet it has been through debates over universal legal norms and the empirical realities of contested collective difference that the problems of culture have been most acute.

Indeed, part of the ambiguity has come from the fact that the meaning of culture itself has changed over time.[9] An illustrative example of this is the way in which the meaning of culture has shifted within major human rights instruments, beginning with the UDHR. "Culture" appears in the UDHR as a modifier, in Articles 22 and 27, in which a person is recognized as having both "cultural rights indispensable for his dignity" and the "right freely to participate in the cultural life of the community." As Johannes Morsink (1999) has explained, in his comprehensive history of the drafting of the UDHR, the invocation of culture in these two articles (by John P. Humphrey, the author of the first and most important draft of the UDHR) was a reference to what would have been known in Canadian polite society in the late 1940s as "the arts": that is, those leisure activities that were believed to enrich the human spirit and provide an outlet for creative expression.[10]

The meaning of culture within international law underwent an important change with the 1972 Convention Concerning the Protection of the World Cultural and Natural Heritage. Here, culture became a symbol of past human achievements within a competitive (and political) hierarchy of legal classification through which only those markers of "outstanding universal value" were considered worthy of protection as "cultural heritage."[11] A final example of how the meanings of culture have both shifted and have remained diverse within international law is the 2001 UNESCO Universal Declaration on Cultural Diversity. This intriguing and relatively obscure international declaration was "adopted unanimously in a most unusual context. It came in the wake of the events of 11 September 2001. . . . It was an opportunity for States to reaffirm their conviction that intercultural dialogue is the best guarantee of peace and to reject outright the theory of the inevitable clash of cultures and civilizations" (UNESCO 2002 [2001]).[12] The declaration adopts a version of what might be thought of as a classical anthropological definition of culture,[13] but then confirms the problematic place of this broad approach to culture within international law by asserting that "no one may invoke cultural diversity to infringe upon human rights guaranteed by international law, nor to limit their scope" (Art. 4).

And as we have seen in several places in this book (notably in chapters 4 and 7), regardless of how culture is *defined* in international law, yet another category of conflicts that has received sustained ethnographic attention involves the practice of international law, in which vernacularization, localization, and resistance are often grounded in arguments for or against culture. But in cases in which cultural norms are closely associated with ethnonational identity, particularly within international criminal tribunals, the lines of tension can be drawn quite differently. This is because the relationship between culture and law can go straight to the core of questions of guilt, innocence, and mitigation within broader processes of conflict transformation that involve nothing less than the future of fractured societies.

In a number of studies of "epistemological confrontations" over the meanings and legal implications of culture in international criminal tribunals, Nigel Eltringham (e.g., 2004, 2013) argues that the openness and fluidity of legal rules in these novel forums create an opening through which legal knowledge about culture and culpability can evolve less through antagonism and more through "strategic ambivalence" (2013: 347). Focusing on the role of expert witnesses, including anthropologists, at the International Criminal Tribunal for Rwanda (ICTR), Eltringham shows how the nature of the violations themselves—crimes either by or against collectivities, or both, such as genocide and crimes against humanity—demand the introduction of legal knowledge about both cultural values and the more ambiguous causal relationship between these values and massive human rights violations.

For example, would a particular set of cultural beliefs make a group of people more likely to engage in ultra-violence against their neighbors if these beliefs were manipulated by politicians through relentless propaganda? Eltringham concludes that the emergence of apparently distinct and often opposing epistemologies of culture in international criminal tribunals should be understood to be the result of the practice of "judicial economy" (2013: 352) rather than a result of the clash between universal legal principles and local norms.

In his ethnography of judicial practice in Lebanon's shari'a courts, Morgan Clarke examines another way in which epistemologies of culture are shaped in revealing ways in the course of legal processes. For shari'a judges in Beirut, the application of legal rules of procedure can come into conflict with a parallel set of imperatives, those imposed by an overlapping set of historical, religious, and moral categories. Clarke conducted research among Lebanon's intricate network of religious courts, which emerged from "Lebanon's communitarian legal and political settlement" (2012: 107) among the country's eighteen official religious communities. The specific conflict he focuses on revolves around what might be called different cultures of moral reasoning within the religious courts. Judges are both religious specialists and state functionaries and these two roles demand different kinds of ethical frames. Yet these two frames must be present to greater or lesser degrees at the same time. As he puts it, "an Islamic judge can, in practice, ignore neither the demands of legal consistency and bureaucratic efficiency nor those of a truly religious vocation" (2012: 107).

Clarke observed as religious court judges applied these alternative modes of reasoning in the course of attempting to resolve family law matters like domestic disputes, spousal support, and property settlement among siblings. In one revealing ethnographic passage, Clarke shows how the tension between legal efficiency and cultural values in their courtrooms leads judges to display the proper approach to this tension through their outward appearance and manner of living. As he describes one judge, he was

> [n]ot a man of great material extravagance. Nevertheless, conforming to expectations, his personal appearance is polished and his mobile telephone a new enough model not to look dowdy in what is a competitive field in Lebanon. . . . He drives a Mercedes of classic vintage rather than the most luxurious and latest model; he lives in a popular neighborhood. One can see, then, as a lawyer pointed out to me with approval, that he is honest and not on the take. (2012: 110–111)

As Clarke explains, for Beirut's judges of Islamic law, the relationship between law and culture was really one between bureaucratic efficiency and the application of rules tempered by "humanity," by which they meant rules anchored in religious doctrine and invoked so as to lead the parties in court "back to the right way" (111). Rather than an opposition between theories of knowledge per se, for Clarke the struggle over which modes of reasoning to emphasize in court was even more a struggle over "what sort of ethical self must a judge cultivate" (116). Thus, Clarke's study suggests that we must tease out the ways in which "culture" encompasses multiple categories in legal settings—identity (ethnic, religious, class), moral practice, and what might be thought of as bureaucratic psychology.

Finally, in her ethnographic study of Gypsy (*Tsigane*) society and dispute resolution procedures in Andalusia (Spain), Caterina Pasqualino (1999) examines the ways in which Spain's Gypsy population is subject to a "double negation" (617). On the one hand, Spanish Gypsies—like Gypsy populations throughout Europe—are denied legal recognition as an ethnic group or distinct nationality by the nation-state because they are said to lack functioning institutions, territorial stability, and clear ethnic boundary markers that distinguish them from both other Gypsy populations and Spain's non-Gypsies. But on the other hand, Spain's Gypsies resist the call to develop precisely those institutions and clear boundary markers that would make it more likely that they would receive legal recognition by the state.[14] As a result, according to one study, "[d]espite a 600 year history in Spain . . . [Gypsies] are not recognized either as an ethnic minority, or as one of the 'peoples of Spain'" (Open Society Institute 2002).

As Pasqualino's study shows, disputes within Spanish Gypsy communities are typically resolved by a group of "influential heads of family who have the right to intervene in their personal capacity," that is, not as heads of Gypsy legal institutions that are known elsewhere in Europe as *kris* (1999: 620).[15] However, these groups of men do not remain assembled for purposes of either hearing subsequent disputes or, more generally, as the basis for claims making against the Spanish state. Pasqualino concludes that the central factor in the ongoing marginalization of Gypsies in Spain is the fact that their collective identity and cultural practices clash with European ideologies of legal nationalism.

As she puts it, "they do not claim rights to territory, unlike the Basque and Catalan 'peoples'" (624). Spain's Gypsies refuse to conform to legal expectations of collective identity, especially those that involve confrontation with or attempts to subvert the state. As a result, they are pushed into a legal and political void in ways that make it much more likely that they will continue to suffer social discrimination, quotidian violence, and, at the extremes, collective expulsion or confinement.[16]

## Being Seen Like the State

Anthropologists have studied another important dynamic in the relationship between law, nationalism, and the state, one through which marginalized collectivities develop institutions that emulate those of the state. As we will see, these acts of mimesis have uncertain consequences. In some cases, the process of reproducing (or creating new) institutions, particularly legal institutions, in forms that are recognizable to the state, can create spaces of action and legitimacy for cultural and national minorities. These might or might not be within a general sociolegal context in which the state recognizes legal pluralism as part of restructuring after conflict or as a result of political pressure from global institutions. Yet in other cases, the process of producing institutional forms and modes of governance that imitate the state can lead to less room for maneuver by vulnerable populations. This is because these new institutions create a governance wormhole that connects peoples and regions that were formally isolated from the state directly to its instruments of control.

In his ethnography of "emulations of legal culture" among Bugis migrants in East Kalimantan, Indonesia, Jaap Timmer (2010) argues that in certain cases, "people may not be so much interested in how the state sees them (Scott 1999) but may be keen to be seen like a state through their own statelike regulation" (2010: 704). Timmer studied the relationship between different cultural and labor collectivities in the contested Mahakam delta, in which small-scale shrimp farming coexists uneasily next to massive oil and gas exploration led by a subsidiary of a Franco-Belgium energy company. Timmer critiques the literature on legal pluralism that assumes the state and the nonstate are "separate worlds," a distinction that might serve theoretical ends but which also "overlook[s] the ways in which people themselves forge middle grounds by emulating state categories and arrangements to strengthen and legitimize nonstate justice, though certainly not for all" (2010: 704).

But this "middle ground" that is carved out for themselves by Bugis migrants results in an ambiguous act of simulation through which local justice mechanisms are created strategically among a population that has faced discrimination by both the Indonesian state and other local populations. As Timmer explains, the Bugis devise legal institutions so that they will be seen like a state, but:

> They do not, however, become like the state in the sense of providing justice and controlling authority according to the state's ideal of the rule of law. In emulating state categories and regulations, Bugis do not introduce common principles of the state to protect the marginalized. In other words, the kind of middle ground they forge does not prevent the unchecked exercise of social authority. To the contrary, Bugis in the delta of the Mahakam River are keen to be seen like the state to legitimize the continuation of long-standing modes of patron-client labor organization and natural resource exploitation that disadvantage many. (704)

The conclusion that Timmer draws from the ethnography of Bugis "legal emulation" is that the state can be both present and absent in ways that must be understood through quite local sets of interests. As he puts it, in the Mahakam delta the state is "virtually absent . . . , not in terms of discourse but, rather, in terms of service provision and law enforcement" (2010: 711). This has created a space in which a cultural and labor minority has been able to imitate state power through local justice institutions that are created not for a broader social good or because they believe that their cultural norms are more authentic, but "for the advancement of their concerns" (711).

But as Daniel Goldstein's (2003) ethnography of lynching, justice, and the law in Bolivia demonstrates, emulations by marginalized collectivities can take the form of more general modes of governance and control that are normally attributed to the state, even when they are expressed in ways that violate legal norms and challenge the state's formal monopoly over the use of violence. Goldstein's study of local justice mechanisms in the periurban barrios of Cochabamba took place at a significant time in Bolivian history.

In the early 2000s, the Bolivian state was in the midst of a profound crisis of identity and legitimacy that was fueled by pressures from both above and below. From above, the thoroughly neoliberalized state was well along in the process of withdrawing from its role in the provisioning of public goods, a form of retreat that was also accompanied by the outsourcing of governance to transnational companies in areas like water services and the exploitation and transportation of natural resources. Yet from below, the evacuation of the state coupled with growing levels of urban and periurban poverty created conditions of ever-present insecurity among people who had migrated to the city from the countryside and who had maintained links with their indigenous rural villages.

The result was the prevalence of collective acts of neighborhood justice that were normalized, familiar, but noninstitutional. Goldstein gives a vivid depiction of the crisis of "citizen security" at the time in Cochabamba's forgotten margins:

> Murders, rapes, and other violent crimes are common in the barrio, as are alcoholism, domestic abuse, and abandonment. Because most people work in the city center, they must leave their homes unattended during the day and so are vulnerable to the predations of thieves, who often steal the most basic of household goods: clothing, food stores, canisters of cooking gas. For people who can count themselves among the poorest in the Western hemisphere, such losses are devastating. (2003: 24)

Because Bolivian police officers did not see vigorous investigation and the enforcement of the law as part of their responsibilities,[17] residents responded by imposing—or attempting to impose—the harshest of punishments on those suspected of the kinds of everyday thievery that Goldstein describes. In a typical act of community justice, suspects were captured by a quickly mobilized group of residents; the suspects (some of whom were caught in the act of committing crimes) were beaten, tortured, and subjected to humiliations with symbolic import (like having their heads shaved or being stripped of their clothes, since nakedness is highly shameful among Bolivia's highland peoples); and finally the suspects were led to a public space, where they were put to death by various means including hanging and being doused with gasoline and burnt alive.

In Goldstein's analysis, these acts of "vigilante" justice are "inherently contradictory" (25) forms of mimesis. On the one hand, residents of Bolivia's state governance-free zones took it upon themselves to exercise modes of social control that should have been exercised exclusively by the state. In this sense, their actions reaffirmed the Weberian conception of the state, which depends on its ability to "identity itself as the only source of legitimate violence in society, to define its law and the enforcement thereof as legitimate while consigning all other forms of violence to the realm of irrationality, of savagery, of chaos" (25).

But on the other hand, Goldstein argues that violent community actions against suspected criminals can shift over time from the reaffirmation of state power to the rejection of it. By acting like the state (albeit one in which there are no judicial trials and suspects go directly from capture to capital punishment), barrio residents deny the actual state's legitimacy, including its power over citizenship and its obligations, the granting of rights, and the use of coercion. As he puts it, what he describes elsewhere (2004) as "spectacular violence" "represents a simultaneous embrace and rejection of the official order; it reaffirms the power of the state to enforce the law, while at the same time suggesting that justice may be attained apart from the law, that the two are, perhaps, separable" (2003: 25).

## Conclusion: The Anthropology of Law in a World of Exclusion

Contemporary anthropological studies of the relationships between law, ethnonationalism, the state, and conflict encompass some of the most transformative and troubling dynamics of our time. Indeed, as the research surveyed in this chapter suggests, the years after the end of the post–Cold War have been marked by a set of struggles that portend a future in which ideologies of inclusion, solidarity, and universal aspirations will continue to confront opposing movements based on exclusion, suspicion of the other, and (collective) self-interest. To return to Aryeh Neier's vigorous and confident rejection of Singapore's anti–human rights defense of "Asian values," it is remarkable how clearly his vision of a world community governed by "open society" values of human rights, individual freedom, and a pervasive respect for diversity failed to materialize. Writing before China proved once and for all that democracy and human rights protections were not preconditions for a well-functioning capitalist economy, he praises Japan as Asia's "mightiest economic power" in large part because it "respects the rights of its own citizens" (1993: 44). The entire tone of his intervention indicates that from the perspective of 1993, he was certain that the world was on the cusp of a human rights revolution that would soon sweep antediluvian alternatives of all kinds into the dustbin of history.

Yet from a current perspective, not only is this particular dustbin not full of these alternatives, but they remain thick upon the global landscape. This fact carries significant implications for the recent anthropology of law, which, as we have seen throughout this book, emerged at a historical moment—fleeting as it turned out to be—when the Kantian "sweet dream" of perpetual peace was being grounded in a cosmopolitan legal imaginary to an extraordinary degree. But as we have seen in this chapter, the rise of a global juristocracy, the apotheosis of law as the mechanism par excellence of social and political transformation, could cut both ways. As Robert Hayden observed about what some have called "revolution by constitution," "constitutionalism itself can be antidemocratic" (1992: 673).

And in perhaps the most important contemporary example of the use of law to shepherd radical social, political, and economic change (Bolivia, which was "refounded" by a revolutionary constitution in 2009), the most recent ethnographic research is pointing to a mixed record (see Fabricant 2012; Goodale n.d.; McNeish 2013). In certain areas, the new constitution and follow-on legislation are indeed redistributing wealth to vulnerable populations and restructuring basic norms of governance around ethnic and regional autonomy. Yet in other areas, the instruments of law are being used by the ruling political party—the *Movimiento al Socialismo* or Movement to Socialism—to consolidate power in the political capital of La Paz, suppress the opposition by dividing it and then incorporating its dispersed elements into the institutions of government, and menace potentially critical NGOs by forcing them to submit to a laborious process of bureaucratic oversight.

At the same time that cosmopolitan, transnational, and revolutionary legal projects are facing challenges in practice, violent ideologies of exclusion are taking root and shaping global political and moral discourse in striking ways. From the repression of the Rohingya minority by Buddhist nationalists in the newly democratic Myanmar to Italy's declaration of an *emergenza nomadi*, which led to the creation of ghettoes and increasing acts of persecution against the country's Roma population; from the reemergence of the "extreme right" in Europe as a political and social force to the appearance of U.S. politicians who seem to be straight out of Sinclair Lewis's 1935 novel *It Can't Happen Here*, a book that shows how fascism comes just after patriotic exceptionalism; and from Russia's panethnic interventions in neighboring Ukraine to the global wave of violence by apocalyptic religious movements guided by handbooks with titles like the "The Management of Savagery"—what is clear is that broad structures of socioeconomic inequality, legacies of colonialism, and competition for resources in a world threatened by depletion and the looming transformations of climate change, do not necessarily give rise, as some notable theories of history supposed, to progressive movements committed to pluralism, equality, inclusion, and peace on Earth.

On the one hand, the recognition of these stark realities creates a dilemma for anthropologists of law, many of whom studied the rise of cosmopolitan legality in the early and middle years of the post–Cold War as a form of "engaged anthropology" that was conceived partly in solidarity with interlocutors who were themselves in the midst of different progressive struggles. What are scholars to do, now that new legal forms are emerging to justify modes of social and political action that appear to be antithetical to these earlier (and still ongoing) struggles? But on the other hand, anthropology's ways of knowing still remain among the best points of access for capturing the "hold life has" for people and for contextualizing the ideologies that shape their actions. In the current conjuncture, therefore, anthropologists must broaden their frames of research and analysis to locate the place of law at those points of departure where ideologies of liberation, counterhegemony, and solidarity diverge from those of exclusion, violent difference, and apocalyptic sacrifice.

# Conclusion

## Law in a Post-Utopian World

As we have seen throughout this book, the intellectual history of the anthropology of law reveals a domain of research, theory, and participatory action that has often found itself at the leading edge of debates over the foundations of social control and resistance, the relationship between law and different forms of governance (e.g., colonialism, human rights, constitutionalism, tribal rule, postconflict truth commissions, international criminal justice), the role of law in legitimating ideology, the capacity of law to facilitate movements for social change, and the limitations of law as a mechanism for the resolution of protracted social conflicts, among many others.

Yet what runs as a common epistemological thread throughout the full sweep of this rich legacy, from Maine's study of ancient law to Merry's multisited ethnography of the global CEDAW monitoring system, from Schapera's programmatic survey of Tswana law and custom to Darian-Smith's research on English legal identity in a changing Europe, is the reframing of law away from its apparent institutional and normative isolation toward a theoretical vision of the legal as a mode through which society reproduces itself in terms of always-contested "vital motifs of cultural identity," to recall Alain Pottage's description from chapter 2. But to make this claim about a uniquely anthropological orientation to law is not the same as to say that the anthropology of law is simply the study of law *and* society in the key of ethnography, or that it is the comparative version of what has more recently been called "empirical legal studies."

Rather, the anthropology of law has represented one of the few systematic attempts over the *longue durée* to unpeel the layers of law from the inside out; to unfold law's charts on the table of ethnographic scrutiny and examine its topographies and distortions; and to study law as a moral register that is not, as Aristotle claimed, free from passion, but instead infused with will, desire, madness, and the indelible traces of human suffering. In short, the anthropology of law is a *sui generis* optic, a lens through which one might view the hold that law has for people.

Each of this book's chapters has surveyed some of the most important ways in which the anthropology of law has made its far-reaching, if at times unacknowledged, contributions. Despite necessary soundings in the longer history of the anthropology of law, the book has focused on the body of research that has developed since the end of the Cold War. The argument has been that like social, political, and economic relations more generally, the warp and woof of law was deeply affected by the openings and closures of this liminal moment in history, particularly the emergence and diffusion of international and transnational legal orders.

Anthropologists of law responded to these broader realignments with methodological creativity and analytical rigor and thereby reestablished the field yet again. Yet in comparison with earlier periods, this regrounding was one that was more responsive to the wider centrifugal forces of which law formed an essential vector. That is to say, what I described in the Introduction as the new anthropology of law was not one that sought to penetrate ever deeper into the essence of law as such, whether by focusing on rules or dispute processes or the regulation of social deviance or "principles extracted from legal decisions" (Pospisil 1971). On the contrary, scholars insisted on following the capillary networks of law wherever they led, from sessions of new supranational tribunals to the various landscapes on which the "protean forms of social action assembled, by convention, under a portal named 'human rights'" (Baxi 2002: v) crystallized as a problematic assemblage of contemporary world making.

But as the chapters in this book have also demonstrated, the liminal period of the post–Cold War through which the new anthropology of law could emerge eventually ended, as all periods of liminality must. If the "interstructural character of the liminal" (Turner 1967: 99) opens up the possibility for reordering social hierarchies and reconfiguring lines of power, it also anticipates what comes after, in which what is new is always, crucially, made in part from what was old. Indeed, a cynical—or perhaps materialist—reading of Turner's anthropological theory of liminality would say that historical periods of creativity and apparently limitless possibility merely serve to obscure the very deepest fault lines of power by draping them in the cloak of transformation. In any case, as Turner explained, the "reformulation of old elements in new patterns" (1967: 99) was the eventual outcome of periods of transition in which new institutions and cultural logics were forged.

As we have seen, the trajectory of the new anthropology of law roughly tracked the opening and gradual closing of the historical period in which law and the legal became hegemonic, from the rise of "juristocracy" (Hirschl 2004) to the "juridification of politics" (Brown 2010; or even the "hyper-juridification of politics," Sircar and Jain 2015) to the emergence of global "cultures of legality"(Couso, Huneeus, and Sieder 2010) to revolution by constitution. What marked these signs of law's apotheosis was the presence of legal institutions, philosophies, and procedural logics across a wide and unprecedented range of processes, from the transition to a postapartheid society in South Africa to debates over the use of torture in the so-called War on Terror, from the resolution of a Maoist insurgency in Nepal to the emergence of a global regime to monitor and regulate "all forms" of discrimination against women.

But as the years of the post–Cold War stretched on, the limits to these "novel appropriations of the law in the pursuit of political and social change" (Domingo 2010) became increasingly clear. The "reformulation of old elements in new patterns" marked the end of law's term of service as the handmaiden of triumphal challenges to the nation-state and of dreams of more inclusive social communities based on equality, tolerance, and appeals to the concept of human dignity. The expansion of economic inequality, both at a global level and within countries; the devolution of human rights revolutions into ethnic and religious conflicts; the failure of international legal regimes to deter or prevent the naked annexation of countries by more powerful neighbors; the misappropriation of categories of collective identity to make dubious claims of discrimination, legal exclusion, and "micro-aggression"; and the undermining of a fragile system of international criminal justice by postcolonial plutocrats masquerading as postcolonial martyrs—all these and more were signposts pointing to the fact that law had been "cut down to size," as Harri Englund (2013) put it, in his critique of human rights.

Anthropologists were thus confronted with a changing landscape of law once again, a landscape on which the cosmopolitan legal imaginaries forged in the early years after the end of the Cold War coexisted with, or in some cases were overwhelmed by, those oriented to radically different logics—of apocalyptic theology, of resurgent nationalism, of the invisible hand of the free market. This, then, is where the arc of intellectual history catches up to the present, since the period *after* the end of the post–Cold War remains the one in which anthropologists of law must conduct research and continue to track the changing ways and means of law in a post-utopian world.

In this final chapter, therefore, the focus shifts largely away from the body of existing research to consider what the future might hold for the anthropology of law. Compared with earlier chapters, the sections here will take up challenges and potential areas of inquiry in a more speculative fashion. The chapter is not meant to summarize the book as a whole but rather to make its own distinct contribution to ongoing debates about law—partly with reference to some of the most recent studies, partly in reference to current conflicts, and partly in reference to what anthropologists have observed coming into view just over the horizon.

In the next section, the chapter explores the problem of law and knowledge. What can we know about the empirical relationship between law and social justice, between the implementation of human rights laws and something like gender violence, between international criminal tribunals and long-term social and economic transformation? As we will see, anthropologists have recently begun to subject basic questions of measurement to critical scrutiny. Yet if it is in a sense impossible to measure the capacity of law to fulfill the broader social and political goals demanded of it, does this mean law should be "cut down to size" or reconfigured as simply one among a range of instruments of social control?

After that, the chapter considers the place of law, particularly international and transnational law, in the face of rapidly growing global inequalities. Does the promotion of the rule of law actually facilitate global inequality in certain ways? If so, what are the alternatives? Next, the chapter turns to the rise and fall of the law of concentric circles, that is, legal ideologies that challenged the nation-state from above and encouraged the formation of categories of identity framed at large, maximally inclusive, scales. From the vantage point of the present, the utopian

dreams of a world of global citizenship based on human rights and respect for moral differences appear increasingly distant, even naïve. The
section will examine some of the likely reasons for this growing disenchantment with legal cosmopolitanism.

The chapter concludes on a provocative note. Recent anthropology
has challenged institutional and ideological human-centrism in the face
of coming conflicts over changes to the environment, competition for
natural resources, and the continuing exponential growth of the global
population. This final section of the chapter (and book) suggests that
law has a key role to play in responding to these conflicts, but from a
grounding in a legal ecology that implies a different kind of holism.

## Law at the Limits of Knowledge, Knowledge at the Limits of Law

In her introduction to a collection of ethnographic essays on the rise of
the global "audit culture" in the post–Cold War period, Marilyn Strathern (2000) argues that this culture is one in which the "financial and
the moral meet," a crossroads at which the criteria of economic efficiency and those of good governance come together under the banner
of "accountability." What are the characteristics of the audit culture? As
Strathern explains:

> Audit regimes accompany a specific epoch in Western international af-
> fairs, a period when governance has become reconfigured through a veri-
> table army of "moral fieldworkers" (NGOs), when environmental liability
> has been made an issue of global concern . . . , when the ethics of ap-
> propriation has been acknowledged to an unprecedented scale in respect
> of indigenous rights, and when transparency of operation is everywhere
> endorsed as an outward sign of integrity. At the same time the apparently
> neutral "market" provides a ubiquitous platform for individual interest
> and national politics alike, while "management" is heard everywhere as
> an idiom of regulation and organization. (2000: 2)

But if from the viewpoint of the late 1990s, the underlying principles of the audit culture were "almost impossible to criticize," since they
"advance[d] values that academics generally hold dear, such as responsibility, openness about outcomes and widening of access" (2000: 3), the

critical evaluation of how "rituals of verification" (Power 1997) shaped the world had taken a less sanguine turn by the beginning of the 2010s. Yet rather than focusing on the underlying intentions behind the spread of audit culture in many domains of contemporary life, much of the literature has explored the way in which specific theories of knowledge ground the push for accountability and rely on techniques of measurement that depict a warped image of the social world (e.g., Davis, Fisher, Kingsbury, and Merry 2012; Merry, Davis, and Kingsbury 2015; Rottenburg, Merry, Park, and Mugler 2016).

The pervasive demand to measure the effectiveness of a wide range of governance strategies revolves around "indicators," which Davis, Fisher, Kingsbury, and Merry (2012: 73) define as "a named collection of rank-ordered data that purports to represent the past or projected performance of different units. The data are generated through a process that simplifies raw data about a complex social phenomenon." Indicators are expressed through quantification, which reflects a "trust in technical rationality, in the legibility of the social world through measurement and statistics, and in the capacity of numbers to render different social worlds commensurable," as Sally Engle Merry (2016: 9–10) puts it, in her ethnographic study of the production of indicators on different categories of human rights compliance and violation.

The rise of "governance by indicators" (Davis, Fisher, Kingsbury, and Merry 2012) not coincidentally took place during the same historical period in which the broader neoliberal world order was emerging. Much like the assumptions about the market underlying the expansion of capitalism, those underlying the ideology of global commensurability likewise purported to reveal the world as it was through "different kinds of numerical representation" (Merry 2016: 13).

Yet as Shore and Wright (2015) have argued, indicators do not so much reveal the world as "reassemble" it in an image consistent with logics of governance that preserve global inequalities of power, access to resources, and ideological capital. Arguably the most significant consequence of the growing dominance of "evidence-based governance" is the fact that the ideology of commensurability masks a powerful regime of "lateral reason" (Maurer 2005): through the "seductions of quantification" (Merry 2016), abstract concepts such as "freedom," "poverty," "transparency," and "rule of law" are conceptually flattened so that "all things can be measured and that those measures provide an ideal guide to decision making" (Merry 2016: 10).

But as the critical ethnography of evidence-based governance has demonstrated, the production of quantitative indicators depends on a vast political economy of bureaucratic knowledge production in which data proxies for something like violence against women in Fiji stand in for data proxies for something like compliance with CEDAW in Fiji, which is then aggregated with other indicators that stand in collectively for something like human rights compliance in Fiji, which is then finally represented by a numerical value, say 5.5 on scale of 1 to 10 (a number which itself might be aggregated in international policy making to stand in for something like human rights compliance in Melanesia).

Yet at each stage an act of what might be called "vertical reason" takes place, in which an empirical slippage from below is reconciled to an empirical slippage from above. The result is a steady distancing from the complicated social realities that are the apparent object of measurement as the "microprocesses through which surveys are created, categories defined, phenomena named, [and] translations enacted . . . are, in turn, shaped by the actors, institutions, funding, and forms of expertise at play" (Merry 2016: 6).

As studies have shown, the production and circulation of indicators for international and transnational law have become a signal example of how social and economic conflict, reconciliation, gender relations, and political agency, among many others, are rendered measurable through the very act of measurement itself. Even more, through the "quiet power of indicators" (Merry, Davis, and Kingsbury 2015), what is not measured is not measurable and what is not measurable does not, in an important sense, exist. Thus, the global indicator culture becomes a self-reproducing, recursive mechanism through which what is ultimately measured is not anything like human rights compliance, let alone something like "freedom," but rather compliance with the terms and conditions of indicator culture itself.

And even more troubling is the fact that there is something like an inverse correlation between the development of indicator culture and the capacity to interconnect broad legal policies to social, political, and economic change at the microlevel. As regimes of quantitative governance become more self-contained and self-referential, their relation to the practice of everyday life becomes more tenuous, more hypothetical. Merry and Wood (2015) have described this dynamic as the "paradox of measurement." Among other things, this paradox points to the ultimate limits in our capacity to know whether or not the didactic logics of the post–Cold War legal revolution ever served what Eleanor Roosevelt, looking far into the future, imagined as their "frankly educational" purposes (1948: 477).[1]

Indeed, the new anthropology of law has developed on the edges of these limits of knowledge, where "hard law" trails into "soft law" and "soft law" trails into diffuse forms of normative discourse in which the "connotative power" (Goodale 2007) of law is harnessed as part of an ambiguous process of identity (re)formation and incipient agency. But if, for example, we can simply count the number of people prosecuted under a new domestic statute intended to implement a provision of international human rights law, can we also count the number of people whose moral consciousness has been shaped by the idea of human dignity, or for whom the fact of universal human rights creates a single, overarching category of collective belonging, or who would agree (perhaps marking "5" in a survey with "5" meaning "strongly agree") with the statement that "recognition of the inherent dignity and of the equal and inalienable rights of all members of the human family is the foundation of freedom, justice and peace in the world"?

And even if it were possible, despite what the wide-ranging anthropological critique of indicators has taught us, to measure these intransitive dimensions of law, what would we do if the regression analysis showed only partial correlation, or even worse, negative correlation? What use is a new juridical or moral grammar if it is never put into practice, if the speaker never speaks? In the end, the anthropology of law suggests that an inevitable epistemological gap will remain between the "accidental truths" of human rights and other cosmopolitan legalities and the "necessary truths" demanded by policy makers and so-called empirical legal scholars, to paraphrase the eighteenth-century German philosopher Lessing. Thus, like Kierkegaard (who was influenced by Lessing's 1777 essay "On the Proof of the Spirit and of Power"), we are left with a choice: whether or not to take a leap of faith, to "surrender" (Goodale 2009) to the transformative promises of human rights, truth and reconciliation, and the need to "think and feel beyond the nation" (Cheah and Robbins 1998), even if the "ugly, broad ditch" remains as wide as ever.[2]

## The Law, in Its Majestic Equality

In his 1894 novel *The Red Lily*, Anatole France wrote, "In its majestic equality, the law forbids rich and poor alike to sleep under bridges, beg in the streets and steal loaves of bread. It is one of the blessings of the Revolution" (1894: 117).[3] As recent anthropological studies have demonstrated, the significance of France's trenchantly ironic critique of law's "majestic equality" took on new urgency in the years after the end of the Cold War. As different chapters have shown, law and the legal were burdened with the task of shepherding forms of economic and social transformation that traditionally would have come within the sphere of politics expressed through varying strategies of indirect and direct action.

Although anthropologists (e.g., Graeber 2004) have observed the extent to which political movements remain a potent instrument of confrontation, subversion, and defiance, from New York's Occupy Wall Street to Spain's Movimiento 15-M to Greece's Syriza, the broader impact of these movements remains marginal. Instead, the much more pervasive legacy of the post–Cold War was the juridification of politics, identity (such as indigenous rights), and social organization, at the same time in which global inequality was growing steadily to the point at which, in 2015, 1 percent of the world's population controlled more than 50 percent of global wealth (Oxfam 2015).

The effects of the absorption of both relations of production and social relations into law are obviously variable from an ethnographic perspective. For example, in her study of the "(un)rule of law" in Guatemala, Rachel Sieder (2010) examines the ways in which peasant and indigenous peoples, encouraged by transnational human rights activists, engaged in paralegal strategies to protest national mining legislation that

> [i]ncreased tax breaks and investment opportunities for transnational capital and reduced the royalties payable to the Guatemalan state from 6 to 1 percent. The reform constitute[d] part of a global trend of legal

adjustment concerning natural resource exploitation that [was] part and
parcel of the neoliberal development model. (2010: 170)

And yet the overarching presence of law on both sides of the conflict
led to a result that underscored the dilemma of juridification, the consequences of requiring social relations to be "textured by formal legal
rules" (2010: 161; quoting O'Donnell 2005: 293).

Although invocations of indigenous rights norms by communities reflected a challenge to the use of law by the state to encourage transnational
capitalist accumulation in the country, these remained mostly symbolic
appropriations. On the other side, however, the full, material force of the
law was applied. This was in part because the neoliberal Guatemalan state
exercised formal legal sovereignty in the country despite the presence of
a robust tradition of legal pluralism. But it was also because the state was
embedded in other legal regimes that reproduced the linkages between
law and economic power at larger scales. As she puts it, "[o]ther areas
of law, such as those related to foreign investment and intellectual property rights [were] effectively extraterritorialized or denationalized via free
trade agreements and the legal processes associated with global economic
integration, often with minimum or zero transparency" (2010: 179). In
her analysis, these uneven consequences of law's majestic equality show
that "[u]nder prevailing global conditions, law continues to be one of the
principal tools of neocolonial power" (178).[4]

So what exactly are these prevailing global conditions and what does
anthropology have to say about law's role in challenging or reinforcing
them? Writing in 1990, David Harvey looked back on the global market
crash of October 1987 and thought he could glimpse promising "cracks
in the mirrors, fusions at the edges." Cracks in the mirrors, because the
1987 crash, in which "nearly a third of the paper value of assets worldwide was written off within a few days" (1990: 356), exposed the "crisis-
tendencies of capitalism." These are starkly visible when accumulating
debt, commodity inflation, and the "fantastic world of booming paper
wealth and assets" create the conditions in which "banks write off bil-
lions of dollars of bad loans, governments default, [and] international
currency markets remain in perpetual turmoil" (357). And as the system
inevitably fractures through the weight of its own internal contradictions, fusions at the edges take place, meaning the assembling of alter-

natives that represent a "counter-attack of narrative" (359; interestingly, as examples of such fusions, he points to Jesse Jackson's "charismatic politics," strong unionism among British automobile workers, and the fight against "racism, apartheid, and world hunger").

Yet in retrospect, it appears that Harvey read far too much transformative potential in the evolution from Fordism to "flexible accumulation" (1990: 147). That is, the "contradictory experiences acquired under capitalism" have not proven to be inconsistent with the "[m]echanical reproduction of value systems, beliefs, cultural preferences, and the like" (345), despite the supposed generativity to be found in the "speculative grounding of capitalism's inner logic" (345). Thus, twenty years after Black Monday, the global economic system experienced a much more significant and pervasive moment of crisis during the Great Recession that began around 2007. Nevertheless, even with widespread unemployment, political instability, and the massive intervention of states into private markets, the powerful centers of the global capitalist system endured and even prospered, as a collective of the world's largest economies (the Group of Twenty, or G-20) met for the first time in 2008 to ensure the recapitalization of global markets and the repair of the cracks to its mirrors.

By 2016, despite a "slowdown and rebalancing of the Chinese economy, lower commodity prices, and strains in some large emerging market economies" (IMF 2016), the global capitalist system was growing once again under the steady watch of the G-20, which began meeting every year beginning in 2011 to guarantee even greater control over the functioning of global capitalist networks. And even more ominous, at least from a certain perspective, the reinforced post–Great Recession capitalist system does not even need to use its mirrors to create the illusion of middle-class prosperity, since it is, as David Graeber (2014) has lamented, the "only game in town." The result is the return of "savage capitalism," in which "a miserly 1% presid[es] over a social order marked by increasing social, economic and even technological stagnation."[5]

Given this broader account of a global political economy marked by deep capitalist resilience and the reproduction of inequality at all scales (Global North–Global South, intra–Global North, intra–Global South, North-North, South-South, and so on), it is not surprising that it is typically only the poor who find themselves subject to laws against begging, vagrancy, and other examples of "crimes of poverty" (Braithwaite 1991).

On balance, recent anthropological research paints a sobering picture of the role of law more generally on this global socioeconomic landscape. At the largest of levels, the law forms an essential institutional and conceptual architecture to the global capitalist system through business contracts, international trade agreements, bilateral treaties, and the articles of incorporation that serve as the legal DNA that constitutes corporations and determines their actions. And at the smallest of levels, those at which people react—sometimes violently, sometimes out of a sense of frustration—to the structural impediments and inequalities that define this global economic system, the law stands ready to clean up the sociological mess. It might be true, as Aristotle claimed in the *Politics*, that "poverty is the parent of revolution and crime," but the post–Cold War period has shown that it is crime, rather than revolution, that is the more common response and that law occupies an essentially conservative position in relation to these causes and effects.

This is not to say that law does not have an important function in contemporary processes of economic redistribution (that is, toward the middle and bottom, not toward the top), but these are still peripheral experiments that only prove the broader rule. For example, at least since the adoption of its 2009 constitution, Bolivia had been in the midst of a process of "refoundation" that has been described as a revolution by political leaders and scholars alike (e.g., Hylton and Thomson 2007). If so, despite the legacy of popular street mobilizations that paved the way for the Bolivian revolution (often inspired doctrinally by Trotskyism), it has been law that has become its bedrock. The law (through the constitution) is the blueprint for the revolution; the law was the means through which important sectors of the economy were nationalized and put under the control of the revolutionary state; and it is the law through which a portion of the earnings from these new state industries are redistributed by right to categories of the population that are considered in particular need (the elderly, pregnant women, young students).

But even here, at the very heart of Bolivia's revolution by law, the role of law itself is more complicated than it would appear. At many points, the law seems to be working at cross-purposes. From one side, it is facilitating the redistribution of wealth within a "postneoliberal" (Goodale and Postero 2013) socioeconomic model that carries important lessons for a world that has no use for them (the global economic system is much more likely to tolerate an authoritarian capitalist regime like China than a democratic socialist one like Bolivia).

Yet from the other side, the vast body of existing law—in the form of codes, presidential decrees, and administrative orders—continues to regulate what might be thought of as prerevolutionary norms. Indeed, as Cecila Urquieta, the young government lawyer in charge of reconciling these legal tensions, explained, in Bolivia more than 85 percent of all law (as of 2011) in force comes from the dead hand of past epochs. As she acknowledged, the government has accepted that it will take "at least ten years" (from 2015) before the law in Bolivia will catch up to the country's revolutionary aspirations (Goodale n.d.).

## The Law of Concentric Circles

In a series of fragments that come down to us from the second century C.E., the Stoic philosopher Hierocles outlined a theory of ethics based on a conception of identity expressed through concentric circles. In describing "how we ought to conduct ourselves towards our kindred," he imagines an ontology of interconnection that is the basis for moral action. As he puts it, "each of us is . . . circumscribed by many circles; some of which are less, but others larger." The first circle is the self, with "mind as a centre." From there, the circles of identity and moral action get ever larger, passing through extended family, "those of the same tribe," and "those of the same province." "But the outermost and greatest circle," Hierocles argues, "and which comprehends all the other circles, is that of the whole human race." Given the fact that all humans share the largest circle of belonging, one should strive to "collect . . . the circles . . . to one centre, and always to endeavour earnestly to transfer himself from the comprehending circles to the several particulars which they comprehend" (quoted in Taylor 1822: 106–108).

In Hierocles, we have a very early expression of cosmopolitanism, one that captures both its powerful appeal for different visionaries over the centuries and its most problematic characteristics. Although Hierocles recognizes that "something of benevolence must be taken away from those who are more distant from us by blood" (Taylor 1822: 110), nevertheless we must acknowledge our kinship with all others in the "whole human race" and act toward them as we would act toward ourselves, to see all humans in a sense as constituents of one, vast collective self. Yet it is this very moral imperative to reverse, as it were, the experience of identity, by prioritizing the outermost circle of belonging, that is the greatest weakness of cosmopolitanism. This is particularly true as cosmopolitanism develops from moral imperative to become the basis for institutional action.

The German political philosopher Thomas Pogge argued that one must distinguish between moral and legal approaches to cosmopolitanism. Moral cosmopolitanism, like Hierocles's, simply "holds that all persons stand in certain moral relations to one another: we are required to respect one another's status as ultimate units of moral concern" (Pogge 1992: 49). Legal cosmopolitanism, by contrast, "is committed to a concrete political ideal of a global order under which all persons have equivalent rights and duties, that is, are fellow citizens of a universal republic" (49). The move from moral to legal cosmopolitanism depends on the extent to which "human rights are activated . . . through the emergence of social institutions" (51). In this way, the realization of the cosmopolitan ideal in practice is highly contingent. As Pogge puts it, "[i]t is only because all human beings are now participants in a single, global institutional scheme—involving such institutions as the territorial state and a system of international law and diplomacy as well as a world market for capital, goods, and services—that all human rights violations . . . come to be . . . everyone's concerns" (51).[6]

To a certain extent, a significant part of the anthropology of law since the early 1990s can be read as the first systematic evaluation of the practice of legal cosmopolitanism. If so, it would be difficult to draw anything but uncertain conclusions from this ethnographic record. On the one hand, it is possible to say that "all human beings . . . participa[te] in a single, global institutional scheme" in only the most general of ways. Yes, there is the United Nations in which most countries participate, and yes, there is a growing system of international law that includes human rights declarations and treaties, international and regional courts, and institutional mechanisms for monitoring compliance at a global level. But as we have seen at different places in this book, the emergence of this global institutional scheme has been marked by political manipulation by global powers, including strategic opting out by countries like the United States and China; structural conflict between state sovereignty and supranational norms in which sovereignty normally trumps; and sheer bad faith, as in the case of attacks on the International Criminal Court by African leaders who wield charges of neocolonialism to protect themselves from prosecution.

Yet if we leave this problematic institutional history aside and examine the moral legacy of post–Cold War cosmopolitanism, the picture that emerges is even more disquieting. Indeed, the Hierocletian ideal never took root as a pervasive global ethics; the "worldwide overlapping consensus" envisaged by Pogge and many others seems as distant as ever, perhaps even more so, from our contemporary vantage point. But if the counterintuitive demand to prioritize the outermost circle of belonging before all others appears as sheer fantasy in light of the ethnographic and historical record, what is more worrying is the fact that cosmopolitanism from the other direction has proven to be nearly as tenuous. Even if it is understood that "something of benevolence must be taken away" with distance from self, the violent, catastrophic extremes to which this proved to be true could scarcely have been imagined. From Srebrenica to Rwanda, from Abu Ghraib to the ethnic cleansing in Darfur, the tragic unwillingness to extend the hand of benevolence across lines of difference has haunted the "age of human rights" (Mutua 2016).

A response from the anthropology of law to the failure of cosmopolitanism would focus on the extent to which Hierocles's early vision, which acknowledged multiplicity and accepted the fact that the pull of close relations—family, community, religion, tribe—exerted itself differently from the pull of an abstract humanity, had been replaced by a much starker ethical vision. Here, pluralism is the enduring nemesis of human dignity, since the actual range of cultural beliefs and practices cannot be contained within the tight normative arc of something like the UDHR's thirty articles. The result is a take-it-or-leave-it ethics in which one is left with the outermost circle of the "human family," or nothing. Not surprisingly, this austere form of cosmopolitanism has been largely ignored or left behind to be replaced by various alternative visions of belonging with dubious ethical purchase, including nationalism, religious fundamentalism, class domination, and racial politics.

In 1999, the American Anthropological Association made an effort to reconcile the diversity revealed by the long sweep of ethnographic research with the either/or normative vision of contemporary human rights. Its "Declaration on Anthropology and Human Rights" asserts that the "capacity for culture is tantamount to the capacity for humanity" and, more legally, that "[p]eople and groups have a generic right to realize their capacity for culture." Yet although it "founds its approach on anthropological principles of respect for concrete human differences . . . rather than the abstract legal uniformity of Western tradition," the Declaration's attempt to distinguish between the *capacity* for culture and culture itself—that is, those "concrete human differences" that are the bane of human rights advocacy—was simply unconvincing.

Nevertheless, the anthropology of law does suggest another possible resource grounded in "[a]nthropology's cumulative knowledge of human cultures" that offers a different approach to the problem of how to reimagine legal—and perhaps moral—belonging in a world increasingly marked by exclusion. As we saw in chapter 2, an important part of the intellectual history of the anthropology of law has been the study of legal pluralism. Although much of the notable research was conducted under problematic conditions of colonialism at the service of different regimes of direct and indirect rule, the fact of legal pluralism was always much thicker and more consequential than these particular cases. In many ways, the true potential of legal pluralism was always to be found apart from formal policies to bring the "semi-autonomous social field [which] has rule-making capacities . . . but . . . is simultaneously set in a larger social matrix" (Moore 1973: 720) to heel under the institutional surveillance of the state.

This is what might be called de facto or actually existing legal pluralism. It often develops in the shadows of a formal monopoly on law that does not tolerate as a matter of doctrine the existence of "rule-making" legal orders outside the boundaries of the state. In practice, particularly in states marked by a minimal institutional presence in rural regions or in certain urban zones, or by a weak national legal infrastructure, multiple legal orders proliferate precisely because they have not been coopted by the state. As anthropologists have shown, the relationship between these different legal orders is typically one of interdependence and contingency.

This is not to say that systems of informal legal pluralism are necessarily egalitarian. They are usually regulated by sets of flexible norms that determine which points of legal intervention take precedence for certain conflicts or certain categories of legal actors. For example, in highland Bolivia, an extremely dense network of legal pluralism regulates conflicts based on social fields that are rooted in rural peasant organizations, the outer edges of state law, and *ayllus*, which are large-scale indigenous kinship and economic networks with pre-Columbian origins (see Fernández Osco 2000; Goodale 2008a).[7] Conflicts—from homicide to property disputes, from allegations of witchcraft to calumny—are moments in social time shaped by their circulation within these "interlegal" (Santos 1987, 1995) webs.

Yet equally important is the fact that this legal multiplicity is experienced by people not only as a form of local social organization but also as a form of social identity based on an ethics of pluralism that accommodates different norms, different sanctions, and different lines of legal authority. And this phenomenology of actually existing legal pluralism is as much intransitive as it is transitive, as much a part of the self as it is a social fact, since it is "superimposed, interpenetrated and mixed in our minds, as much as in our actions, either on occasions of qualitative leaps or sweeping crises in our life trajectories, or in the dull routine of eventless everyday life" (Santos 1995: 473).

Thus, the ethnographic account of legal pluralism suggests a radically different conception of the relationship between law and belonging. Instead of the self-contained concentric circles of Hierocles, neatly nested in an ethical hierarchy that stretches from the individual mind out to "all members of the human family" and ideally back again, we are presented with a model that is based on flexible norms, what might be called simultaneous legal identities, and an abiding tolerance for "relational justice" (Robbins 2010). Instead of a shallow account of equality based on an abstract cosmopolitan ideal like "human dignity," the study of living legal pluralism reveals practices of interconnection grounded in social relations, juridical modesty, and moral creativity.

## Conclusion: Thinking Like a Conflict

To conclude this chapter (and the book itself), let us return to Maine's theory of sociolegal history. In the Introduction, I playfully adopted Maine's schema in arguing that recent anthropology has tracked the development of law from its basis in contracts within nation-states to the emergence of international and transnational legal orders, which unfold beyond state borders. Yet in the move from contract to cosmopolitanism, the law ceased to be simply an instrument of governance or social control or financial regulation. Instead, in the manifold spaces in which so-called soft law was deployed, law often became a logic through which an abstract conception of the person was made the basis for a problematic global ethics.

I have also suggested at different points throughout this book, but particularly in this last chapter, that the phase in history—to keep with Maine, as a kind of *hommage*—in which law is marked by its cosmopolitanism is passing away. In looking to the future, what might be the new forms that law is likely to take in the face of a wide range of present and looming problems, from the rise of theological death cults to staggering rates of global inequality, from the slow disintegration of transnational experiments like the European Union to coming upheavals wrought by human-induced climate change? Or, to be even more direct, what might be the new forms that law *should* take?

In his provocative rewriting of the postwar history of human rights, Samuel Moyn (2010) argues that they express the latest in a long line of Western utopian projects through which the world's conflicts and many forms of structural violence would finally be overcome through a sheer act of global moral will. But what appeared as a moment of endless possibility in the halcyon days of the early post–Cold War now appear in retrospect to have been more a time of ethical hubris, when the utopian project of universal human rights got too close to the sun of "concrete human differences" and then fell to the sea. Although he did not write about human rights, there is no question but that the great theorist of failed universalisms, Isaiah Berlin, would not have been surprised by this fate, since all universalisms share a common weakness: the claim to resolve once and for all the world's many contradictions, follies, and cruelties in one grand synthesis.

But rather than staking our future on a set of "values without qualities" (Goodale 2016), the response from the anthropology of law should be to double down on our knowledge of how human societies have organized relations, including conflicts, in ways that fundamentally challenge the human chauvinist dogmas that underlie the dominant contemporary ideologies, from capitalism to nationalism.

These radical alternatives are likely to be found at the margins of global power, since what they imply threatens the neoliberal world order. They are mostly embedded in "epistemologies of the South" (Santos 2014) and reflect *cosmovisiones* and deep ecologies in which humans occupy profoundly interdependent positions with nonhuman animals, cosmological forces, and the land. In his moving, revelatory study of "how forests think," based on long-term ethnographic research among the Runa of Ecuador's Upper Amazon, Eduardo Kohn (2013) explores the subversive implications and possibilities in one such epistemology of the South. He argues that an ecological vision in which humans are reimagined within "formations . . . [that have] a kind of reality beyond the human" (2013: 193), carries important lessons for our collective survival. So what does a "living-future logic of a thinking forest" (195) point to for the future of law?

If law has developed from status to contract and from contract to cosmopolitanism, the stage beyond could be described as the ecological. Here, instead of thinking (or feeling) like a human rights victim, or even less like a plaintiff, a legal ecology would encourage us to think like a conflict, that is, like a social formation—following Kohn—that has a reality "beyond the human." There is of course no indication that the emergence of such a legal imaginary is imminent. At present, the consequences of humancentrism are all too apparent. (But even so, on the day I write these words, scientists have just announced that they have confirmed the ideas about the *real* universe of someone pondering over a century ago in an office about an hour by train from where I sit now, ideas about a postgeological future that render these concerns ultimately meaningless.)

Still, the many ethnographic reports from the margins demonstrate that an ecological vision of law and life lives on in small places. To paraphrase Arundhati Roy, on a quiet day one can hear it breathing. As Rita Kesselring's (2017) study of embodied suffering in postapartheid South Africa reveals, it was not the protection of "human dignity" through human rights in which people found a way to come to terms with their experiences of racial injustice, but rather through the quotidian social formations of neighborhood child care, mutual aid associations, and other everyday places in which a living solidarity could flourish.

# NOTES

## INTRODUCTION

1 Friedrich Engels's *The Origin of the Family, Private Property, and the State: In Light of Lewis H. Morgan's Research* (1884), published a year after Karl Marx's death, used Morgan's writings to argue that the historical record showed class struggle to be at the base of human history. The incorporation of Morgan's work into the canon of Marxist ideology made him an intellectual hero in the Soviet Union. As Moses puts it, quoting the Russian anthropologist Y. I. Semenov, "one can come to the objective truth only going along the road laid by L. H. Morgan and Frederick [*sic*] Engels. All other ways only lead to the deviation from the creation of unified and genuine teaching about primordial society" (Moses 2009: 285).

2 Although a complete study of the Society of Legal Anthropology has not yet been published, further information on its objectives and key members can be found in Del Olmo 1981; González-Leandri 2008; and Rodriguez 2006.

3 It should be emphasized that Malinowski was not criticizing the earlier historical comparativists like Maine, McLennan, or Morgan here, nor obviously the arch-armchair anthropologist Sir James Frazer, author of *The Golden Bough*, to whom the lecture is dedicated (and who wrote a glowing Preface to Malinowski's 1922 *Argonauts*). Instead, Malinowski was distinguishing ethnography from the work of the verandah anthropologists like W. H. R. Rivers and the other members of the 1898 Torres Strait Expedition, which included, somewhat uncomfortably for Malinowski, his mentor and teacher C. G. Seligman. Nevertheless, some historians of anthropology have questioned the extent to which Malinowski's work represented a true paradigm shift (see, e.g., Urry 1993).

4 As Moore put it, "Gluckman's critics . . . fixed on the Reasonable Man as if he were some sort of Piltdown hoax made up of unsuitably joined parts, and usually impl[ied] that he [was] a construct of the observer" (1969: 264).

5 The 1964 conference led to the publication of a special issue on the ethnography of law in *American Anthropologist*; the 1966 Wenner-Gren conference in Austria led to the edited volume *Law in Culture and Society* (1969).

6 Roberts finished *Order and Dispute* in the summer of 1978 (Roberts 1979: 10); the *RAIN* article appeared in April 1978.

7 As Fuller notes, "[i]n some respects, the argument concurrently raging between formalists and substantivists in economic anthropology, in which Bohannan played a leading role on the substantivist side, had its legal equivalent in the

dispute between Bohannan and Gluckman, even if the latter's advocacy of cross-cultural legal comparison is not strictly formalist" (Fuller 1994: 3).

8   Other anthropologies of law were also developing over this period within their own trajectories in places like the Netherlands and France. As the von Benda-Beckmanns explain, "the years from the mid-1970s were characterized by a dynamic expansion of the anthropology of law in The Netherlands and generally by an increasing interest in legal systems in the Third World" (F. von Benda-Beckmann and K. von Benda-Beckmann 2002: 704; see also Griffiths 1983, 1986). For developments in the French anthropology of law, see Le Roy 2006; Rouland 1988.

9   Outside academia, the sense of paradigm crisis and transition was also palpable. For example, at the press conference at the end of the Malta summit in December 1989, a meeting between the United States and the U.S.S.R that many consider the technical end of the Cold War, the Soviet leader, Mikhail Gorbachev, concluded that "the world is leaving one epoch and entering another" (BBC, "Malta Summit Ends Cold War," 1989).

10  For example, "human rights" does not appear as a topic for research or discussion in *History and Power*, except in one short reference to the American and French revolutions (Aubert 1989: 56, 61). And even in the next major international compilation of essays in the anthropology of law, which was based on a 1991 meeting, the question of human rights—as discourse, as practice, as politics, as law—is barely mentioned (Lazarus-Black and Hirsch 1994). At this point, human rights was still not an anthropological problem as such; rather, it appears as one among several concepts used to address problems of violation and vulnerability.

11  In her 2001 review article on the anthropology of law, Sally Falk Moore identified the following "new questions" that had emerged over the previous fifty years: law as culture; law as domination; and law as problem solver (Moore 2001: 96–97).

12  Perhaps frustrated by the unwillingness of anthropologists of law to critically examine this "many-threaded fabric," Nader eventually directed her arguments to the field of anthropology more generally. See, e.g., her 1972 essay "Up the Anthropologist: Perspectives Gained from Studying Up," which was published in *Reinventing Anthropology*, a collection of essays edited by Dell Hymes.

13  Coincidently, Maine wrote and delivered the lectures that were the basis of *Ancient Law* during the same years and less than two kilometers away from where the greatest critic of capitalism, Karl Marx, was hard at work on his own magnum opus.

14  As Niezen explains, "indigenism" is used to "describe the international movement that aspires to promote and protect the rights of the world's 'first peoples'" (2003: 4). Indigenism, in this sense, is to be distinguished from *indigeneity*, the legally and historically constructed identity that forms the basis of indigenism. Other anthropologists who have used "indigenism" in this way include Dombrowski 2002 and Sylvain 2002.

15 On the enduring problem of economic inequality within capitalism, see Thomas Piketty's (2014) longitudinal study of the relationship between returns on capital and the rate of economic growth.

## CHAPTER 1. SPEAKING THE LAW

1 Other major figures in the anthropology of law present at that "turbulent" and "tumultuous" 1966 international meeting, during which participants "disagreed on both personal and intellectual levels" (Nader 1996: ix), were Philip Gulliver, E. Adamson Hoebel, Sally Falk Moore, Leopold Pospisil, Isaac Schapera, and Nader herself.

2 See also Conley and O'Barr (1990: 4–9), where they discuss in particular Bohannan's contributions to this debate from the perspective of linguistic anthropology.

3 Also as a matter of making connections in the intellectual history of the anthropology of law, it should be noted that Greenhouse's 1982 *Man* article was framed as a direct response to Simon Roberts's 1978 *RAIN* piece, in which, as was discussed in the Introduction, Roberts made the case against an anthropology of law per se, preferring instead "to let the study of social control be resorbed into the rest of sociocultural anthropology" (Greenhouse 1982: 58). In addition, Greenhouse studied at Harvard in the late 1960s and early 1970s with, among others, Klaus-Friedrich Koch, who was one of Laura Nader's three graduate students to participate (as rapporteurs) in the 1966 Wenner-Gren conference in Austria (Nader 1996: ix).

4 Indeed, the title of the chapter is "Dialogues in Legal Anthropology."

5 Interestingly, Foucault's writings are only cited by one scholar in the 1989 Starr and Collier volume, the Dutch anthropologist Anton Blok, and then only as a source on the history of executions in Europe!

6 In a later interview about the origins of the research that formed the basis for the 1990 *Rules versus Relationships*, O'Barr relates that it was at a lunch with Sally Engle Merry during the 1983 American Anthropological Association meetings in Denver that he decided to begin the ethnography of legal discourse in small claims courts. In fact, despite the "inedible" food on offer at the "dumpy little restaurant," O'Barr's meeting with Merry was apparently so inspiring that he walked right across the street and into a court and began recording sessions (Halliday and Schmidt 2009: 119).

7 Nesper describes how a fight between a "very prominent spiritual leader" and another tribal elder was resolved through a process of mediation and the sharing of tobacco among the disputants (2007: 679).

8 For another important study of the relationship between law, language, and cultural identity, see James Clifford's essay on the 1977 trial in Boston Federal Court, in which the descendants of Wampanoag Indians living in Mashpee, Massachusetts, "Cape Cod's Indian Town," were forced to prove their identity and continuous occupation of the region from the seventeenth century in order to secure legal rights (Clifford 1988).

9 Moreover, Haviland notes that the court translator was a native speaker of Cuban Spanish, a dialect quite different from the Mexican Spanish that the Mixtec participants in the trial struggled to utilize (774, fn. 7).

10 The defendant was released on appeal after spending five years in prison because the court of appeal found his right to adequate counsel had been violated since his lawyer did not let him testify in his own defense. "The state, obliged to bring the case to a new jury, simply chose not to reprosecute" (773).

11 As Lipset explains, Darapap was "not in receptivity mode, awaiting the imminent arrival of modernity; it [was] instead a place where modernity ha[d] already come and gone, leaving in its wake a few services and then moving on" (68).

12 As Muehlmann explains, during the Mexican revolution (1910–1920), many Cucapá lost a "significant portion" of their land because at the time they were mostly monolingual Cucapá speakers and therefore could not effectively "represent themselves legally or even fully understand the processes that were taking place" (2008: 36). According to indigenous rights law, however, it is the inability to speak Cucapá, not Spanish, that makes members of the community legally vulnerable.

13 Muehlmann cites to the work of the widely read public anthropologist and social advocate Hugh Brody, who made the argument—in his 2000 book *The Other Side of Eden: Hunters, Farmers, and the Shaping of the World*—that the indigenous language Inuktitut is one without swearwords, the capacity to invoke the supernatural "to express dismay or insult," and the words of "polite obeisance" that in other languages mark the fact of social hierarchy (Brody 2000: 44).

14 For more on this dynamic, see chapter 6.

15 For more on E. P. Thompson's study of law, see chapter 5.

## CHAPTER 2. HISTORY, HERITAGE, AND LEGAL *MYTHOI*

1 It is perhaps less well known that the kind of functionalism that Malinowski developed in anthropology went well beyond the epistemological to encompass what might be seen as a personal or even spiritual quest. As he put it in the wistful final section of *Argonauts*, "[i]n the roamings over human history, and over the surface of the earth, it is the possibility of seeing life and the world from the various angles, peculiar to each culture, that has always charmed me most, and inspired me with real desire to penetrate other cultures, to understand other types of life. . . . We cannot possibly reach the final Socratic wisdom of knowing ourselves if we never leave the narrow confinement of the customs, beliefs and prejudices into which every man is born" (1922: 517, 518).

2 For a later, more theoretical, critique of the idea of societies without history, see Fabian 1983, which argues that the very act of writing about ethnographic fieldwork in a tense that suggests a never-ending present denies the possibility of chronological coexistence, or "coevalness." In an earlier study of the effects of cultural relativism, Ernst Bloch described the warped image of the chronological other that emerged from such a "denial of coevalness" as one of "cultural monads,

that is, culture souls without windows, with no links among each other, yet full of mirrors facing inside" (Bloch 1962 [1932]: 326, quoted in Fabian 1983: 45).

3 The region in which Evans-Pritchard conducted research among the Nuer was at the time part of the Anglo-Egyptian Sudan "condominium," a rare form of colonial jurisdiction in which multiple powers agree to share control, or "dominion," over a defined territory. In fact, the British Empire exercised most of the control over the colonial territory, especially in the south (see Sharkey 2003). The condominium ended on January 1, 1956, when Sudan gained its independence through a treaty signed by Britain and Egypt.

4 As Mamdani explains, British colonial officials led the way in using manufactured forms of local legal tradition as a strategy of rule: "Britain . . . keenly glimpsed authoritarian possibilities in culture. Not simply content with salvaging every authoritarian tendency from the heterogeneous historical flow that was precolonial Africa, Britain creatively sculpted tradition and custom as and when the need arose. . . . By this dual process, part salvage and part sculpting, they crystallized a range of usually district-level Native Authorities, each armed with a whip and protected by the halo of custom" (1996: 49).

5 In their later study of Tswana dispute processes, John Comaroff and Simon Roberts (who was at the time "acting as Adviser on Customary Law to the Botswana Government") distanced themselves from Schapera's Handbook to the extent to which its focus on Tswana legal rules depicted a neat and tidy, internally coherent, legal system. By contrast, their own ethnography revealed a "loosely constructed repertoire rather than an internally consistent code, that Tswana were not unduly concerned if these rules sometimes contradicted one another, and that almost any conduct or relationship was potentially susceptible to competing normative constructions" (Comaroff and Roberts 1981: 18).

6 See, e.g., *Mashabane v. Molosankwe*, 2000 (1) BLR 185 (HC), in which, after discussing conflicting legal opinions, the high court justice resolves the case with reference to a section of Schapera's Handbook as controlling authority: "In this ruling here I am inclined to follow Schapera's book, op. cit., more so that the question as to the existence or content of a rule of customary law is a question of law to be determined by this court," 2000 (1) BLR 193–194.

7 For an extended discussion of the historical and ideological debates around the definition of "adat," see F. von Benda-Beckmann and K. von Benda-Beckmann 2011, 2013.

8 As Isaac Schapera put it, "[i]n the field of ethnological jurisprudence, there is no literature so rich and abundant as the studies of Van Vollenhoven, that great architect of Indonesian Adat law" (Schapera 1950: 82).

9 "Lawfare" is the turn to law's very structures of order to exert power over a population that is bound by the terms of political belonging to comply. Or, as they define it, lawfare is the use by a regime of "its own rules—of its duly enacted penal codes, its administrative law, its states of emergency, its charters and mandates and warrants, its norms of engagement—to impose a sense of order upon its sub-

ordinates by means of violence rendered legible, legal, and legitimate by its own sovereign word" (Comaroff and Comaroff 2006: 30).

10   "The Supreme Court of British Columbia is the province's superior trial court. The Supreme Court is a court of general and inherent jurisdiction which means that it can hear any type of case, civil or criminal. It hears most appeals from the Provincial Court in civil and criminal cases and appeals from arbitrations. A party may appeal a decision of the Supreme Court to the Court of Appeal" (Province of British Columbia 2016).

11   "*Adaawk* are Gitksan oral histories comprised of a collection of sacred reminiscences about ancestors, histories and territories that document House ownership of land and resources. The Wet'suwet'en *kungax* is a song, or songs, about trails between territories" (Culhane 1998: 120).

12   Although Allan McEachern, a "short, barrel-chested man noted for his clenched jaw and Columbo-inspired wardrobe" (Times Colonist 2008), was reviled for his legal reasoning in the 1991 *Delgamuukw* case and accused of racism and of being a juridical shill for the timber industry, he nevertheless went on to a distinguished career, serving as Chief Justice of the British Columbia Court of Appeal and later as Chancellor of the University of British Columbia, a post he held at the time of his death in 2008.

13   As UNESCO further explains, the "Convention is not intended to ensure the protection of all properties of great interest, importance or value, but only for a select list of the most outstanding of these from an international perspective" (UNESCO 2015: 12).

14   This was a 2013 special issue of *Gradhiva*, edited by David Berliner and Chiara Bortolotto, which featured anthropological studies of a number of specialized problems within the UNESCO world heritage regime, from the fact that only certain kinds of culture are seen as "correct" (Nielsen 2013) to the emergence of "hyper-sites" (Berliner and Istasse 2013) on the list.

15   For an anthropological study that emphasizes a different set of dynamics within the global heritage regime, see Brumann 2014.

16   In 2014, Palestine had its second site added to the list, the terraced hillsides of Battir, in the Central Highlands between Nablus and Hebron.

17   Nevertheless, this is not to say that extraordinary pressures do not shape the working of international courts at what might be called the macropolitical level. For example, in his otherwise strong argument for the development of a robust ICC, Kenneth Roth (2014), Executive Director of Human Rights Watch, acknowledges the serious "limits on the reach of international justice," most important of which is the fact that the leaders of many countries who might very well be subject to prosecution are effectively immune, either because their country is not a state party to the Rome Statute or because they receive protection from members of the UN Security Council, which has the legal power to grant jurisdiction to prosecutions in countries that are not part of the statute.

18  Fitzpatrick argues that modern law is both shaped by its reliance on the logic of myth—particularly in the way legal texts are mythologized—and repelled by it at the same time, in that modern law denies the legitimacy of the "myth-ridden" legal Other. This dualism is represented most clearly through modern law's association with colonialism and legal categories of race.

CHAPTER 3. JUSTICE BETWEEN THE DEVIL AND THE DEEP BLUE SEA

1  Because the girl was part of Kima'i's totemic clan, she was called "sister" and "forbidden as such" (79).

2  For an ethnographic study of the relationship between justice and gender, see Griffiths 1998.

3  The 1948 Convention on the Prevention and Punishment of the Crime of Genocide came into force in 1951.

4  The jurisdictional requirements of the 1998 Rome Statute are slightly more complicated than this, particularly in the fact that the UN Security Council can refer cases to the Court that involve individuals from states that are not parties to the statute. To date (2015), the ICC has begun investigations in two nonstate parties in this way: Darfur, Sudan (2005), and Libya (2011).

5  The corresponding phrases in Kinyarwanda are *itsembabwoko n'itsembatsemba* (genocide and massacres) and *jenoside yakorewe aba Tutsi* (genocide against the Tutsis) (Burnet 2011: 103).

6  The German situation is an intriguing one in the history of national commissions, since the Commission of Inquiry for the Assessment of History and Consequences of the SED Dictatorship (1992–1994) was established before the South African TRC as a largely research-based investigation of state repression in East Germany between 1949 and 1989 (see Hayner 2011: 52–53). The impact of this narrow, non-national commission was limited. As Hayner explains, "The commission held no subpoena power, and most former government officials who were invited to give testimony declined, in part fearing their testimony could be used against them in court" (2011: 52). More broadly, however, Germany never established a national commission to account for crimes committed by the Nazi regime, a form of collective silence that postwar German authors like Günter Grass and Heinrich Böll explored with such sensitivity and power.

7  As Dwyer notes, this museum complex was still open to the public as of 2011 (2011: 246). In 2012, the Academy Award-nominated documentary *The Act of Killing* was released, which reveals an Indonesian society in which "'Communist' [is] still a dirty word" (Hoang 2014) and in which paramilitary leaders who participated in the killings—many of whom still wield power in the country—discuss at length on camera (with "delight rather than remorse," as Hoang puts it) the various atrocities they committed.

8  The American Anthropological Association (AAA) formed a commission to study the rise of security anthropology during war and concluded in 2007 that it

was both unethical and likely to place anthropologists and their interlocutors in a position of danger (AAA 2007).

9 Even at the most basic of definitional levels, the opposition between justice-as-reason and justice-as-power was always problematic. For example, *The Oxford Universal Dictionary* from 1955 defines "justice" as "the quality of being (morally) just" as well as the "exercise of authority of power . . . by assignment of reward or punishment."

10 As the Preamble to the Universal Declaration of Human Rights puts it, the "recognition of the inherent dignity and of the equal and inalienable rights of all members of the human family is the foundation of . . . justice . . . in the world."

## CHAPTER 4. HUMAN RIGHTS AND THE POLITICS OF ASPIRATION

1 Important examples of the process through which anthropologists come to take a professional interest in human rights as a consequence of prior or ongoing human rights activism would include Shannon Speed's earlier work in Central America (described in Speed 2008); Winifred Tate's time with human rights NGOs in Colombia (described in Tate 2007), and Terence Turner's longtime activism on behalf of the Kayapo that preceded his academic contributions to the question of human rights and anthropology.

2 The critical examination of the ideological dimensions of this historiography has been undertaken elsewhere (see Goodale 2009, especially chapter 2). However, the point should be made that the precise contours of the prehistory of human rights, and of anthropology's role in it, are still being defined.

3 The information in this section is based on archival research in UNESCO's archives in Paris and in the special collections of the University of Chicago Library. The revised history of UNESCO's role in the drafting of the UDHR is being published in several places, including Goodale 2017a and Goodale 2018, a volume that updates and in a sense completes the information presented in a much-misunderstood symposium book published by UNESCO itself in 1949.

4 Despite the fact that the AAA was then, as it is now, the world's largest association of professional anthropologists, the AAA of 1946–1947 would be nearly unrecognizable compared to the organization today. For example, although there were around 600 professional anthropologists in the United States at the time, only 200 actually belonged to the AAA, a majority of whose members were instead "amateurs, students, [and] interested persons from other fields and libraries" (AAA Executive Committee Minutes, 1946). By contrast, the AAA in 2015 had around 11,000 individual and institutional members from around the world and could legitimately be thought of as an international anthropology association.

5 In fact, as archival research has revealed, Herskovits was not actually asked by Huxley or Havet to produce a response on behalf of anthropology. Instead, he was contacted from a list of potential American respondents created by Richard McKeon, then Dean of Humanities at the University of Chicago and someone who would play a key role in the process. Moreover, Herskovits sent his "State-

ment" directly to McKeon, who forwarded it to Havet in Paris along with a batch of others from the United States. Because *none* of the responses to the UNESCO survey were sent directly to the Commission on Human Rights, the appended note in the 1947 *American Anthropologist* article that has led to so much confusion must now be seen simply as an erroneous attempt by the editor of *AA* at the time to describe what had previously been done with the document.

6  A detailed record of these interventions can be found at the website of the Committee for Human Rights (CfHR): http://www.americananthro.org/ParticipateAndAdvocate/CommitteeDetail.aspx?ItemNumber=2218. The following gives a sense of the range of activities: "CfHR strongly urges the Government of Guatemala to move forward with the trial of former General Efraín Ríos Montt on the charge of genocide" (2013); "CfHR writes letter of support to the Brazilian Anthropological Association (ABA) concerning endangered indigenous land rights by Act# 303" (2012); "Model letter to Kenyan authorities concerning police assaults on Samburu villages" (2010); "CfHR letter concerning the impact of global warming" (2009); "CfHR Statement on the protests in Tibet" (2008); "Letter to New Zealand Prime Minister Helen Clark concerning the arrest of Maori activists" (2007); and "Letter to Armenian President Kocharian regarding the detention of anthropology graduate student Yektan Turkyilmaz" (2005).

7  That these volumes were a turning point for anthropology can be seen in the fact that an earlier work, on "human rights in cross-cultural perspective" (An-Na'im 1992), was framed by the perspectives of international lawyers and philosophers. Moreover, the three anthropologists (Diane Bell, Manuela Carneiro da Cunha, Tom G. Svensson) who appeared among the sixteen contributors could not base their interventions in systematic ethnographic research on human rights because it did not exist at the time (the volume stemmed from a 1989 conference held in Canada).

8  If, in Nader's classic formulation, studying up is both a method and a call to arms for anthropologists to turn the ethnographic lens toward powerful institutions, the idea of studying human rights networks sideways is a recognition that the nodes of power and influence within these networks are not always clear or where they might be expected to be.

9  In the process of developing an insider's approach to human rights networks, Riles's study problematized the one taken by the political scientists Keck and Sikkink, whose widely referenced work on human rights advocacy had just been published (1998).

10  For another anthropological study of law within the Israeli-Palestinian conflict, see Kelly 2006.

11  That the high point in the wider postwar history of human rights was reached some years ago and that we have entered a period of general anxiety and even doubt can be seen even within the UN itself. For example, each year Human Rights Day (December 10) is given a formal theme that is meant to capture the general state of human rights, partly in retrospect but partly with a view to the fu-

ture. As recently as 2011, the theme was the ebullient "Celebrate Human Rights!" since it appeared that powerful human rights movements were suddenly sweeping the globe "from Tunis to Madrid, from Cairo to New York." But by 2013, the Arab Spring had imploded (with the exception perhaps of Tunisia) and Occupy Wall Street had done nothing to stop the force of global capitalism (it turned out that even the ubiquitous Guy Fawkes masks were made under sweatshop labor conditions in the Global South). As a consequence, the theme for Human Rights Day 2013 was the much more restrained and even bureaucratic "Working for Your Rights" (www.un.org).

12 The topic of anthropology of law and indigenous peoples is taken up at length in chapter 6.

## CHAPTER 5. SHAPING INCLUSION AND EXCLUSION THROUGH LAW

1 Although Graeber's ambitious writings on value have had influence well beyond the boundaries of anthropology, a comprehensive handbook (Hirose and Olson 2015) on value theory makes no mention of the anthropology of value, Graeber's book, or any of the subsequent debates, thereby illustrating one of Graeber's key arguments, which is that questions of value have been historically balkanized within particular disciplines—such as philosophy, political theory, and economics—to the detriment of theory and potential applications.

2 Bowen argues that *laïcité* should not be used as an analytical category by anthropologists or others seeking to understanding the role of legal regulation in French society. As he puts it, "the word came late to the French language, and it does not appear in the major law (of 1905) regulating the status of religions. . . . It makes no sense for a social scientist or historian to ask, 'Does this policy reinforce *laïcité*?'— although it makes great sense for a politician to do so" (2007: 2–3).

3 Thoreson's multisited ethnography (New York City and Cape Town, South Africa) focused on the activism of the International Gay and Lesbian Human Rights Commission (IGLHRC), which was founded in 1990 as the first NGO devoted to advancing LGBT human rights worldwide.

4 As Mainsant explains, "France has what's called an 'abolitionist' legal system, that is to say, one that does not regulate or prohibit prostitution: prostitution is authorized by virtue of the fact that it is not mentioned in the penal code in which soliciting and pimping are [formally] prohibited" (2013: 486).

## CHAPTER 6. LAW AND THE FOURTH WORLD

1 Nevertheless, this ambiguity has also proven to be a mechanism through which indigenous legal practices have been able to flourish in unexpected ways. For a wide-ranging study that argues that customary law must be understood as a form of "living law" that is essential to any intercultural approach to justice, see Tobin 2014.

2 It is worth pointing out that Standing is both an economist and someone who worked for the ILO itself for over thirty years, eventually rising to become the Director of the ILO's Socio-Economic Security Program.

3   For a discussion of the historical circumstances surrounding the creation of ILO Convention 107 in relation to later developments, see Allen and Xanthaki 2011 and Pulitano 2012.

4   The legal status of indigenous rights within India remains an important part of the broader history, since India has by far the largest population of indigenous people of any country in the world, around 120 million, according to the International Work Group for Indigenous Affairs (www.iwgia.org). For comparison, India's indigenous population is nearly three times greater than those of all the countries of Latin America and the Caribbean *combined* (www.iwgia.org).

5   In addition, as of 2015, only one African country had ratified ILO 169 (the Central African Republic); no South-East or East Asian country was a state party; and other countries with important indigenous populations that were not states parties included Australia, New Zealand, Canada, and the United States.

6   As Niezen explains, the outcome of this "apparently arcane" debate had serious consequences indeed, since the use of "peoples" was "associated with self-determination, which, in turn, is associated in international law with a right of independent statehood" (2003: 38; citing to Anaya 1996). Despite the fact that "peoples" was eventually adopted in the convention, it was qualified (in Article 1.3) so that the term implied no additional legal rights.

7   In 2010, Canada issued a statement clarifying its earlier vote against the Declaration in which it explained that it had decided to endorse the Declaration because it was an "aspirational document" and therefore did not have any legal consequences for the country. In 2016, Canada fully adopted the Declaration and committed to implement its provisions consistent with the Canadian Constitution.

8   The treaty included "a CAN $190 million cash settlement and [it] makes the Nisga'a owners in fee simple of 2,000 square kilometers of land." In addition, the treaty "includes a guaranteed allocation of Nass River salmon, amounting to approximately 26 percent of the total allowable catch, a set of wildlife harvesting entitlements, and rights to all surface and subsurface resources, including timber and minerals, on treaty lands" (2009: 67).

9   Chave-Dartoen uses this phrase in French to translate this category of local Wallisian officials within the chiefdom, but the conventional English translation of *maître d'œuvre* as "project manager" likely loses too much of the meaning from the original Faka'uvea word/category to prove useful. Thus, Chave-Dartoen's French translation is left as it is.

10  Interestingly, Jackson's use of the term "hyper-Indian" to describe this particular effect of indigenous rights mobilization on identity was independent of Ramos's use of "hyperreal Indian." Although both anthropologists were working on the problem of representation at the same time, even in relation to the same indigenous population (although Ramos's article is based on research among Tukano-ans in Brasilia, Brazil's capital city), neither scholar knew of the work of the other (Jean Jackson, personal communication).

11 The 1993 Native Title Act was a landmark piece of indigenous rights legislation through which the Australian government created a framework for recognizing and enforcing native land titles in the aftermath of the 1992 High Court of Australia decision in *Mabo v Queensland (No. 2)*, which extended legal protection to native land titles in part by rejecting the legal doctrine of *terra nullius*, or "empty land." For an extended anthropological history and critique of the concept of *terra nullius*, see Culhane 1998.

12 In general, contemporary theorists in anthropology who work on questions of identity and power have followed and incorporated the insights of theorists like Charles Taylor (1992) and Axel Honneth (1996), in which the "moral grammar of social conflicts" must be understood in terms of struggles over recognition and self-worth rather than over redistribution (but see Li 2010; Goodale 2017b). As Fraser put it, perhaps a bit too dismissively, it "is no accident that both of the major contemporary theorists of recognition, Honneth and Taylor, are Hegelians" (1995: 72).

13 As James Scott explained, despite the fact that his study of "weapons of the weak" challenged prevailing theoretical approaches of the time, which tended to elide the ethnographic complexities of resistance in everyday life, the "economic origins of the petty class relations examined [in his book] . . . might easily be traced all the way to the board rooms of New York City and Tokyo" (1985: xix).

14 As Olivia Harris put it, in a study of ethnicity, markets, and migration in the history of the indigenous Andes, "Otavaleños have become prosperous entrepreneurs but have not abandoned their Indian identity, partly because in the second half of the twentieth century they have made it a source of income through the sale of weavings and handicrafts to tourists. But few other Indian groups have been able to capture and control a market . . . in this way" (1995: 370).

15 For a superb example, see Eduardo Kohn's ethnographic study of what it means to "think like a forest" (2013), which is discussed in more detail in the Conclusion.

CHAPTER 7. LAW AND THE MORAL ECONOMY OF GENDER

1 For an anthropological critique and rereading of Maine's *Ancient Law* that surveys the controversies over Maine's scholarship and his use of the *Institutes* of Gaius, see Starr 1989.

2 Interestingly, in the section on "the domestic relations" in his monumental *The Principles of Sociology* (published in three volumes in 1898), Herbert Spencer rejected McLennan's argument about the role of women in bride capture because it denied them agency (again, using a contemporary framing).

3 In her review of Colson's book in *American Anthropologist*, Hortense Powdermaker (1959) criticized an otherwise "excellent and detailed" ethnography for its failure to examine patterns of male labor migration between southern Africa and Europe, as these both reflected and influenced relations within families.

4 Because they were intended as a window into central concepts of the time in at least transatlantic thought, it is perhaps worth noting that "gender" does not

appear as one of Raymond Williams's "keywords" in either 1976 or 1983 on a list that included class, culture, ethnic, family, Man, racial, and sex ("gender" does appear in the entry for "sex," but only to mention that gender has been used as a synonym for sex to refer to one of the two biological categories of humans). By the time Tony Bennett, Lawrence Grossberg, and Meaghan Morris published a list of "new keywords" in 2005, "gender" had made the list.

5 Indeed, his influential *Europe and the People without History* had recently been published.

6 In their introduction to Starr's contribution, the editors describe it as a "reanalysis of selected Roman legal categories [that] demonstrates that unchallenged ideas can dominate theoretical assumptions" (1989: 10).

7 As we will see in the next section, violence against women and gender violence are by no means the same thing. Most violence against women is gender violence but not all gender violence is violence against women.

8 For example, Hillary Clinton, then the First Lady of the United States, gave a widely publicized speech in which she discussed the problem of violence against women in detail and memorably argued that "[i]f there is one message that echoes forth from this conference, it is that human rights are women's rights. . . . And women's rights are human rights."

9 Breton-Le Goff emphasizes the fact that cases like the Democratic Republic of Congo, in which gender violence takes place in the context of protracted civil war and systematic atrocity, create unique and serious challenges to the use of law as the main strategy of "elimination of all forms of discrimination against women."

10 Kazakhstan acceded to CEDAW in August 1998. As a former republic of the Soviet Union, it had been under the terms of the treaty from January 1981 to 1991.

11 As Snajdr emphasizes in a footnote, despite state discourses about "primordial" Kazakh culture, in fact the question of cultural beliefs in the country must be understood in relation to a sequence of historical changes, including "Islamic conversion and integration . . . , tsarist Russian subjugation, and the formalization of Central Asian ethnicity under the Soviets in the mid-1930s (2007: 617; fn. 5).

12 For another important study of gender, ethnicity, and the law, see Julie Billaud's (2015) ethnography of Afghan women living under conditions of humanitarian intervention and military occupation.

13 The CEDAW Committee's meetings were held in New York City until 2008, when the treaty body was moved to Geneva as part of a wider process to consolidate all the UN's human rights treaty bodies within the Office of the High Commissioner for Human Rights (OHCHR).

14 For another set of studies of "gender and culture at the limit of rights," see Hodgson 2013.

15 For a stimulating debate over the history of anthropology's study of incest, see the exchange between Borneman and an international group of scholars at the end of Borneman's article (2012: 194–201).

16 For an important anthropological study of international antitrafficking initiatives, see Warren 2007.

17 "[A]lso known as female circumcision or by activists as female genital mutilation (FGM)" (Shell-Duncan 2008: 226). As Shell-Duncan explains, attempts to resolve the "ongoing contentious nature of naming the practices" have been largely unsuccessful. For example, a move in the mid-2000s by several key UN agencies to use the hybrid acronym "FGM/C" was opposed by many African organizations, which insisted on using only "FGM." Shell-Duncan, who has played a leading role in these debates, "prefer[s] the less value-laden term *female genital cutting*" but uses "the acronym *FGM* . . . when referring to the views and work of scholars and activists who strategically employ this term" (2008: 233–234; emphases in original).

18 Even if a "number of scholars have reached the conclusion that the most promising rights-based claim for opposing FGC is the right to health and bodily integrity," the close connections with the earlier nonrights based health strategies still create "numerous problems" (2008: 228).

## CHAPTER 8. ETHNONATIONALISM AND CONFLICT TRANSFORMATION

1 In a December 2005 speech in Philadelphia, a location carefully chosen for its association with the linkage between violent military action and the fact that "all men are created equal, that they are endowed by their Creator with certain unalienable Rights," George. W. Bush asked, "[t]he fundamental question is, do we have the confidence [in our] values to help change a troubled part of the world?" (*Washington Post*, December 12, 2005).

2 For an impassioned response to the Singaporean defense of "Asian values," see Neier 1993, arguing that the culturalist opposition to human rights was really an effort to "deligitimate [*sic*] international efforts to address the abuses that particularly characterize [Singapore's] government and its regional allies: detention without trial and denial of press freedoms" (1993: 51).

3 The use of "curious grapevine" by Eleanor Roosevelt to imagine a future in which human rights and concepts of human dignity would shape the global landscape comes from a 1948 *New York Times* article on the work of the UN Commission on Human Rights, quoted in Korey 1998 (48).

4 This is not to say that one should try and pinpoint the passage from the post–Cold War to the period after with any degree of historical certainty, but one could underscore certain symbolic markers of the end of post–Cold War optimism and liminal possibility, including revelations about systematic torture at Abu-Ghraib (2003), the global financial crisis (2008), and the devolution of the so-called Arab Spring into regional crisis, state violence, and political repression (around 2012).

5 Keucheyan writes about the extraordinary ways in which the threat of climate change has been "financialized" by private companies and governments, for example, through the issuance of massive catastrophe bonds or "cat bonds." As he

puts it, a "world of environmental desolation and conflict will work for capitalism, as long as the conditions for investment and profit are guaranteed" (2014).

6  For reasons that would be obvious to many, given both the underlying topics and stakes involved, the wide-ranging debates over the concepts and historical realities of nations and nationalism, both within and outside anthropology, have been heated. For example, Ernest Gellner's influential 1983 study has been the subject of sustained critique along historical, interpretive, and theoretical lines, leading one scholar to pose the rhetorical question "should we still read Ernest Gellner?" (Conversi 2007). At the same time, Walker Connor's alternative approach, which sees ethnicity and the emotional power of "felt history" as the basis of nationalism, has itself come under sustained criticism. For example, Ian Bremmer has argued that Connor conflates ethnonationalism with other categories of nationalism and thereby ignores the role of "other types of 'glue' (territoriality, shared history, occupation)" (1995: 1133). My use of "ethnonationalism" in this chapter does not represent a distinct position vis-à-vis these debates.

7  For an exchange that involves many of these competing approaches to nations and nationalism and the position of anthropology in relation to them, see Hayden 2007 and the accompanying comments.

8  Alison Dundes Renteln, who is a leading authority on the "cultural defense" in U.S. domestic law in particular, notes that debates over the relationship between culture and law have taken place in countries such as Australia, Belgium, the Netherlands, and South Africa (2005: 47). See also Renteln 2004.

9  To say nothing of the problem of translation between different languages. Unfortunately, this dimension of the place of culture within international law must be put to the side, but for an expansive reconsideration of how the process of "translating worlds" opens up new epistemological spaces (for anthropologists and others), see Severi and Hanks 2015.

10  In Morsink's analysis of the appearance of culture in the UDHR, it is important to note that Humphrey, a distinguished law professor at McGill University, was deeply involved (with his wife Jeanne) in the "cultural life of Montreal and other places they lived." They hosted "numerous intellectuals and artists" at their house, they helped establish the Contemporary Arts Society of Montreal, and they regularly patronized art galleries and attended plays and concerts (Morsink 1999: 218; see also Humphrey 1984).

11  See chapter 2.

12  Although the UNESCO Director-General at the time, the Japanese diplomat Kōichirō Matsuura, expressed the hope that the UNESCO Universal Declaration on Cultural Diversity would come to shape global thinking and action with "the same force as the Universal Declaration of Human Rights" (UNESCO 2002), the following fifteen years saw little evidence of widespread "intercultural dialogue"; scant mobilization around the idea that "cultural diversity . . . [is] the common heritage of humanity"; and almost no indication that UNESCO's promotion of cultural diversity had "prevent[ed] segregation and fundamentalism."

13 For example, in the definition given to first-year anthropology students since time immemorial (or at least since 1871), E. B. Tylor writes that "culture . . . taken in its broad, ethnographic sense, is that complex whole which includes knowledge, belief, art, morals, law, custom, and any other capabilities and habits acquired by man as a member of society" (1871: 1).

14 The legal persecution of Gypsies in Europe has a long history. Writing about this history in France, for example, Shannon Fogg explains that Gypsies were "pushed to the edges of society in medieval Europe due to their dark skin, strange language, indifference to established religion, and perceived threat to guilds, [and] the first anti-Gypsy legislation in France appeared in 1539" (2007: 87).

15 Pasqualino reviews debates within the Gypsy studies literature over whether the *kris*, where it is present, should be understood primarily as a legal institution or rather as a political or civic institution (1999: 619–620).

16 In a fascinating doctoral study, Sara Memo (2013) analyzes the legal status of Gypsies/Roma at a European level. After revealing patterns in the legal exclusion of Roma throughout Europe, Memo argues that the problem is at its core one of mismatch between the "Westphalian paradigm" of majority and minority peoples bound to defined territories, and the Roma's essential transnationality. She suggests that the best solution to this mismatch would be for European institutions to look to international legal instruments covering indigenous people and apply them to the Roma as a "European transnational people."

17 As he explains, "mistrust of the police and suspicions about their allegiances are endemic in the marginal barrios of Cochabamba. . . . [I]t is widely accepted that the police are in league with the criminals, taking money to look the other way in the event of a crime" (2003: 31).

## CONCLUSION

1 In an article in the spring of 1948, before the UN General Assembly had voted on the UDHR, Eleanor Roosevelt reflected on the "promise of human rights," which was not, in her opinion, the fact that a new international legal or political regime had been created (it hadn't, in any case). Rather, it was that a new moral-didactic vision had been codified, even if its realization in practice would have to wait for at least several decades. As she explained, "We have found that the conditions of our contemporary world require the enumeration of certain protections which the individual must have if he is to acquire a sense of security and dignity in his own person. The effect of this is frankly educational. Indeed, I like to think that the Declaration will help forward very largely the education of the peoples of the world" (1948: 477).

2 As Lessing described his inability to reconcile faith with reason, "[t]hat, then, is the ugly, broad ditch which I cannot get across, however often and however earnestly I have tried to make the leap. If anyone can help me over it, let him do it, I beg him, I adjure him. He will deserve a divine reward from me" (1957 [1777]: 55).

3  "[L]a majestueuse égalité des lois, qui interdit au riche comme au pauvre de coucher sous les ponts, de mendier dans les rues et de voler du pain. C'est un des bienfaits de la Révolution."

4  For an insightful study of how indigenous women in Ecuador confronted legacies of inequality, including those expressed through rights discourses, see Radcliffe 2015. As she shows, indigenous women drew from local and alternative epistemologies as both a critique of development policies and as a resource in the face of endemic poverty and institutional disempowerment.

5  Graeber's article contains a devilish critique of Thomas Piketty's 2014 *Capital in the Twenty-First Century*, which proposes new international tax regulations as a response to the structural gap between rates of return on investments and economic growth: "having demonstrated [that] capitalism is a gigantic vacuum cleaner sucking wealth into the hands of a tiny elite, [Piketty] insists that we do not simply unplug the machine, but try to build a slightly smaller vacuum cleaner sucking in the opposite direction." As Graeber goes on, "the sheer fact that in 2014 a left-leaning French intellectual can safely declare that he does not want to overthrow the capitalist system but only to save it from itself is the reason [fundamental challenges to the system] will never happen."

6  Pogge's study of cosmopolitanism and human rights expressed the liminal optimism of its time (1992). As he says, "The recent development of, and progress within, both governmental and nongovernmental international organizations supports the hope, I believe, that such a conception might, in our world, become the object of a worldwide overlapping consensus" (49, fn. 4).

7  For a study of *ayllus* and cosmopolitics that has far-reaching implications for the development of alternative legal imaginaries, see de la Cadena 2015.

# REFERENCES

LEGAL CASE
2000 Mashabane v. Molosankwe. Vol. 1. Pp. 185: High Court of Botswana.

BOOKS AND ARTICLES
Adcock, Fleur
  2014 Rights through the United Nations: The Domestic Influence of the Special
    Rapporteur on the Rights of Indigenous Peoples. Paper presented at the Ameri-
    can Anthropological Association Annual Meeting. Washington, D.C.
Allen, Lori A.
  2009 Martyr Bodies in the Media: Human Rights, Aesthetics, and the Poli-
    tics of Immediation in the Palestinian Intifada. American Ethnologist
    36(1):161–180.
  —
  2013 The Rise and Fall of Human Rights: Cynicism and Politics in Occupied Pales-
    tine. Stanford: Stanford University Press.
Allen, Stephen, and Alexandra Xanthaki, eds.
  2011 Reflections on the UN Declaration on the Rights of Indigenous Peoples. Ox-
    ford: Hart Publishing.
American Anthropological Association (AAA)
  1946 Executive Committee Minutes. Suitland, Maryland: National Anthropological
    Archives.
  —
  1947 Statement on Human Rights. American Anthropologist 49(4):539–543.
  —
  1999 Committee for Human Rights. Declaration on Anthropology and Human
    Rights. www.aaanet.org.
  —
  2001 Committee for Human Rights. 1995–2001 Cumulative 5-Year Report. www.
    aaanet.org.
  —
  2006 Committee for Human Rights. Committee Charge. www.americananthro.org.
  —
  2007 Executive Board Statement on the Human Terrain System Project. http://
    s3.amazonaws.com; www.aaanet.org.

An-Na'im, Abdullahi Ahmed, ed.

1992 Human Rights in Cross-Cultural Perspective: A Quest for Consensus. Philadelphia: University of Pennsylvania Press.

Anaya, James

1996 Indigenous Peoples in International Law. Oxford: Oxford University Press.

Aoki, Keith

1998 Neocolonialism, Anti-Commons Property, and Biopiracy in the (Not-So-Brave) New World Order of International Property Protection. Indiana Journal of Global Legal Studies 6(1):11–58.

Arendt, Hannah

1963 Eichmann in Jerusalem: A Report on the Banality of Evil. New York: Viking Press.

Arias, Enrique Desmond, and Daniel M. Goldstein, eds.

2010 Violent Democracies in Latin America. Durham: Duke University Press.

Asdar Ali, Kamran

2010 Voicing Difference: Gender and Civic Engagement among Karachi's Poor. Current Anthropology 51(S2):S313–S320.

Atlani-Duault, Laëtitia

2007 *Goluboi* ou la difficulté d'être "bleu." Homosexualité et aide internationale en Asie centrale. Anthropologie et Sociétés 31(2):91–111.

Aubert, Vilhelm

1989 Law and Social Change in Nineteenth-Century Norway. *In* History and Power in the Study of Law: New Directions in Legal Anthropology. June Starr and Jane F. Collier, eds. Pp. 55–80. Ithaca: Cornell University Press.

Bachofen, Johann Jakob

1861 Das Mutterrecht: eine Untersuchung über die Gynaikokratie der alten Welt nach ihrer religiösen und rechtlichen Natur Stuttgart: Verlag von Krais & Hoffman.

Baer, Monika

2010 L'invisible visible. Genre, sexualité et société civile. Ethnologie française 40(2):245–255.

Bakhtin, Mikhail

1981 [1934/35] The Dialogic Imagination: Four Essays. Slavic Series. Austin: University of Texas Press.

—

1984a Problems of Dostoevsky's Poetics. Minneapolis: University of Minnesota Press.

—

1984b Rabelais and His World. H. Iswolsky, transl. Bloomington: Indiana University Press.

Banaker, Reza

2009 Law through Sociology's Looking Glass: Conflict and Competition in Sociological Studies of Law. *In* The ISA Handbook in Contemporary Sociology. Ann Denis and Devorah Kalekin-Fishman, eds. London: Sage.

Bass, Gary
    2000 Stay the Hand of Vengeance: The Politics of War Crimes Tribunals. Princeton:
        Princeton University Press.
Baxi, Upendra
    2002 The Future of Human Rights. New Delhi: Oxford University Press.
BBC
    1989 Malta Summit Ends Cold War. http://news.bbc.co.uk.
Beckman, Ludvig, and Eva Erman, eds.
    2012 Territories of Citizenship. London: Palgrave Macmillan.
Bell, Lynda S.
    2001 Who Produces Asian Identity? Discourse, Discrimination, and Chinese Peas-
        ant Women in the Quest for Human Rights. In Negotiating Culture and Human
        Rights. Lynda S. Bell, Andrew J. Nathan, and Ilan Peleg, eds. Pp. 21–42. New
        York: Columbia University Press.
Berlin, Isaiah
    1991 The Crooked Timber of Humanity: Chapters in the History of Ideas. New
        York: Alfred A. Knopf.
—
    1996 The Sense of Reality: Studies in Ideas and Their History. New York: Farrar,
        Straus and Giroux.
Berliner, David, and Manon Istasse
    2013 Les hyper-lieux du patrimonie mondial. Gradhiva 18:124–145.
Billaud, Julie
    2015 Kabul Carnival: Gender Politics in Postwar Afghanistan. Philadelphia: Univer-
        sity of Pennsylvania Press.
Biolsi, Thomas
    1995 Bringing the Law Back In: Legal Rights and the Regulation of Indian-White
        Relations on Rosebud Reservation. Current Anthropology 36(4):543–571.
—
    2005 Imagined Geographies: Sovereignty, Indigenous Space, and American Indian
        Struggle. American Ethnologist 32(2):239–259.
Blackburn, Carole
    2007 Producing Legitimacy: Reconciliation and the Negotiation of Ab-
        original Rights in Canada. Journal of the Royal Anthropological Institute
        13(3):621–638.
—
    2009 Differentiating Indigenous Citizenship: Seeking Multiplicity in Rights, Iden-
        tity, and Sovereignty in Canada. American Ethnologist 36(1):66–78.
Blaser, Mario
    2004 Life Projects: Indigenous Peoples' Agency and Development. In In the
        Way of Development: Indigenous Peoples, Life Projects and Globalization.
        Mario Blaser, Harvey A. Feit, and Glenn McRae, eds. Pp. 52–71. London: Zed
        Books.

Bloch, Ernst

1962 [1932] Ungleichzeitigkeit und Pflicht zu ihrer Dialektik. *In* Erbschaft dieser Zeit. Pp. 104–126. Frankfurt: Suhrkamp.

Bohannan, Paul

1957 Justice and Judgment among the Tiv. Oxford: Oxford University Press.

— 1969 Ethnography and Comparison in Legal Anthropology. *In* Law in Culture and Society. Laura Nader, ed. Pp. 401–418. Chicago: Aldine.

Borneman, John

2012 Incest, the Child, and the Despotic Father. Current Anthropology 53(2):181–203.

Borras, Saturino M., and Jennifer Franco

2010 Contemporary Discourses and Contestations around Pro-Poor Land Policies and Land Governance. Journal of Agrarian Change 10(1):1–32.

Borras, Saturino M., Ruth Hall, Ian Scoones, Ben White, and Wendy Wolford

2011 Towards a Better Understanding of Global Land Grabbing: An Editorial Introduction. Journal of Peasant Studies 38(2):209–216.

Bowen, John

2003 Islam, Law and Equality in Indonesia: An Anthropology of Public Reasoning. Cambridge: Cambridge University Press.

— 2007 Why the French Don't Like Headscarves: Islam, the State, and Public Space. Princeton: Princeton University Press.

— 2010 Can Islam Be French? Pluralism and Pragmatism in a Secularist State. Princeton: Princeton University Press.

— 2016 On British Islam: Religion, Law, and Shari'a Councils. Princeton: Princeton University Press.

Braithwaite, John

1991 Poverty, Power, White-Collar Crime and the Paradoxes of Criminological Theory. Australian & New Zealand Journal of Criminology 24(1):40–58.

Bremmer, Ian

1995 Review of Ethnonationalism: The Quest for Understanding. Slavic Review 54(4):1132–1134.

Breton-Le Goff, Gaëlle

2013 Aux confins du droit positif. Socio-anthropologie de la production normative non gouvernementale en république démocratique du Congo. Anthropologie et Sociétés 37(1):75–95.

Brody, Hugh

2000 The Other Side of Eden: Hunters, Farmers, and the Shaping of the World. New York: North Point Press.

Brown, Wendy
    2010 We Are All Democrats Now. . . . Theory & Event 13(2).
Brumann, Christoph
    2014 Shifting Tides of World-Making in the UNESCO World Heritage Convention:
        Cosmopolitans Colliding. Ethnic and Racial Studies 37(12):2176–2192.
Brunnegger, Sandra
    2016 The Craft of Justice-Making: The Permanent Peoples' Tribunal in Colombia.
        *In* A Sense of Justice: Legal Knowledge and Lived Experience in Latin America.
        Sandra Brunnegger and Karen Faulk, eds. Pp. 123–146. Stanford: Stanford Uni-
        versity Press.
Brunnegger, Sandra, and Karen Faulk, eds.
    2016 A Sense of Justice: Legal Knowledge and Lived Experience in Latin America.
        Stanford: Stanford University Press.
Buckler, Sal
    2007 Same Old Story? Gypsy Understandings of the Injustices of Non-Gypsy
        Justice. *In* Paths to International Justice: Social and Legal Perspectives. Marie-
        Bénédicte Dembour and Tobias Kelly, eds. Pp. 243–261. Cambridge: Cambridge
        University Press.
Burnet, Jennie E.
    2011 (In)Justice: Truth, Reconciliation, and Revenge in Rwanda's *Gacaca*. *In* Tran-
        sitional Justice: Global Mechanisms and Local Realities after Genocide and
        Mass Violence. Alexander L. Hinton, ed. Pp. 95–118. New Brunswick: Rutgers
        University Press.
Burrell, Jennifer
    2010 In and Out of Rights: Security, Migration, and Human Rights Talk in
        Postwar Guatemala. Journal of Latin American and Caribbean Anthropology
        15(1):90–115.
Cabot, Heath
    2014 On the Doorstep of Europe: Asylum and Citizenship in Greece. Philadelphia:
        University of Pennsylvania Press.
Cadena, Marisol de la
    2015 Earth Beings: Ecologies of Practice across Andean Worlds. Durham: Duke
        University Press.
Caldeira, Teresa
    2001 City of Walls: Crime, Segregation, and Citizenship in São Paulo. Berkeley:
        University of California Press.
Camp, Roderic A.
    1985 Intellectuals and the State in Twentieth-Century Mexico. Austin: University of
        Texas Press.
Campbell, C. M., and Paul Wiles
    1976 The Study of Law in Society in Britain. Law and Society Review
        10(4):547–578.

Casey, Conerly
    2011 Remembering Genocide: Hypocrisy and the Violence of Local/Global "Justice" in Northern Nigeria. *In* Transitional Justice: Global Mechanisms and Local Realities after Genocide and Mass Violence. Alexander Hinton, ed. Pp. 119–136. New Brunswick: Rutgers University Press.

Castells, Manuel
    1996 The Rise of the Network Society. Oxford: Blackwell.

Cavallar, Georg
    2012 Cosmopolitanisms in Kant's Philosophy. Ethics & Global Politics 5(2):95–118.

CEDAW (Convention on the Elimination of All Forms of Discrimination Against Women)
    1979 www.ohchr.org.

Charbonnier, Georges
    1969 Conversations with Claude Lévi-Strauss. London: Jonathan Cape.

Chave-Dartoen, Sophie
    2002 Le paradoxe wallisien: une royauté dans la République. Ethnologie française 32(4):637–645.

Cheah, Pheng
    1998 The Cosmopolitical—Today. *In* Cosmopolitics: Thinking and Feeling beyond the Nation. Pheng Cheah and Bruce Robbins, eds. Pp. 20–44. Minneapolis: University of Minnesota Press.

Cheah, Pheng, and Bruce Robbins, eds.
    1998 Cosmopolitics: Thinking and Feeling beyond the Nation. Minneapolis: University of Minnesota Press.

Chesterman, Simon
    2001 Just War or Just Peace? Humanitarian Intervention and International Law. Oxford: Oxford University Press.

Christen, Kimberly
    2006 Tracking Properness: Repackaging Culture in a Remote Australian Town. Cultural Anthropology 21(3):416–446.

Clarke, Kamari Maxine
    2009 Fictions of Justice: The International Criminal Court and the Challenge of Legal Pluralism in Sub-Saharan Africa. Cambridge: Cambridge University Press.

Clarke, Kamari Maxine, and Mark Goodale, eds.
    2010 Mirrors of Justice: Law and Power in the Post–Cold War Era. New York: Cambridge University Press.

Clarke, Morgan
    2012 The Judge as Tragic Hero: Judicial Ethics in Lebanon's Shariʿa Courts. American Ethnologist 39(1):106–121.

Clay, Jason
    1982 Editor's Note. Cultural Survival Quarterly 6(1):1.

Clifford, James

1988 The Predicament of Culture: Twentieth-Century Ethnography, Literature, and Art. Cambridge: Harvard University Press.

Colloredo-Mansfeld, Rudi

1999 The Native Leisure Class: Consumption and Cultural Creativity in the Andes. Chicago: University of Chicago Press.

— 2002 "Don't Be Lazy, Don't Lie, Don't Steal": Community Justice in the Neoliberal Andes. American Ethnologist 29(3):637–662.

Colson, Elizabeth

1958 Marriage and the Family among the Plateau Tonga of Northern Rhodesia. New York: Humanities Press.

— 1966 Land Law and Landholdings among the Valley Tonga of Zambia. Southwestern Journal of Anthropology 22(1):1–8.

Comaroff, John, and Simon Roberts

1981 Rules and Processes: The Cultural Logic of Dispute in an African Context. Chicago: University of Chicago Press.

Comaroff, John L.

1994 Foreword. In Contested States: Law, Hegemony, Resistance. Mindie Lazarus-Black and Susan Hirsch, eds. Pp. ix–xiii. New York: Routledge.

Comaroff, John L., and Jean Comaroff

2006 Law and Disorder in the Postcolony: An Introduction. In Law and Disorder in the Postcolony. Jean Comaroff and John L. Comaroff, eds. Pp. 1–56. Chicago: University of Chicago Press.

Conley, John M., and William O'Barr

1985 Litigant Satisfaction versus Legal Adequacy in Small Claims Court Narratives. Law and Society Review 19(4):661–702.

— 1990 Rules versus Relationships: The Ethnography of Legal Discourse. Chicago: University of Chicago Press.

— 1998 Just Words: Law, Language, and Power. Chicago: University of Chicago Press.

— 2002 Back to the Trobriands: The Enduring Influence of Malinowski's *Crime and Custom in Savage Society*. Law & Social Inquiry 27(4):847–874.

— 2004 A Classic in Spite of Itself: "The Cheyenne Way" and the Case Method in Legal Anthropology. Law & Social Inquiry 29(1):179–217.

Connor, Walker

1994 Ethnonationalism: The Quest for Understanding. Princeton: Princeton University Press.

Conversi, Daniele
    2007 Homogenisation, Nationalism, and War: Should We Still Read Ernest Gellner?
        Nations and Nationalism 13(3):371–394.
Coombe, Rosemary
    1998 The Cultural Life of Intellectual Properties: Authorship, Appropriation, and
        the Law. Durham: Duke University Press.
Couso, Javier, Alexandra Huneeus, and Rachel Sieder, eds.
    2010 Cultures of Legality: Judicialization and Political Activism in Latin America.
        Cambridge: Cambridge University Press.
Coutin, Susan
    1994 Enacting Law through Social Practice: Sanctuary as a Form of Resistance. *In*
        Contested States: Law, Hegemony, Resistance. Mindie Lazarus-Black and Susan
        Hirsch, eds. Pp. 282–303. New York: Routledge.
Cowan, Jane
    2006 Culture and Rights after *Culture and Rights*. American Anthropologist 108(1):9–24.
Cowan, Jane, and Julie Billaud
    2015 Between Learning and Schooling: The Politics of Human Rights Monitoring at
        the Universal Periodic Review. Third World Quarterly 36(5):1175–1190.
Cowan, Jane, Marie-Bénédicte Dembour, and Richard A. Wilson, eds.
    2001 Culture and Rights: Anthropological Perspectives. Cambridge: Cambridge
        University Press.
Crăciun, Magdalena
    2012 Rethinking Fakes, Authenticating Selves. Journal of the Royal Anthropological
        Institute 18(4):846–863.
Culhane, Dara
    1998 The Pleasure of the Crown: Anthropology, Law, and First Nations. Burnaby,
        B.C.: Talon Books.
Curtis, Jennifer
    2014 Human Rights as War by Other Means. Peace Politics in Northern Ireland.
        Philadelphia: University of Pennsylvania Press.
Darian-Smith, Eve
    1999 Bridging Divides: The Channel Tunnel and English Legal Identity in the New
        Europe. Berkeley: University of California Press.
Davis, Kevin E., Angelina Fisher, Benedict Kingsbury, and Sally Engle Merry, eds.
    2012 Governance by Indicators: Global Power through Classification and Rankings.
        Oxford: Oxford University Press.
Davis, Mike
    2006 Planet of Slums. London: Verso.
Day, Sophie
    2010 The Re-Emergence of "Trafficking": Sex Work between Slavery and Freedom.
        Journal of the Royal Anthropological Institute 16(4):816–834.
Del Olmo, Rosa
    1981 América Latina y su criminología. Madrid: Siglo Veintiuno Editores.

Dombrowski, Kirk
2002 The Praxis of Indigenism and Alaska Native Timber Politics. American Anthropologist 104(4):1062–1073.

Domingo, Pilar
2010 Novel Appropriations of the Law in the Pursuit of Political and Social Change in Latin America. *In* Cultures of Legality: Judicialization and Political Activism in Latin America. Javier Couso, Alexandra Huneeus, and Rachel Sieder, eds. Pp. 254–278. Cambridge Studies in Law and Society. New York: Cambridge University Press.

Doostdar, Alireza
2004 "The Vulgar Spirit of Blogging": On Language, Culture, and Power in Persian Weblogestan. American Anthropologist 106(4):651–662.

Duménil, Gérard, and Dominque Lévy
2004 Capital Resurgent: Roots of the Neoliberal Revolution. Cambridge: Harvard University Press.

Dwyer, Leslie
2011 Building a Monument: Intimate Politics of "Reconciliation" in Post-1965 Bali. *In* Transitional Justice: Global Mechanisms and Local Realities after Genocide and Mass Violence. Alexander L. Hinton, ed. Pp. 227–248. New Brunswick: Rutgers University Press.

—

2017 "A World in Fragments": Aftermaths of Violence in Bali, Indonesia. Philadelphia: University of Pennsylvania Press.

Eberhard, Christoph
2009 Au-delà de l'universalisme et du relativisme. L'horizon d'un pluralisme responsable. Anthropologie et Sociétés 33(3):79–100.

Eckert, Julia, ed.
2008a The Social Life of Anti-Terrorism Laws. The War on Terror and the Classifications of the "Dangerous Other." Bielefeld: transcript Verlag.

—

2008b Law for Enemies. *In* The Social Life of Anti-Terrorism Laws. The War on Terror and the Classifications of the "Dangerous Other." Julia Eckert, ed. Pp. 7–32. Bielefeld: transcript Verlag.

Eckert, Julia, Brian Donahoe, Christian Strümpell, and Zerrin Özlem Biner, eds.
2012 Law against the State: Ethnographic Forays into Law's Transformations. Cambridge: Cambridge University Press.

Eltringham, Nigel
2004 Accounting for Horror: Post-Genocide Debates in Rwanda. London: Pluto.

—

2010 Judging the "Crime of Crimes": Continuity and Improvisation at the International Criminal Tribunal for Rwanda. *In* Transitional Justice: Global Mechanisms and Local Realities after Genocide and Mass Violence. Alexander Hinton, ed. Pp. 206–226. New Brunswick: Rutgers University Press.

—

2013 "Illuminating the Broader Context": Anthropological and Historical Knowledge at the International Criminal Tribunal for Rwanda. Journal of the Royal Anthropological Institute 19(2):338–355.

Engle, Karen

2001 From Skepticism to Embrace: Human Rights and the American Anthropological Association from 1947–1999. Human Rights Quarterly 23:536–559.

Englund, Harri

2006 Prisoners of Freedom: Human Rights and the African Poor. Berkeley: University of California Press.

—

2013 Cutting Human Rights Down to Size. In Human Rights at the Crossroads. Mark Goodale, ed. Pp. 198–209. New York: Oxford University Press.

Epstein, A. L.

1974 Moots on Matupit. In Contention and Dispute: Aspects of Law and Social Control in Melanesia. A. L. Epstein, ed. Pp. 93–112. Canberra: Australian National University Press.

Evans-Pritchard, E. E.

1940 The Nuer: A Description of the Modes of Livelihood and Political Institutions of a Nilotic People. Oxford: Oxford University Press.

Fabian, Johannes

1983 Time and the Other: How Anthropology Makes Its Object. New York: Columbia University Press.

Fabricant, Nicole

2012 Mobilizing Bolivia's Displaced: Indigenous Politics and the Struggle over Land. Chapel Hill: University of North Carolina Press.

Ferguson, James

2006 Global Shadows: Africa in the Neoliberal World Order. Durham: Duke University Press.

Ferme, Mariane

2001 The Underneath of Things: Violence, History, and the Everyday in Sierra Leone. Berkeley: University of California Press.

Fernández Osco, Marcelo

2000 La ley del ayllu. Práctica de jach'a justicia y jisk'a justicia (Justicia Mayor y Justicia Menor) en comunidades aymaras. La Paz, Bolivia: PIEB.

Ferrándiz, Francisco

2013 Exhuming the Defeated: Civil War Mass Graves in 21st-Century Spain. American Ethnologist 40(1):38–54.

Finnström, Sverker

2010 Reconciliation Grown Bitter? War, Retribution, and Ritual Action in Northern Uganda. In Localizing Transitional Justice: Interventions and Priorities after Mass Violence. Rosalind Shaw and Lars Waldorf, eds. Pp. 135–156. Stanford: Stanford University Press.

Fish, Stanley
    1989 Doing What Comes Naturally: Change, Rhetoric, and the Practice of Theory
        in Literary and Legal Studies. Durham: Duke University Press.
Fitzpatrick, Peter
    1992 The Mythology of Modern Law. London: Routledge.
Flower, John
    2009 Ecological Engineering on the Sichuan Frontier: Socialism as Development
        Policy, Local Practice, and Contested Ideology. Social Anthropology 17(1):40–55.
Foblets, Marie-Claire
    1994 Les familles maghrébines et la justice en Belgique: Anthropologie juridique et
        immigration. Paris: Karthala.
Foblets, Marie-Claire, and Nadjma Yassari, eds.
    2013 Approches juridiques de la diversité culturelle/Legal Approaches to Cultural
        Diversity. Leiden: Martinus Nijhoff.
Fogg, Shannon L.
    2007 The Politics of Everyday Life in Vichy France: Foreigners, Undesirables, and
        Strangers. Cambridge: Cambridge University Press.
France, Anatole
    1894 Le Lys rouge. Paris: Calmann Lévy.
Fraser, Nancy
    1995 From Redistribution to Recognition? Dilemmas of Justice in a "Post-Socialist"
        Age. New Left Review 212 (June/August):68–93.
Freeman, Michael, and David Napier, eds.
    2009 Law and Anthropology: Current Legal Issues. Volume 12. Oxford: Oxford
        University Press.
French, Jan Hoffman
    2004 Mestizaje and Law Making in Indigenous Identity Formation in Northeast-
        ern Brazil: "After the Conflict Came the History." American Anthropologist
        106(4):663–674.

    —
    2009 Legalizing Identities: Becoming Black or Indian in Brazil's Northeast. Chapel
        Hill: University of North Carolina Press.
Fuller, Chris
    1994 Legal Anthropology, Legal Pluralism and Legal Thought. http://eprints.lse.
        ac.uk. London: LSE Research Online.
Galtung, Johan
    1964 Editorial. Journal of Peace Research 1(1):1–4.
Garriott, William
    2011 Policing Methamphetamine: Narcopolitics in Rural America. New York: NYU
        Press.
Geertz, Clifford
    1983 Local Knowledge: Further Essays in Interpretive Anthropology. New York:
        Basic Books.

Gellner, Ernest

1983 Nations and Nationalism. Ithaca: Cornell University Press.

Giordano, Cristiana

2008 Practices of Translation and the Making of Migrant Subjectivities in Contemporary Italy. American Ethnologist 35(4):588–606.

Glendon, Mary Ann

2001 A World Made New: Eleanor Roosevelt and the Universal Declaration of Human Rights. New York: Random House.

Gluckman, Max

1955 The Judicial Process among the Barotse of Northern Rhodesia. Manchester: Manchester University Press.

—

1962 African Jurisprudence. Advancement of Science 75:439–454.

—

1965 The Ideas of Bartose Jurisprudence. Manchester: Manchester University Press.

—

1969 Concepts in the Comparative Study of Tribal Law. In Law in Culture and Society. Laura Nader, ed. Pp. 349–373. Chicago: Aldine.

Goldstein, Daniel M.

2003 "In Our Own Hands": Lynching, Justice, and the Law in Bolivia. American Ethnologist 30(1):22–43.

—

2004 The Spectacular City: Violence and Performance in Urban Bolivia. Durham: Duke University Press.

—

2010 Toward a Critical Anthropology of Security. Current Anthropology 51(4):487–517.

—

2012 Outlawed: Between Security and Rights in a Bolivian City. Durham: Duke University Press.

Golub, Alex

2014 Leviathans at the Gold Mine: Creating Indigenous and Corporate Actors in Papua New Guinea. Durham: Duke University Press.

González-Leandri, Ricardo

2008 José María Ramos Mejía: Médico, intelectual y funcionario del Estado. In Saberes y prácticas médicas en la Argentina: Un recorrido por historias de vida. Adriana Alvarez and Adrían Carbonetti, eds. Pp. 95–134. Mar del Plata: Editorial de la Universidad Nacional de Mar del Plata.

Goodale, Mark

2007 The Power of Right(s): Tracking Empires of Law and New Modes of Social Resistance in Bolivia (and Elsewhere). In The Practice of Human Rights: Tracking Law between the Global and the Local. Mark Goodale and Sally Engle Merry, eds. Pp. 130–162. Cambridge: Cambridge University Press.

— 2008a Dilemmas of Modernity: Bolivian Encounters with Law and Liberalism. Stanford: Stanford University Press.

— 2008b Legalities and Illegalities. *In* A Companion to Latin American Anthropology. Deborah Poole, ed. Pp. 214–229. Malden, Mass.: Blackwell.

— 2009 Surrendering to Utopia: An Anthropology of Human Rights. Stanford: Stanford University Press.

—, ed.

2013a Human Rights at the Crossroads. New York: Oxford University Press.

— 2013b Human Rights *after* the Post–Cold War. *In* Human Rights at the Crossroads. Mark Goodale, ed. Pp. 1–28. New York: Oxford University Press.

— 2016 Values without Qualities: *Pathos* and *Mythos* in the Universal Declaration of Human Rights. *In* The Routledge Companion to Literature and Human Rights. Sophia McClennen and Alexandra Schultheis Moore, eds. Pp. 441–449. London: Routledge.

— 2017a UNESCO and the UN Rights of Man Declaration: History, Historiography, Ideology. Humanity 8(1).

— 2017b Dark Matter: Toward a New Political Economy of Indigenous Rights and Aspirational Politics. Critique of Anthropology 37(2).

— 2018 UNESCO Surveys the World: A Prehistory of Human Rights. Stanford: Stanford University Press.

— N.d. The Enchantments of Law: Rendering the Logics of Justice in Revolutionary Bolivia.

Goodale, Mark, and Kamari Maxine Clarke
2010 Understanding the Multiplicity of Justice. *In* Mirrors of Justice: Law and Power in the Post–Cold War Era. Kamari Maxine Clarke and Mark Goodale, eds. Pp. 1–27. New York: Cambridge University Press.

Goodale, Mark, and Sally Engle Merry, eds.
2007 The Practice of Human Rights: Tracking Law between the Global and the Local. Cambridge: Cambridge University Press.

Goodale, Mark, and Nancy Postero, eds.
2013 Neoliberalism Interrupted: Social Change and Contemporary Governance in Contemporary Latin America. Stanford: Stanford University Press.

Goodrich, Peter
1999 Anti-Teubner: Autopoiesis, Paradox, and the Theory of Law. Social Epistemology 13(2):197–214.

Gossiaux, Jean-François
    2002 La fin des Yougoslaves ou l'ethnicité toujours recommencée. Anthropologie et
        Sociétés 26(1):53–68.
Gossman, Lionel
    2000 Basel in the Age of Burckhardt: A Study in Unseasonable Ideas. Chicago:
        University of Chicago Press.
Graeber, David
    2001 Toward an Anthropological Theory of Value: The False Coin of Our Own
        Dreams. New York: Palgrave Macmillan.
—
    2004 Fragments of an Anarchist Anthropology. Chicago: Prickly Paradigm Press.
—
    2014 Savage Capitalism Is Back––and It Will Not Tame Itself. In The Guardian.
        www.theguardian.com.
Greenhouse, Carol J.
    1982 Looking at Culture, Looking for Rules. Man (New Series) 17(1):58–73.
—
    1986 Praying for Justice: Faith, Order and Community in an American Town.
        Ithaca: Cornell University Press.
—
    1992 Signs of Quality: Individualism and Hierarchy in American Culture. American
        Ethnologist 19(2):233–254.
—
    2005 Nationalizing the Local: Comparative Notes on the Recent Restructuring of
        Political Space. In Human Rights in the "War on Terror." Richard A. Wilson, ed.
        Pp. 184–208. Cambridge: Cambridge University Press.
Griffiths, Anne
    1998 In the Shadow of Marriage: Gender and Justice in an African Community.
        Chicago: University of Chicago Press.
Griffiths, John
    1983 Anthropology of Law in the Netherlands in the 1970s. Nieuwsbrief voor
        nederlandstalige rechtssociologen, rechtsantropologen en rechtspsychologen
        4(2):132–240.
—
    1986 Recent Anthropology of Law in the Netherlands and Its Historical Background.
        In Anthropology of Law in the Netherlands. Keebet von Benda–Beckmann and A.
        K. J. M. Stribosch, eds. Pp. 11–66. Dordrecht/Cinnaminson: Foris Publications.
Gulliver, Philip H.
    1963 Social Control in an African Society. London: Routledge and Kegan Paul.
Guy, Donna J.
    1991 Sex and Danger in Buenos Aires: Prostitution, Family, and Nation in Argen-
        tina. Lincoln: University of Nebraska Press.

Halliday, Simon, and Patrick Schmidt
2009 Conducting Law and Society Research: Reflections on Methods and Practices. New York: Cambridge University Press.

Halme-Tuomisaari, Miia, and Pamela Slotte
2015 Introduction: Revisiting the Origins of Human Rights. *In* Revisiting the Origins of Human Rights. Pamela Slotte and Miia Halme-Tuomisaari, eds. Pp. 1–38. Cambridge: Cambridge University Press.

Hammett, Ian, ed.
1977 Social Anthropology and Law. London: Academic Publishers.

Hardt, Michael, and Antonio Negri
2000 Empire. Cambridge: Harvard University Press.

Harris, Olivia
1995 Ethnic Identity and Market Relations: Indians and Mestizos in the Andes. *In* Ethnicity, Markets, and Migration in the Andes: At the Crossroads of History and Anthropology. Brooke Larson, Olivia Harris, and Enrique Tandeter, eds. Pp. 351–390. Durham: Duke University Press.

Harvey, David
1990 The Condition of Postmodernity: An Enquiry into the Origins of Cultural Change. Malden, Mass.: Blackwell.

—
2003 The New Imperialism. Oxford: Oxford University Press.

Haviland, John B.
2003 Ideologies of Language: Some Reflections on Language and U.S. Law. American Anthropologist 105(4):764–774.

Hayden, Cori
2003 When Nature Goes Public: The Making and Unmaking of Bioprospecting in Mexico. Princeton: Princeton University Press.

Hayden, Robert M.
1992 Constitutional Nationalism in the Formerly Yugoslav Republics. Slavic Review 51(4):654–673.

—
1996 Imagined Communities and Real Victims: Self-Determination and Ethnic Cleansing in Yugoslavia. American Ethnologist 23(4):783–801.

—
1999 Blueprints for a House Divided: The Constitutional Logic of the Yugoslav Conflicts. Ann Arbor: University of Michigan Press.

—
2007 Moral Vision and Impaired Insight: The Imagining of Other Peoples' Communities in Bosnia. Current Anthropology 48(1):105–131.

Hayner, Priscilla B.
2011 Unspeakable Truths: Transitional Justice and the Challenge of Truth Commissions, 2nd ed. London: Routledge.

Hertz, Ellen

    1998 The Trading Crowd: An Ethnography of the Shanghai Stock Market. Cambridge: Cambridge University Press.

Hinton, Alexander

    2004 Why Did They Kill? Cambodia in the Shadow of Genocide. Berkeley: University of California Press.

—, ed.

    2011 Transitional Justice: Global Mechanisms and Local Realities after Genocide and Mass Violence. New Brunswick: Rutgers University Press.

Hirose, Iwao, and Jonas Olson, eds.

    2015 The Oxford Handbook of Value Theory. Oxford: Oxford University Press.

Hirsch, Susan

    1998 Pronouncing and Persevering: Gender and the Discourses of Disputing in an African Islamic Court. Chicago: University of Chicago Press.

Hirschl, Ran

    2004 Towards Juristocracy: The Origins and Consequences of the New Constitutionalism. Cambridge: Harvard University Press.

Hoang, Lien

    2014 "Communist" Still a Dirty Word in Indonesia. Voice of America News.

Hobsbawm, Eric

    1975 The Age of Capital: 1848–1875. London: Weidenfeld and Nicolson.

Hodgson, Dorothy L.

    2002 Precarious Alliances: The Cultural Politics and Structural Predicaments of the Indigenous Rights Movement in Tanzania. American Anthropologist 104(4):1086–1097.

—

    2011 Being Maasai, Becoming Indigenous: Postcolonial Politics in a Neoliberal World. Bloomington: Indiana University Press.

—, ed.

    2013 Gender and Culture at the Limit of Rights. Philadelphia: University of Pennsylvania Press.

Hoebel, E. Adamson

    1954 The Law of Primitive Man: A Study in Comparative Legal Dynamics. Cambridge: Harvard University Press.

Holleman, J. F.

    1973 Trouble-Cases and Trouble-Less Cases in the Study of Customary Law and Legal Reform. Law and Society Review 7(4):585–610.

Holston, James

    2007 Insurgent Citizenship: Disjunctions of Democracy and Modernity in Brazil. Princeton: Princeton University Press.

Honneth, Axel

    1996 The Struggle for Recognition: The Moral Grammar of Social Conflicts. Cambridge, Mass.: MIT Press.

Hopgood, Stephen
　2013 The Endtimes of Human Rights. Ithaca: Cornell University Press.
Horkheimer, Max, and Theodor W. Adorno
　2002 [1947] Dialectic of Enlightenment: Philosophical Fragments. E. Jephcott,
　　transl. Stanford: Stanford University Press.
Hounet, Yazid Ben, and Mickaële Latin Mallet
　2017 Teaching Anthropology of Law at the École des hautes études en sciences sociales
　　(Paris). In The Trials and Triumphs of Teaching Legal Anthropology. Marie-Claire
　　Foblets, Anthony Bradney, and Gordon Woodman, eds. Farnham, U.K.: Ashgate.
Humphrey, John P.
　1984 Human Rights and the United Nations: A Great Adventure. New York: Trans-
　　national Publishers.
Hylton, Forrest, and Sinclair Thomson
　2007 Revolutionary Horizons: Past and Present in Bolivian Politics. London: Verso.
IMF
　2016 World Economic Outlook (WEO) Update. www.imf.org.
International Council of Museums
　2004 Declaration on the Importance and Value of Universal Museums. ICOM
　　News 57(1):4.
Iriye, Akira, Petre Goedde, and William I. Hitchcock, eds.
　2012 The Human Rights Revolution: An International History. New York: Oxford
　　University Press.
Ivison, Duncan
　2002 Postcolonial Liberalism. Cambridge: Cambridge University Press.
IWGIA
　2015 Indigenous Peoples in China. www.iwgia.org.
Jackson, Jean E.
　1995 Culture, Genuine and Spurious: The Politics of Indianness in the Vaupés,
　　Colombia. American Ethnologist 22(1):3–27.
Jakobson, Roman
　1960 Closing Statement: Linguistics and Poetics. In Style in Language. Thomas
　　Sebeok, ed. Pp. 350–377. Cambridge: MIT Press.
Jefremovas, Villia, and Padmapani L. Perez
　2011 Defining Indigeneity: Representation and the Indigenous Peoples' Rights
　　Act of 1997 in the Philippines. In Identity Politics in the Public Realm: Bring-
　　ing Institutions Back In. Avigail Eisenberg and Will Kymlicka, eds. Pp. 79–103.
　　Vancouver: UBC Press.
Keck, Margaret, and Kathryn Sikkink
　1998 Activists beyond Borders: Advocacy Networks in International Politics. Ithaca:
　　Cornell University Press.
Kelly, Tobias
　2006 Law, Violence and Sovereignty among West Bank Palestinians. Cambridge:
　　Cambridge University Press.

—

2011 This Side of Silence: Human Rights, Torture, and the Recognition of Cruelty. Philadelphia: University of Pennsylvania Press.

Kelly, Tobias, and Marie-Bénédicte Dembour

2007 Introduction: The Social Lives of International Justice. *In* Paths to International Justice: Social and Legal Perspectives. Marie-Bénédicte Dembour and Tobias Kelly, eds. Pp. 1–25. Cambridge: Cambridge University Press.

Kennedy, David

2004 The Dark Sides of Virtue: Reassessing International Humanitarianism. Princeton: Princeton University Press.

Kesselring, Rita

2017 Bodies of Truth: Law, Memory, and Emancipation in Post-Apartheid South Africa. Stanford: Stanford University Press.

Keucheyan, Razmig

2014 Not Even Climate Change Will Kill Off Capitalism. *In* The Guardian. www.theguardian.com.

Kirsch, Stuart

2012 Juridification of Indigenous Politics. *In* Law against the State: Ethnographic Forays into Law's Transformations. Julia Eckert, Brian Donahoe, Christian Strümpell, and Zerrin Özlem Biner, eds. Pp. 23–43. Cambridge: Cambridge University Press.

—

2014 Mining Capitalism: The Relationship between Corporations and Their Critics. Berkeley: University of California Press.

Kleinman, Arthur, Veena Das, and Margaret Lock, eds.

1997 Social Suffering. Berkeley: University of California Press.

Kohn, Eduardo

2013 How Forests Think: Toward an Anthropology beyond the Human. Berkeley: University of California Press.

Korey, William

1998 NGOS and the Universal Declaration of Human Rights: "A Curious Grapevine." New York: St. Martin's Press.

Kymlicka, Will

1995 Multicultural Citizenship: A Liberal Theory of Minority Rights. Oxford: Oxford University Press.

—

1996 The Good, the Bad, and the Intolerable: Minority Group Rights. Dissent 43(3):22–30.

Labov, William

1966 The Social Stratification of English in New York City. Washington D.C.: Center for Applied Linguistics.

Latour, Bruno

1987 Science in Action: How to Follow Scientists and Engineers through Society. Cambridge, Mass.: Harvard University Press.

— 1999 Pandora's Hope: Essays on the Reality of Science Studies. Cambridge, Mass.: Harvard University Press.

— 2004 Scientific Objects and Legal Subjectivity. *In* Law, Anthropology, and the Constitution of the Social: Making Persons and Things. Alain Pottage and Martha Mundy, eds. Pp. 73–114. Cambridge: Cambridge University Press.

Lazarus-Black, Mindie
   2001 Law and the Pragmatics of Inclusion: Governing Domestic Violence in Trinidad and Tobago. American Ethnologist 28(2):388–416.

— 2007 Everyday Harm: Domestic Violence, Court Rites, and Cultures of Reconciliation. Urbana-Champaign: University of Illinois Press.

Lazarus-Black, Mindie, and Susan F. Hirsch, eds.
   1994a Contested States: Law, Hegemony and Resistance. New York: Routledge.

— 1994b Performance and Paradox: Exploring Law's Role in Hegemony and Resistance. *In* Contested States: Law, Hegemony, and Resistance. Mindie Lazarus-Black and Susan Hirsch, eds. Pp. 1–31. New York: Routledge.

Le Roy, Étienne
   2006 Juridicités: approches du droit au Laboratoire d'anthropologie juridique de Paris: témoignages réunis à l'occasion de son quarantième anniversaire. Paris: Karthala.

Leeman, Esther
   2014 Global Discourse, Local Realities: The Paradoxical Outcomes of Indigenous Land Titling Efforts in Cambodia. Paper presented at the Swiss Anthropological Association Annual Meeting. Basel, Switzerland.

Lentz, Carola
   2003 "This Is Ghanaian Territory!" Land Conflicts on a West African Border. American Ethnologist 30(2):273–289.

Lessing, Gotthold
   1957 Lessing's Theological Writings. H. Chadwick, transl. Stanford: Stanford University Press.

Li, Tania
   2007 The Will to Improve: Governmentality, Development, and the Practice of Politics. Durham: Duke University Press.

— 2010 Indigeneity, Capitalism, and the Management of Dispossession. Current Anthropology 51(3):385–414.

— 2014a What Is Land? Assembling a Resource for Global Investment. Transactions of the Institute of British Geographers (12065):1–14.

—

2014b Land's End: Capitalist Relations on an Indigenous Frontier. Durham: Duke University Press.

—

2015 Transnational Farmland Investment: A Risky Business. Journal of Agrarian Change 15(4):560–568.

Lipovec Čebron, Uršula

2012 Exclusion politique et sanitaire. Le corps des "effacés" slovènes. Ethnologie française 42(2):241–249.

Lipset, David

2004 "The Trial": A Parody of the Law amid the Mockery of Men in Post-Colonial Papua New Guinea. Journal of the Royal Anthropological Institute 10(1):63–89.

Llewellyn, Karl N., and E. Adamson Hoebel

1941 The Cheyenne Way. Norman: University of Oklahoma Press.

Lorway, Robert

2008 Defiant Desire in Namibia: Female Sexual-Gender Transgression and the Making of Political Being. American Ethnologist 35(1):20–33.

Low, Setha M., and Sally Engle Merry

2010 Engaged Anthropology: Diversity and Dilemmas: An Introduction to Supplement 2. Current Anthropology 51(S2):S203–S226.

Macfarlane, Alan

2000 The Riddle of the Modern World: Of Liberty, Wealth, and Equality. London: Palgrave.

Mahmood, Saba

2012 Sectarian Conflict and Family Law in Contemporary Egypt. American Ethnologist 39(1):54–62.

Maine, Henry Sumner

1861 Ancient Law: Its Connection with the Early History of Society, and Its Relation to Modern Ideas. London: John Murray.

Mainsant, Gwénaëlle

2013 Contrôle policier et définitions de la prostitution. Ethnologie française 43(3):485–493.

Makaremi, Chowra

2008 Les "zones de non-droit." Un dispositif pathétique de la démocratie. Anthropologie et Sociétés 32(3):81–98.

Makdisi, Ussama

2002 Spectres of Terrorism. Interventions 4(2):265–278.

Malagón Barceló, Javier

1961 The Role of the *Letrado* in the Colonization of America. The Americas 18(1):1–17.

Malinowski, Bronislaw

1922 Argonauts of the Western Pacific: An Account of Native Enterprise and Adventure in the Archipelagoes of Melanesian New Guinea. London: Routledge & Kegan Paul.

—
1926 Crime and Custom in Savage Society. London: Kegan Paul.

—
2002 [1926] Myth in Primitive Psychology. London: Routledge.

Mamdani, Mahmood
1996 Citizen and Subject: Contemporary Africa and the Legacy of Late Colonialism. Princeton: Princeton University Press.

Mattei, Ugo, and Laura Nader
2008 Plunder: When the Rule of Law Is Illegal. Malden, Mass.: Blackwell.

Maurer, Bill
2005 Mutual Life, Limited: Islamic Banking, Alternative Currencies, Lateral Reason. Princeton: Princeton University Press.

McFate, Montgomery
2005 The Military Utility of Understanding Adversary Culture. Joint Force Quarterly 38:42–48.

McGovern, Mike
2010 Proleptic Justice: The Threat of Investigation as a Deterrent to Human Rights Abuses in Côte d'Ivoire. *In* Mirrors of Justice: Law and Power in the Post–Cold War Era. Kamari Maxine Clarke and Mark Goodale, eds. Pp. 67–86. New York: Cambridge University Press.

McLennan, John
1865 Primitive Marriage. An Inquiry into the Origin of the Form of Capture in Marriage Ceremonies. Edinburgh: Adam and Charles Black.

McNeish, John-Andrew
2013 Extraction, Protest and Indigeneity in Bolivia: The TIPNIS Effect. Latin American and Caribbean Ethnic Studies 8(2):221–242.

Medina, Laurie
2014 Law, Jurisprudence, and the Production of Indigenous Land Rights: Maya Indigenous Communities v. Belize. Paper presented at the American Anthropological Association Annual Meeting. Washington, D.C.

—
2015 Governing through the Market: Neoliberal Environmental Government in Belize. American Anthropologist 117(2):272–284.

Melhuus, Marit
2012 Problems of Conception: Issues of Law, Biotechnology, Individuals and Kinship. Oxford: Berghahn Books.

Memo, Sara
2013 The Legal Status of Roma in Europe: Between National Minority and Transnational People. Ph.D. dissertation, Department of International Studies, University of Trento.

Merry, Sally Engle
1990 Getting Justice and Getting Even: Legal Consciousness among Working-Class Americans. Chicago: University of Chicago Press.

—

1992 Anthropology, Law, and Transnational Processes. Annual Review of Anthropology 21:357–377.

—

1994 Courts as Performances: Domestic Violence Hearings in a Hawai'i Family Court. *In* Contested States: Law, Hegemony, Resistance. Mindie Lazarus-Black and Susan Hirsch, eds. Pp. 35–58. New York: Routledge.

—

2006a Human Rights and Gender Violence: Translating International Law into Local Justice. Chicago: University of Chicago Press.

—

2006b Transnational Human Rights and Local Activism: Mapping the Middle. American Anthropologist 108(1):38–51.

—

2009 Gender Violence: A Cultural Perspective. Malden, Mass.: Wiley-Blackwell.

—

2010 Beyond Compliance: Toward an Anthropological Understanding of International Justice. *In* Mirrors of Justice: Law and Power in the Post–Cold War Era. Kamari Maxine Clarke and Mark Goodale, eds. Pp. 28–42. New York: Cambridge University Press.

—

2011 Measuring the World: Indicators, Human Rights, and Global Governance. Current Anthropology 52(S3):S83–S95.

—

2016 The Seductions of Quantification: Measuring Human Rights, Gender Violence, and Sex Trafficking. Chicago: University of Chicago Press.
Merry, Sally Engle, Kevin E. Davis, and Benedict Kingsbury, eds.
2015 The Quiet Power of Indicators: Measuring Governance, Corruption, and Rule of Law. New York: Cambridge University Press.
Merry, Sally Engle, and Rachel E. Stern
2005 The Female Inheritance Movement in Hong Kong: Theorizing the Local/Global Interface. Current Anthropology 46(3):387–409.
Merry, Sally Engle, and Summer Wood
2015 Quantification and the Paradox of Measurement: Translating Children's Rights in Tanzania. Current Anthropology 56(2):205–229.
Mertz, Elizabeth
1994 Legal Language: Pragmatics, Poetics, and Social Power. Annual Review of Anthropology 23:435–455.

—

2007 The Language of Law School: Learning to "Think Like a Lawyer." New York: Oxford University Press.

Meskell, Lynn

2013 UNESCO's World Heritage Convention at 40: Challenging the Economic and Political Order of International Heritage Conservation. Current Anthropology 54(4):483–494.

2014 States of Conservation: Protection, Politics, and Pacting within UNESCO's World Heritage Committee. Anthropological Quarterly 87(1):217–244.

2015 Introduction: Globalizing Heritage. *In* Global Heritage: A Reader. Lynn Meskell, ed. Pp. 1–21. Malden, Mass.: Wiley-Blackwell.

Messer, Ellen

1993 Anthropology and Human Rights. Annual Review of Anthropology 22:221–249.

Messick, Brinkley

1993 The Calligraphic State: Textual Domination and History in a Muslim Society. Berkeley: University of California Press.

Moore, Sally Falk

1969 Law and Anthropology. Biennial Review of Anthropology 6:252–300.

1973 Law and Social Change: The Semi-Autonomous Social Field as an Appropriate Subject of Study. Law and Society Review 7(4):719–746.

1978 Law as Process: An Anthropological Approach. London: Routledge & Kegan Paul.

1986 Social Facts and Fabrications: "Customary" Law on Kilimanjaro, 1880–1980 (Lewis Henry Morgan Lectures). Cambridge: Cambridge University Press.

2001 Certainties Undone: Fifty Turbulent Years of Legal Anthropology, 1949–1999. Journal of the Royal Anthropological Institute 7(1):95–116.

—, ed.

2004 Law and Anthropology: A Reader. Malden, Mass.: Blackwell

Morgan, Lewis Henry

1851 League of the Ho-dé-no-sau-nee or Iroquois. Rochester, N.Y.: Sage and Brother.

1871 Systems of Consanguinity and Affinity of the Human Family. Washington, D.C.: Smithsonian Institution.

1877 Ancient Society: or, Researches in the Line of Human Progress from Savagery through Barbarism to Civilization. Chicago: C. H. Kerr.

Morsink, Johannes

   1999 The Universal Declaration of Human Rights: Origins, Drafting, Intent. Philadelphia: University of Pennsylvania Press.

Moses, Daniel Noah

   2009 The Promise of Progress: The Life and Work of Lewis Henry Morgan. Columbia: University of Missouri Press.

Moyn, Samuel

   2010 The Last Utopia: Human Rights in History. Cambridge, Mass.: Belknap Press
   of Harvard University Press.

Muehlmann, Shaylih

   2008 "Spread Your Ass Cheeks": And Other Things That Should Not Be Said in
   Indigenous Languages. American Ethnologist 35(1):34–48.

—

   2009 How Do Real Indians Fish? Neoliberal Multiculturalism and Contested Indigeneities in the Colorado Delta. American Anthropologist
   111(4):468–479.

Mundy, Martha

   1995 Review of The Calligraphic State: Textual Domination and History in a Muslim
   Society (Brinkley Messick). Islamic Law and Society 2(3):353–357.

Mutua, Makau

   2016 Is the Age of Human Rights Over? In The Routledge Companion to Literature
   and Human Rights. Sophia McClennen and Alexandra Schultheis Moore, eds.
   Pp. 450–458. London: Routledge.

Nader, Laura

   1965 The Anthropological Study of Law. American Anthropologist 67 (Special Issue) (6):3–32.

—

   1969 Law in Culture and Society. Chicago: Aldine Publishing.

—

   1972 Up the Anthropologist—Perspectives Gained from Studying Up. In Reinventing Anthropology. Dell Hymes, ed. Pp. 284–311. New York: Pantheon.

—

   1990 Harmony Ideology: Justice and Control in a Zapotec Mountain Village. Stanford: Stanford University Press.

—

   1996 Law in Culture and Society. Berkeley: University of California Press.

—

   2002 The Life of the Law: Anthropological Projects. Berkeley: University of California Press.

Nader, Laura, and Duane Metzger

   1963 Conflict Resolution in Two Mexican Communities. American Anthropologist
   65(3):584–592.

Nader, Laura, and Harry F. Todd, Jr., eds.
  1978 The Disputing Process: Law in Ten Societies. New York: Columbia University Press.
National Health Service (NHS)
  2015 Women Involved with the Sex Industry (Praed Street project). www.imperial.nhs.uk.
Navarro, Daniel
  2009 El Positivismo en Argentina. Las primeras publicaciones de criminología. Criminología y psiquiatría forense. https://psiquiatriaforense.wordpress.com.
Neier, Aryeh
  1993 Asia's Unacceptable Standard. Foreign Policy 92(Autumn):42–51.
Nesper, Larry
  2007 Negotiating Jurisprudence in Tribal Court and the Emergence of a Tribal State: The Lac du Flambeau Ojibwe. Current Anthropology 48(5):675–699.
Nielsen, Bjarke
  2013 L'Unesco et le culturellement correct. Gradhiva 18:74–97.
Niezen, Ronald
  2003 The Origins of Indigenism: Human Rights and the Politics of Identity. Berkeley: University of California Press.
—
  2010 Public Justice and the Anthropology of Law. Cambridge: Cambridge University Press.
—
  2013a The Law's Legal Anthropology. In Human Rights at the Crossroads. Mark Goodale, ed. Pp. 185–197. New York: Oxford University Press.
—
  2013b Truth and Indignation: Canada's Truth and Reconciliation Commission on Indian Residential Schools. Toronto: University of Toronto Press.
Niezen, Ronald, and Maria Sapignoli, eds.
  2017 Palaces of Hope: The Anthropology of Global Organizations. New York: Cambridge University Press.
O'Donnell, Guillermo
  2005 Afterword. In The Judicialization of Politics in Latin America. Rachel Sieder, Line Schjolden, and Alan Angell, eds. Pp. 293–298. New York: Palgrave.
Ong, Aihwa
  1996 Cultural Citizenship as Subject-Making: Immigrants Negotiate Racial and Cultural Boundaries in the United States. Cultural Anthropology 37(5):737–762.
Ong, Aihwa, and Stephen Collier, eds.
  2005 Global Assemblages: Technology, Politics, and Ethics as Anthropological Problems. Oxford: Blackwell.
Oomen, Barbara
  2005 Chiefs in South Africa: Law, Power & Culture in the Post-Apartheid Era. Oxford: James Currey.

Open Development Cambodia
    2015 Economic Land Concessions (ELCs). www.opendevelopmentcambodia.net.
Open Society Institute
    2002 The Situation of Roma in Spain. www.romadecade.org.
Osanloo, Arzoo
    2006a Islamico-Civil "Rights Talk": Women, Subjectivity, and Law in Iranian Fam-
        ily Court. American Ethnologist 33(2):191–209.
—

    2006b The Measure of Mercy: Islamic Justice, Sovereign Power, and Human Rights
        in Iran. Cultural Anthropology 21(4):570–602.
Osnos, Evan
    2014 Age of Ambition: Chasing Fortune, Faith, and Truth in the New China. New
        York: Farrar, Straus and Giroux.
Oxfam
    2015 Wealth: Having It All and Wanting More. www.oxfam.org.
Pasqualino, Caterina
    1999 Hors la loi: Les Tsiganes d'Europe face aux institutions. Ethnologie française
        29(4):617–626.
Peebles, Gustav
    2012 Whitewashing and Leg-Bailing: On the Spatiality of Debt. Social Anthropol-
        ogy 20(4):429–443.
Philips, Susan U.
    1994 Local Legal Hegemony in the Tongan Magistrate's Court: How Sisters Fare
        Better Than Wives. In Contested States: Law, Hegemony, and Resistance. Mindie
        Lazarus-Black and Susan Hirsch, eds. Pp. 59–88. New York: Routledge.
—

    2000 Constructing a Tongan Nation-State through Language Ideology in the
        Courtroom. In Regimes of Language: Ideologies, Polities, and Identities. Paul
        Kroskrity, ed. Pp. 229–257. Santa Fe, N. Mex.: School of American Research
        Press.
Piketty, Thomas
    2014 Capital in the Twenty-First Century. Cambridge: Belknap Press of Harvard
        University Press.
Pirie, Fernanda
    2013 The Anthropology of Law. Clarendon Law Series. Oxford: Oxford University
        Press.
Pogge, Thomas W.
    1992 Cosmopolitanism and Sovereignty. Ethics 103(1):48–75.
Pospisil, Leopold
    1971 Anthropology of Law: A Comparative Theory. New York: Harper & Row.
Pottage, Alain
    1993 Review of The Mythology of Modern Law (Peter Fitzpatrick). Modern Law
        Review 56(4):615–619.

2004 Introduction: The Fabrication of Persons and Things. *In* Law, Anthropology, and the Constitution of the Social. Alain Pottage and Martha Mundy, eds. Pp. 1–39. Cambridge: Cambridge University Press.

Pottage, Alain, and Martha Mundy, eds.
2004 Law, Anthropology, and the Constitution of the Social: Making Persons and Things. Cambridge: Cambridge University Press.

Povinelli, Elizabeth A.
2002 The Cunning of Recognition: Indigenous Alterities and the Making of Australian Multiculturalism. Durham: Duke University Press.

Powdermaker, Hortense
1959 Review of *Marriage and the Family among the Plateau Tonga of Northern Rhodesia* (Elizabeth Colson). American Anthropologist 61(6):1119–1121.

Power, Michael
1997 The Audit Society: Rituals of Verification. Oxford: Oxford University Press.

Province of British Columbia
2016 The Courts of British Columbia. www.courts.gov.bc.ca.

Pulitano, Elvira
2012 Indigenous Rights in the Age of the UN Declaration. Cambridge: Cambridge University Press.

Rabinow, Paul
1999 French DNA: Trouble in Purgatory. Chicago: University of Chicago Press.

Radcliffe, Sarah A.
2015 Dilemmas of Difference: Indigenous Women and the Limits of Postcolonial Development Policy. Durham: Duke University Press.

Ramos, Alcida Rita
1994 The Hyperreal Indian. Critique of Anthropology 14(2):153–171.

Renteln, Alison Dundes
2004 The Cultural Defense. New York: Oxford University Press.

—
2005 The Use and Abuse of the Cultural Defense. Canadian Journal of Law and Society 20(1):47–67.

Richards, Donald G.
2004 Intellectual Property Rights and Global Capitalism: The Political Economy of the TRIPS Agreement. Armonk, N.Y.: M. E. Sharpe.

Richland, Justin B.
2008 Arguing with Tradition: The Language of Law in Hopi Tribal Court. Chicago: University of Chicago Press.

Riles, Annelise
1998 Infinity within the Brackets. American Ethnologist 25(3):378–398.

—
2000 The Network Inside Out. Ann Arbor: University of Michigan Press.

—
    2011 Collateral Knowledge: Legal Reasoning in the Global Financial Markets. Chi-
        cago: University of Chicago Press.
Risse, Thomas, Stephen C. Ropp, and Kathryn Sikkink, eds.
    1999 The Power of Human Rights: International Norms and Domestic Change.
        Cambridge: Cambridge University Press.
Rivkin-Fish, Michele
    2003 Anthropology, Demography, and the Search for a Critical Analysis of Fertility:
        Insights from Russia. American Anthropologist 105(2):289–301.
Robbins, Joel
    2010 Recognition, Reciprocity, and Justice: Melanesian Reflections on the Rights
        of Relationships. *In* Mirrors of Justice: Law and Power in the Post–Cold War
        World. Kamari Maxine Clarke and Mark Goodale, eds. Pp. 171–190. New York:
        Cambridge University Press.
Roberts, Simon
    1978 Do We Need an Anthropology of Law? Royal Anthropological Institute News
        25 (April):4–7.
—
    1979 Order and Dispute: Introduction to Legal Anthropology. London: Pelican
        Books.
Rodriguez, Julia
    2006 Civilizing Argentina: Science, Medicine, and the Modern State. Chapel Hill:
        University of North Carolina Press.
Roosevelt, Eleanor
    1948 The Promise of Human Rights. Foreign Affairs 26(3):470–477.
Rose, Nikolas
    2006 The Politics of Life Itself: Biomedicine, Power, and Subjectivity in the Twenty-
        First Century. Princeton: Princeton University Press.
Rosen, Lawrence
    1989 The Anthropology of Justice: Law as Culture in Islamic Society. Cambridge:
        Cambridge University Press.
—
    2006 Law as Culture: An Invitation. Princeton: Princeton University Press.
Rosenblatt, Adam
    2015 Digging for the Disappeared: Forensic Science after Atrocity. Stanford: Stan-
        ford University Press.
Roth, Kenneth
    2014 Africa Attacks the International Criminal Court. New York Review of Books
        61(2) (February 6).
Rottenburg, Richard, Sally Engle Merry, Sung-Joon Park, and Johanna Mugler, eds.
    2016 The World of Indicators: The Making of Governmental Knowledge through
        Quantification. Cambridge: Cambridge University Press.

Rouland, Norbert
  1988 Anthropologie Juridique. Paris: Les Presses universitaires de France.
  —
  1991 Aux confins du droit: Anthropologie juridique de la modernité. Paris: Odile Jacob.
Rubin Museum
  2016 David R. Nalin. http://rubinmuseum.org.
Said, Edward
  1978 Orientalism. New York: Pantheon.
Saillant, Francine
  2007 "Vous êtes ici dans une mini–ONU." Les réfugiés publics au Québec. De l'humanitaire au communautaire. Anthropologie et Sociétés 31(2):65–90.
  —
  2009 Droits, citoyenneté et réparations des torts du passé de l'esclavage. Perspectives du Mouvement noir au Brésil. Anthropologie et Sociétés 33(2):141–165.
Salomon, Frank
  1981 Weavers of Otavalo. In Cultural Transformations and Ethnicity in Modern Ecuador. Norman Whitten, ed. Pp. 420–449. Urbana: University of Illinois Press.
Sanford, Victoria
  2003 Buried Secrets: Truth and Human Rights in Guatemala. New York: Palgrave.
Santos, Boaventura de Sousa
  1987 Law: A Map of Misreading. Toward a Postmodern Conception of Law. Journal of Law and Society 14(3):279–302.
  —
  1995 Toward a New Common Sense: Law, Science and Politics in the Paradigmatic Transition. New York: Routledge.
  —
  2014 Epistemologies of the South: Justice against Epistemicide. London: Routledge.
Sapignoli, Maria
  2009 Indigeneity and the Expert: Negotiating Identity in the Case of the Central Kalahari Game Reserve. In Law and Anthropology. Michael Freeman and David Napier, eds. Pp. 247–268. Oxford: Oxford University Press.
  —
  2015 Dispossession in the Age of Humanity: Human Rights: Citizenship, and Indigeneity in the Central Kalahari. Anthropological Forum 25(3): 285–305.
Sarfaty, Galit
  2012 Values in Translation: Human Rights and the Culture of the World Bank. Stanford: Stanford University Press.
Schabas, William A.
  2009 Genocide in International Law: The Crime of Crimes. Cambridge: Cambridge University Press.

Schapera, Isaac

1938 A Handbook of Tswana Law and Custom: Compiled for the Bechuanaland Protectorate Administration. International African Institute. Oxford: Oxford University Press.

—

1950 Review of *Adat Law in Indonesia* (Barend ter Haar, ed.). American Anthropologist 52(1):82–84.

Schulte-Tenckhoff, Isabelle

1997 La question des peuples autochtones. Brussels: Bruylant/Paris: L.G.D.J.

—, ed.

2002 Altérité et droit: contributions à l'étude du rapport entre droit et culture. Brussels: Bruylant.

Scott, James C.

1985 Weapons of the Weak: Everyday Forms of Peasant Resistance. New Haven: Yale University Press.

—

1999 Seeing Like a State: How Certain Schemes to Improve the Human Condition Have Failed. New Haven: Yale University Press.

Selim, Lala Rukh

2011 On the Possibility of Cultural Property: The Musée Guimet Controversy and Case Study of Events in Bangladesh. Journal of the Royal Anthropological Institute 17:S176–S191.

Selmeski, B. R.

2007 Who Are the Security Anthropologists? Anthropology News 48:11–12.

Severi, Carlo, and William F. Hanks, eds.

2015 Translating Worlds: The Epistemological Space of Translation. Chicago: HAU Books.

Sharkey, Heather J.

2003 Living with Colonialism: Nationalism and Culture in the Anglo-Egyptian Sudan. Berkeley: University of California Press.

Shaw, Rosalind

2007 Memory Frictions: Localizing Truth and Reconciliation in Sierra Leone. International Journal of Transitional Justice 1:183–207.

—

2010 The Production of "Forgiveness": God, Justice, and State Failure in Post-War Sierra Leone. *In* Mirrors of Justice: Law and Power in the Post–Cold War Era. Kamari Maxine Clarke and Mark Goodale, eds. Pp. 208–226. New York: Cambridge University Press.

Shell-Duncan, Bettina

2008 From Health to Human Rights: Female Genital Cutting and the Politics of Intervention. American Anthropologist 110(2):225–236.

Shiva, Vandana

1993 Monocultures of the Mind: Perspectives on Biodiversity and Biotechnology. London: Zed Books.

Shore, Cris, and Susan Wright
    2015 Audit Culture Revisited: Rankings, Ratings, and the Reassembling of Society. Current Anthropology 56(3):421–444.
Shotwell, J. T.
    1933 The International Labor Organization as an Alternative to Violent Revolution. Annals of the American Academy of Political and Social Science 166:18–25.
Sieder, Rachel
    2010 Legal Cultures in the (Un)Rule of Law: Indigenous Rights and Juridification in Guatemala. In Cultures of Legality: Judicialization and Political Activism in Latin America. Javier Couso, Alexandra Huneeus, and Rachel Sieder, eds. Pp. 161–181. New York: Cambridge University Press.
Simpson, Gerry
    2007 Law, War and Crime: War Crimes, Trials and the Reinvention of International Law. Cambridge: Polity Press.
Sircar, Oishik, and Dipika Jain, eds.
    2015 New Intimacies, Old Desires: Law, Culture and Queer Politics in Neoliberal Times. New Delhi: Zubaan Books.
Slotte, Pamela, and Miia Halme-Tuomisaari, eds.
    2015 Revisiting the Origins of Human Rights. Cambridge: Cambridge University Press.
Slyomovics, Susan
    2005 The Performance of Human Rights in Morocco. Philadelphia: University of Pennsylvania Press.
Snajdr, Edward
    2007 Ethnicizing the Subject: Domestic Violence and the Politics of Primordialism in Kazakhstan. Journal of the Royal Anthropological Institute 13(3):603–620.
Speed, Shannon
    2008 Rights in Rebellion: Indigenous Struggle and Human Rights in Chiapas. Stanford: Stanford University Press.
Spencer, Herbert
    1898 The Principles of Sociology. New York: D. Appleton and Company.
Standing, Guy
    2008 The ILO: An Agency for Globalization? Development and Change 39(3):355–384.
Starr, June
    1989 The "Invention" of Early Legal Ideas: Sir Henry Maine and the Perpetual Tutelage of Women. In History and Power in the Study of Law: New Directions in Legal Anthropology. June Starr and Jane F. Collier, eds. Pp. 345–368. Ithaca: Cornell University Press.
Starr, June, and Jane Collier, eds.
    1989 History and Power in the Study of Law: New Directions in Legal Anthropology. Ithaca: Cornell University Press.

—

 1989 Introduction: Dialogues in Legal Anthropology. *In* History and Power in the
 Study of Law: New Directions in Legal Anthropology. June Starr and Jane F.
 Collier, eds. Pp. 1–28. Ithaca: Cornell University Press.

Starr, June, and Mark Goodale, eds.
 2002 Practicing Ethnography in Law: New Dialogues, Enduring Methods. New
 York: St. Martin's Press.

Steiner, Henry J., and Philip Alston, eds.
 2000 International Human Rights in Context: Law, Politics, Morals. 2nd ed. Oxford: Oxford University Press.

Stocking, George W.
 1987 Victorian Anthropology. New York: Free Press.

Strathern, Marilyn
 2000 New Accountabilities: Anthropological Studies in Audit, Ethics and the Academy. *In* Audit Cultures: Anthropological Studies in Accountability, Ethics and
 the Academy. Marilyn Strathern, ed. Pp. 1–18. London: Routledge.

Sylvain, Renée
 2002 "Land, Water, and Truth": San Identity and Global Indigenism. American
 Anthropologist 104(4):1074–1085.

—

 2005 Disorderly Development: Globalization and the Idea of "Culture" in the Kalahari. American Ethnologist 32(3):354–370.

Tate, Winifred
 2007 Counting the Dead: The Culture and Politics of Human Rights Activism in
 Colombia. Berkeley: University of California Press.

Taylor, Charles
 1992 Multiculturalism and "The Politics of Recognition." Princeton: Princeton
 University Press.

Taylor, Thomas
 1822 Political Fragments of Archytas, Charondas, Zaleucus, and Other Ancient
 Pythagoreans, Preserved by Stobaeus, and Also, Ethical Fragments of Hierocles,
 the Celebrated Commentator on the Golden Pythagorean Verses, Preserved by
 the Same Author. Chiswick: Whittingham.

Teubner, Gunther
 1997 The King's Many Bodies: The Self-Deconstruction of Law's Hierarchy. Law and
 Society Review 31 (4):763–788.

Theidon, Kimberly
 2010 Histories of Innocence: Postwar Stories in Peru. *In* Localizing Transitional Justice: Interventions and Priorities after Mass Violence. Rosalind Shaw and Lars
 Waldorf, eds. Pp. 92–110. Stanford: Stanford University Press.

—

 2012 Intimate Enemies: Violence and Reconciliation in Peru. Philadelphia: University of Pennsylvania Press.

Thompson, E. P.
    1977 Whigs and Hunters: The Origin of the Black Act. London: Penguin Books.
Thoreson, Ryan R.
    2014 Transnational LGBT Activism. Working for Sexual Rights Worldwide. Minneapolis: University of Minnesota Press.
Times Colonist
    2008 Obituary: Allan McEachern, 1926–2008––"He Was a Judge's Judge and a Lawyer's Lawyer." www.canada.com.
Timmer, Jaap
    2010 Being Seen Like the State: Emulations of Legal Culture in Customary Labor and Land Tenure Arrangements in East Kalimantan, Indonesia. American Ethnologist 37(4):703–712.
Tobin, Brendan
    2014 Indigenous Peoples, Customary Law and Human Rights—Why Living Law Matters. Abingdon: Routledge.
Todd, Loretta
    1990 Notes on Appropriation. Parallelogramme 16(1):24–33.
Travers, Max
    2001 Sociology of Law in Britain. American Sociologist 32(2):26–40.
Trouwborst, Albert
    2002 Anthropology, the Study of Islam, and Adat Law in The Netherlands and the Netherlands East Indies, 1920–1950. In Tales from Academia: History of Anthropology in the Netherlands, Part 2. Han Vermeulen and Jean Kommers, eds. Pp. 673–694. Saarbrücken: Verlag für Entwicklungspolitik.
Tsing, Anna
    2005 Friction: An Ethnography of Global Connection. Princeton: Princeton University Press.
Turner, Terence
    1997 Human Rights, Human Difference: Anthropology's Contribution to an Emancipatory Cultural Politics. Journal of Anthropological Research 53(3):273–291.
Turner, Victor
    1967 The Forest of Symbols: Aspects of Ndembu Ritual. Ithaca: Cornell University Press.
Tylor, E. B.
    1871 Primitive Culture. New York: J. P. Putnam's Sons.
UNESCO
    1947 Proceedings of the First General Conference, held at UNESCO House, Paris, from 20 November to 10 December 1946. http://unesdoc.unesco.org.
—
    1949 Human Rights: Comments and Interpretations. New York: Columbia University Press.
—
    2002 [2001] Universal Declaration on Cultural Diversity. http://unesdoc.unesco.org.

—

2015 Operational Guidelines for the Implementation of the World Heritage Convention. Paris: UNESCO World Heritage Centre.

United Nations, Human Rights Council
2001 Resolution 2001/57.

UN Special Rapporteur on the Rights of Indigenous Peoples
2015 Biography of Victoria Tauli-Corpuz. http://unsr.vtaulicorpuz.org.

Urry, James
1993 Before Social Anthropology: Essays on the History of British Anthropology. Reading: Harwood Academic Publishers.

Urton, Gary
1981 At the Crossroads of the Earth and the Sky: An Andean Cosmology. Austin: University of Texas Press.

Volkan, Vamik
1997 Bloodlines: From Ethnic Pride to Ethnic Terrorism. Boulder, Colo.: Westview Press.

von Benda-Beckmann, Franz, and Keebet von Benda-Beckmann
2002 Anthropology of Law and the Study of Folk Law in The Netherlands after 1950. *In* Tales from Academia: History of Anthropology in the Netherlands, Part 2. Han Vermeulen and Jean Kommers, eds. Pp. 695–731. Saarbrücken: Verlag für Entwicklungspolitik.

—, eds.
2009 The Power of Law in a Transnational World. Anthropological Enquiries. New York: Berghahn Books

—

2011 Myths and Stereotypes about Adat Law: A Reassessment of Van Vollenhoven in the Light of Current Struggles over Adat Law in Indonesia. Bijdragen tot de Taal-, Land- en Volkenkunde (Journal of the Humanities and Social Sciences of Southeast Asia) 167(2/3):167–195.

—

2013 Political and Legal Transformations of an Indonesian Polity. The Nagari from Colonisation to Decentralisation. Cambridge: Cambridge University Press.

von Benda-Beckmann, Franz, Keebet von Benda-Beckmann, and Anne Griffiths, eds.
2005 Mobile People, Mobile Law: Expanding Legal Relations in a Contracting World. Aldershot: Ashgate.

Waldorf, Lars
2010 "Like Jews Waiting for Jesus." *In* Localizing Transitional Justice: Interventions and Priorities after Mass Violence. Rosalind Shaw and Lars Waldorf, eds. Pp. 183–202. Stanford: Stanford University Press.

Walker, Jeffrey
2000 Rhetoric and Poetics in Antiquity. Oxford: Oxford University Press.

Warren, Kay

    2007 The 2000 UN Human Trafficking Protocol: Rights, Enforcement, Vulnerabilities. *In* The Practice of Human Rights: Tracking Law between the Global and the Local. Mark Goodale and Sally Engle Merry, eds. Pp. 242–269. Cambridge: Cambridge University Press.

Washington Post

    2005 President Bush Delivers Remarks on the War on Terrorism. *In* Washington Post. www.washingtonpost.com.

Weiner, Mark S.

    2006 Americans without Law: The Racial Boundaries of Citizenship. New York: NYU Press.

Wemyss, Martyn

    2016 Human Rights and Legal Subjectivity in Highland Bolivia. Ph.D. dissertation, Department of Anthropology, London School of Economics.

Wenk, Irina

    2014 Indigenous Land Titling and Post-Titling Challenges in Central Mindanao, the Philippines. Paper presented at the Swiss Anthropological Association Annual Meeting. Basel, Switzerland.

White, James Boyd

    1985 Heracles' Bow: Essays on the Rhetoric and Poetics of the Law. Madison: University of Wisconsin Press.

Williams, Raymond

    1976 Keywords: A Vocabulary of Culture and Society. London: Croom Helm.

——

    1977 Marxism and Literature. Oxford: Oxford University Press.

Willock, I. D.

    1974 Getting on with Sociologists. British Journal of Law and Society 1(1):3–12.

Wilson, Richard A., ed.

    1997 Human Rights, Culture and Context: Anthropological Perspectives. London: Pluto Press.

——

    2005 Human Rights in the "War on Terror." New York: Cambridge University Press.

Wilson, Richard A.

    2001 The Politics of Truth and Reconciliation in South Africa. Cambridge: Cambridge University Press.

——

    2011 Writing History in International Criminal Trials. New York: Cambridge University Press.

Wilson, Richard Ashby, and Jon P. Mitchell, eds.

    2003 Human Rights in Global Perspective: Anthropological Studies of Rights, Claims, and Entitlements. London: Routledge.

Wolf, Eric R.

    1982 Europe and the People without History. Berkeley: University of California Press.

Woolford, Andrew
    2011 Genocide, Affirmative Repair, and the British Columbia Treaty Process. *In* Transitional Justice: Global Mechanisms and Local Realities after Genocide and Mass Violence. Alexander Hinton, ed. Pp. 137–156. New Brunswick: Rutgers University Press.
Wyzanski, Charles E.
    1946 Nuremberg: A Fair Trial? A Dangerous Precedent. Atlantic Monthly (April).
Yngvesson, Barbara
    1993 Virtuous Citizens, Disruptive Subjects: Order and Complaint in a New England Court. New York: Routledge.

—

    2010 Belonging in an Adopted World: Race, Identity, and Transnational Adoption. Chicago Series in Law and Society. Chicago: University of Chicago Press.
Zenker, Olaf
    2014 New Law against an Old State: Land Restitution as a Transition to Justice in Post-Apartheid South Africa? Development and Change 45(3):502–523.

—

    2016 Anthropology on Trial: Exploring the Laws of Anthropological Expertise. International Journal of Law in Context 12(3):293–311.

# INDEX

AAA. *See* American Anthropological Association

Aboriginal Title: in Australia, 153–54, 234n11; in Canada, 58–60, 122

Acholi spiritual tradition, 94

*adaawk* (Gitksan oral histories), 59–60, 228n11

*adat* law, 15, 56–57, 227nn7–8

Adcock, Fleur, 112–13

ad hoc tribunals, 68–69, 80

ADR. *See* Alternative Dispute Resolution

adultery, 75–76

agency, law as, 22, 118

age of capital, 27

Agreement on Trade-Related Aspects of Intellectual Property Rights (TRIPS), 143

Alaska Native Claims Settlement Act of 1971 (ANCSA), 159–60

Ali, Kamran Asdar, 109

Allen, Lori, 109

alternative currency, 124–25

Alternative Dispute Resolution (ADR), 6

American Anthropological Association (AAA), 229n8, 230n4; diversity and, 217–18; human rights and, 99–102, 145–46, 231n6

Anaya, S. James, 113, 145

*Ancient Law* (Maine), 9–10, 163, 165, 224n13

*Ancient Society* (Morgan), 11

ANCSA. *See* Alaska Native Claims Settlement Act of 1971

Andean cosmology, 161–62

Anglo-American perspective, on anthropology of law, 7–8, 15

Anglo-Egyptian Sudan "condominium," 227n3

anthropology: of human rights, 23, 96–97, 230n1; of injustice, 86–87; security, 87, 229n8; of world-making, 114–16

*The Anthropology of Justice* (Rosen), 77

anthropology of law: Anglo-American perspective on, 7–8, 15; colonialism and, 8, 14–15, 19, 47–48, 54–57; contributions of, 203–6; death and resurrection of, 17–21; emergent areas in, 25–26, 206–7; golden age of, 12–17; heritage and, 57–58, 63–68; history and, 1, 5–21, 33, 53–54, 62–63, 70–72, 216–17, 224n8; introduction to, 1–6; key themes of, 186; Malinowski and, 12–14, 16, 21, 53, 75–77, 164, 223n3, 226n1; Moore and, 7, 14–15, 33–34, 165, 224n11; proto-anthropologists of, 9–12, 26–27, 53, 163; reenvisioning of, 29; rubrics of, 5–6; three domains of, 21–26; in world of exclusion, 199–201. *See also* ethnonationalism; human rights; indigeneity, law and; justice; moral economy of gender; regulation

antitrafficking movement, 179–80

Arendt, Hannah, 79

Argentinian proto-anthropologists, 11–12

*Argonauts of the Western Pacific* (Malinowski), 12–13, 226n1

armchair anthropologists, 9–12, 223n3

aspiration, politics of, 102–3, 108–10, 147

asylum seekers, 134–35
Atlani-Duault, Laëtitia, 176–78
audit culture, 207–8
Australia, 153–54, 234n11

Bachofen, Johann Jakob, 9–10, 163
Baer, Monika, 175–76
Bakhtin, Mikhail, 51
Bali, 85–86
Banaker, Reza, 7
Bangladesh, 65–68
Barthes, Roland, 70
Beckman, Ludvig, 28
Belize, 113
Berkeley Village Law Project, 17
Berlin, Isaiah, 186, 220
Biolsi, Thomas, 132
bioprospecting, 120–21
Biotechnology Act, Norwegian, 122–24
Black Act of 1723, 117, 120, 137–38
Blackburn, Carole, 148–49
Bloch, Ernst, 226n2
body, contested, 179–82
Bohannan, Paul, 15–17, 27, 33–34, 223n7
Bolivia: Cochabamba, 87–88, 197–98,
    238n17; human rights in, 2–3, 87, 89;
    justice in, 87, 89, 94, 197–99, 219;
    refoundation of, 214–15
Borneman, John, 178
Borras, Saturnino, 157
Botswana, 55–56
Bowen, John, 128–30, 232n2
Bremmer, Ian, 237n6
Breton-Le Goff, Gaëlle, 169–70, 235n9
British Columbia, Supreme Court of, 59–
    60, 228n10
Brody, Hugh, 59, 226n13
Brunnegger, Sandra, 108
Buckler, Sal, 81
Bugis migrants, 196–97
bulubulu, in Fiji, 174
Bunong people, 157–59
Burger, Warren, 6

Burnet, Jennie E., 84
Bush, George W., 184–85, 236n1

calligraphic state, 49
Cambodia, 157–59
Canada: Aboriginal Title in, 58–60, 122;
    Indian residential schools in, 91–92;
    Nisga'a First Nation in, 148–49, 233n8;
    Supreme Court of British Columbia
    in, 59–60, 228n10; UN-DRIP and, 144,
    233n7
capitalism: accumulation in, 28, 118,
    156–61, 212–13; capitalization of life
    in, 121; challenges to, 239n5; climate
    change and, 236n5; donor, 81; equality
    and, 212–15, 225n15; ILO and, 142–45;
    indigenous rights and, 156–61; regula-
    tion and, 118
case study method, 15
CEDAW. See Convention on the Elimina-
    tion of All Forms of Discrimination
    Against Women
Central Asia, 171–73, 176–78
CfHR. See Committee for Human Rights
Channel Tunnel, 60–61
Chave-Dartoen, Sophie, 149–50, 233n9
The Cheyenne Way (Llewellyn and Hoe-
    bel), 2, 15
China, 106, 145, 199
Christen, Kimberly, 153–54
citizen security, 23, 78, 86–89
citizenship: indigeneity and, 148–50; new
    territories of, 28, 86; re-culturalized,
    120; in Slovenia, 191
Clarke, Kamari, 81–82
Clarke, Morgan, 194–95
class relations, 138, 234n13
Clifford, James, 225n8
climate change, 187, 201, 236n5
Clinton, Hillary, 235n8
Cochabamba, Bolivia, 87–88, 197–98,
    238n17
coevalness, denial of, 226n2

Cold War: end of, 2–4, 19, 27, 111, 184, 204–5, 224n9, 236n4; human rights and, 111, 115; international tribunals and, 79–80

collective identity, regulation of, 119–20, 133–36

collective titling, 157–59

Collier, Jane, 20, 35, 166, 225n5

Colloredo-Mansfeld, Rudi, 160–61

Colombia, 108, 146, 151

colonialism: anthropology of law and, 8, 14–15, 19, 47–48, 54–57; British, 55, 227nn3–4; context of, 54–57; Dutch, 14–15, 56–57; indirect rule in, 55–56; international tribunals and, 79; legacies of, 58–62; pluralism and, 57; race and, 229n18; subject regulation and, 131–32

Colson, Elizabeth, 164, 234n3

Comaroff, Jean, 58

Comaroff, John, 18–20, 58, 227n5

Commission of Inquiry for the Assessment of History and Consequences of the SED Dictatorship, 229n6

Commission on Human Rights, UN, 98, 145, 230n5

Committee for Human Rights (CfHR), 101, 145–46, 231n6

comparative legal history, 5, 9

concentric circles, law of, 215–19

conflict resolution. *See* dispute settlement

Conley, John, 39–40

Connor, Walker, 237n6

constitutional nationalism, 185, 189, 200

constitution making, 4–5, 24

contested body, 179–82

contracts, 10, 27

Convention Concerning the Protection of the World Cultural and Natural Heritage, 192

Convention on the Elimination of All Forms of Discrimination Against Women (CEDAW): gender and,

25, 103, 165–69, 172–74, 182, 235n10, 235n13; implementation of, 103

Coombe, Rosemary, 122

Corpuz, Victoria Tauli, 145

cosmopolitanism, 25, 28, 184–87, 239n6; disenchantment with, 207, 215–21; justice and, 94

Côte d'Ivoire, 81

court transcripts, 39–40

Cowan, Jane, 102–3

Crane, David, 91

*Crime and Custom in Savage Society* (Malinowski), 13–14, 75–77, 164

criminal anthropology, 12

Croatia, 189–90

Cucapá, 49–51, 152–53, 226n12

Culhane, Dara, 58–60, 70

cultural authenticity, 150–51, 154

cultural politics, 147–50

cultural relativism, 226n2

Cultural Survival, Inc., 100–101

culture: audit, 207–8; collective belonging and, 136; commodification of, 122; definitions of, 192–93, 238n13; in international law, 187, 192–96, 237n9; justice and, 93; right to, 97–103; in UDHR, 192, 237n10; work, 153–54

*Culture and Rights* (Cowan, Dembour, and Wilson), 102–3

Curtis, Jennifer, 107

Darapap, 48, 226n11

Darian-Smith, Eve, 60–61, 128

Day, Sophie, 179–80

debt, regulation of, 125–26

Declaration of the Rights of Indigenous Peoples (UN-DRIP), 144–45, 233n7

de facto pluralism, 218–19

*Delgamuukw v. The Queen*, 59–60, 228n12

Dembour, Marie-Bénédicte, 102–3

Democratic Republic of Congo (DRC), 169–70, 235n9

democratization, 82

development, human rights and, 2, 109–10, 114

discourse: ethnography of, 39–43; justice as, 78, 87; language, law and, 35–43, 47, 51–52

"Discourse in the Novel" (Bakhtin), 51

dispute settlement: ethnonationalism and, 25, 186, 193; *gacaca* for, 78, 83–84; language and, 40–41, 48; study of, 15–18, 25

*The Disputing Process* (Nader and Todd), 17

Dombrowski, Kirk, 159–60

donor capitalism, 81

DRC. *See* Democratic Republic of Congo

Dutch colonialism, 14–15, 56–57

Dwyer, Leslie, 85–86, 229n7

East Timor Tribunal, 80

Eckert, Julie, 136

economic inequality, 28, 143, 156, 187, 201, 205; capitalism and, 225n15; indigeneity and, 132, 239n4; international law and, 206

Ecuador, 160–61, 234n14, 239n4

education, legal, 46–47

Egypt, 183, 227n3

*Eichmann in Jerusalem* (Arendt), 79

Elkin, A. P., 99

Eltringham, Nigel, 193–94

emergent subjectivities, 119

Engels, Friedrich, 223n1

Englund, Harri, 109–10, 205

equality: capitalism and, 212–15, 225n15; gender, 183; human rights and, 2–3; law and, 132, 206, 211–15, 239n4; marriage, 131. *See also* economic inequality

Erman, Eva, 28

ethnicity, 141, 171–72

ethnographic political economy, of international law, 110–14

ethnography: denial of coevalness and, 226n2; of discourse, 39–43; ethnon-ationalism and, 185–86, 189–91, 193–97, 200; history and, 12–14, 26, 53, 58–62, 64, 69–70, 223n3; human rights and, 97, 102–14, 231nn7–8; indigeneity, law and, 147–50, 152–53, 156–61; justice and, 75–78, 81–85, 87–92, 94; of legal discourse, 39–43; moral economy of gender and, 166–75, 178–83; regulation and, 120–31, 134–35, 138

"Ethno-Historical Models and the Evolution of Law" conference, 20

ethnonationalism: conflict resolution and, 25, 186, 193; constitutional nationalism, 185, 189; debates over, 237n6; ethnography and, 185–86, 189–91, 193–97, 200; exclusion and, 188–91, 199–201; imagined community and, 188–91; key themes of, 186; state and, 196–99; U.S. invasion of Iraq and, 184–85; in Yugoslavia, 185, 189–91

Eurocentric perspective, 8

European Court of Human Rights, 81

Evans-Pritchard, E. E., 55, 227n3

exclusion: ethnonationalism and, 188–91, 199–201; imagined community and, 188–91; indigenous rights and, 153; law shaping, 117–22, 133–34, 138; race and, 188, 190; regulation and, 117–22, 133–34, 138; world of, anthropology of law in, 199–201

female genital cutting (FGC), 181–82, 236nn17–18

Ferrándiz, Francisco, 105

fertility, 180–81

FGC. *See* female genital cutting

Fiji, 173–74

finance, regulation of, 119, 124–27

Finnström, Sverker, 94

Fish, Stanley, 72

Fitzpatrick, Peter, 71, 229n18

Flower, John, 106

Fogg, Shannon, 238n14

forensic scientists, 104–5

Foucault, Michel, 35–36, 225n5

France: in Guimet Affair, 65–68; indirect rule by, 55; *laïcité* in, 128–30, 232n2; prostitution in, 135, 232n4; Wallisian paradox and, 149–50, 233n9; *zones d'attente* in, 134–35

France, Anatole, 211

Franco, Jennifer, 157

Fraser, Nancy, 166–67

*gacaca* (local dispute resolution mechanism), 78, 83–84

Galtung, Johan, 70, 82

Gellner, Ernest, 237n6

gender: CEDAW and, 25, 103, 165–69, 172–74, 182, 235n10, 235n13; concept of, 234n4; equality, 183; identity, 166–68, 175, 182–83; legalization of, 167–68; violence, 104, 166–74, 235nn7–9; women's rights and, 103, 106, 169, 181–82. *See also* moral economy of gender

Generation of '80, 11–12

genocide: international law on, 69, 80, 229n3; justice and, 77, 80; in Rwanda, 25, 83–84, 229n5

Germany, 85, 178, 229n6

Giordano, Cristiana, 131

Gitksan oral histories (*adaawk*), 59–60, 228n11

global heritage, 63–68

Gluckman, Max, 27, 223n4, 223n7; in Gluckman-Bohannan debate, 15–17, 33–34; *The Judicial Process among the Barotse of Northern Rhodesia*, 15

Goldstein, Daniel M., 87–88, 197–99

Gossiaux, Jean-François, 190–91

Graeber, David, 124, 232n1, 239n5

grassroots justice, 82–86

Great Britain: Black Act of 1723 in, 117, 120, 137–38; Channel Tunnel in,

60–61; colonialism of, 55, 227nn3–4; perspective on anthropology of law in, 7–8, 15; Praed Street Project in, 179–80

Greenhouse, Carol, 34, 135–36, 225n3

Guatemala, 112, 211–12

Guimet Affair, 65–68

Gypsy (*Tsigane*) society, 195–96, 238nn14–15

*A Handbook of Tswana Law and Custom* (Schapera), 14, 55–56, 227nn5–6

Harris, Olivia, 234n14

Harvey, David, 212–13

Havet, Jacques, 98, 230n5

Haviland, John B., 43–44, 226n9

Hayden, Cori, 120–21

Hayden, Robert, 185, 189–90, 200

*Heracles' Bow* (White), 33, 47

heritage, 57–58, 63–68, 228nn13–14, 228n16

Herskovits, Melville, 99–100, 115, 230n5

heteroglossia, of law, 51–52

Hierocles, 215–17

Hirschl, Ran, 4, 20

historiography, 97, 230n2

history: anthropology of law and, 1, 5–21, 33, 53–54, 62–63, 70–72, 216–17, 224n8; comparative legal, 5, 9; ethnography and, 12–14, 26, 53, 58–62, 64, 69–70, 223n3; law writing, 68–70; mythological framing of, 70–72; oral, 59–60, 228n11; problems of, 53–54, 56

*History and Power in the Study of Law* (Starr and Collier), 20, 35, 225n5

Hobsbawn, Eric, 27

Hodgson, Dorothy, 147–48

Hoebel, E. Adamson, 2, 15

Hölderlin, Friedrich, 47

Hopi Tribal Court, 44–46

HOUR alternative currency, 124–25

Hugo, Victor, 116

human rights, 224n10, 239n6; AAA and, 99–102, 145–46, 231n6; anthropology of, 23, 96–97, 230n1; in Bolivia, 2–3, 87, 89; Cold War and, 111, 115; Commission on, 98, 145, 230n5; contemporary world-making and, 114–16; cosmopolitanism and, 28; denotative power of, 93; development and, 2, 109–10, 114; equality and, 2–3; ethnography and, 97, 102–14, 231nn7–8; high point of, 231n11; indigenous rights and, 111–14, 133–34, 142–49, 151–62, 211–12, 233n4; Inter-American Commission for, 113; in Iraq, 185; justice and, 87, 89, 92–93; language rights, 43–44; limits of, 108–10, 116; moral creativity in practice of, 105–7; multiplicity of, 96–97, 105–6; networks of, 103–5; politics of aspiration and, 102–3, 108–10, 147; postwar, 220; promise of, 238n1; regulation and, 123, 127, 133–34; right to culture, 97–103; UDHR and, 90, 96, 98–100, 192, 230n3, 230n10, 237n10, 237n12, 238n1; vernacularization, 3, 104, 110; women's rights as, 103, 106, 169, 181–82

*Human Rights, Culture and Context* (Wilson), 102–3

*Human Rights and Gender Violence* (Merry), 104

*Human Rights in Global Perspective* (Wilson and Mitchell), 102–3

human trafficking, 131, 179–80

Huxley, Julian, 98, 230n5

hyperreal Indian, 151–52, 233n10

ICC. *See* International Criminal Court

ICTR. *See* International Criminal Tribunal for Rwanda

ICTY. *See* International Criminal Tribunal for the former Yugoslavia

identity: collective, 119–20, 133–36; gender, 166–68, 175, 182–83; indigeneity and, 141–42, 146–47, 149–56, 160, 234n12,

234n14; justice and, 92; law and, 24–26, 28, 92, 150–56, 203, 206, 215–16, 219; subject regulation and, 128–31

ideologies, language, 43–47

ILO. *See* International Labor Organization

imagined community, exclusion and, 188–91

incest prosecutions, German, 178

inclusion, law shaping, 117–22, 131, 133–34, 138

Indian residential schools, in Canada, 91–92

indicators, governance by, 208–10

indigeneity, law and: capitalist accumulation and, 156–61; citizenship and, 148–50; crossroads of, 161–62; cultural politics and, 147–50; ethnography and, 147–50, 152–53, 156–61; hyperreal Indian and, 151–52, 233n10; identity and, 141–42, 146–47, 149–56, 160, 234n12, 234n14; ILO and, 142–45, 232n2, 233n5; inequality and, 132, 239n4; introduction to, 24–25, 141–46; reassessment of, 162; rights in, 111–14, 133–34, 142–49, 151–62, 211–12, 233n4; strategic maneuvering in, 153–54

indigenism, 28, 160, 224n14

Indigenous and Tribal Peoples Convention, 101

Indigenous Peoples' Rights Act (IPRA), 114, 158

indirect rule, 55–56

Indonesia, 85–86, 196–97, 229n7

inequality. *See* economic inequality

injustice, anthropology of, 86–87

*In lieblicher Bläue* (Hölderlin), 47

intellectual property, 121–22

Inter-American Commission for Human Rights, 113

interlegality, 88

International Criminal Court (ICC): justice and, 68–69, 80–81, 229n4; macropolitical pressure shaping, 228n17

International Criminal Tribunal for Rwanda (ICTR), 68–69, 80, 193–94
International Criminal Tribunal for the former Yugoslavia (ICTY), 68–69, 80
International Labor Organization (ILO), 101, 112, 114; capitalism and, 142–45; indigeneity and, 142–45, 232n2, 233n5
international law: collective identity regulation and, 133; culture in, 187, 192–96, 237n9; development of, 77–79; ethnographic political economy of, 110–14; on genocide, 69, 80, 229n3; indicators for, 209; inequality and, 206; influence of, 4; justice and, 77–78; moral creativity in human rights and, 107; new forms of, 22, 104; prosecutions in, 81
international tribunals: ad hoc, 68–69, 80; Cold War and, 79–80; history and, 68–70. See also specific tribunals
"invisible visible," 167, 175–78
IPRA. See Indigenous Peoples' Rights Act
Iran, 106
Iraq, U.S. invasion of, 184–85
Islam: in France, 128–30; law in, 49, 89, 106, 194–95
Italy, 11–12, 131
Ivison, Duncan, 133

Jackson, Jean, 146, 151–52, 233n10
Jackson, Robert H., 89–90
The Judicial Process among the Barotse of Northern Rhodesia (Gluckman), 15
juristocracy, 4, 20–21, 184, 200, 205
justice: banality of, 79–82; in Bolivia, 87, 89, 94, 197–99, 219; cosmopolitanism and, 94; culture and, 93; definition of, 23, 230n9; as discourse, 78, 87; ethnography and, 75–78, 81–85, 87–92, 94; as framing device, 79; genocide and, 77, 80; grassroots, 82–86; human rights and, 87, 89, 92–93; ICC and, 68–69, 80–81, 229n4; identity and, 92;

international criminal law and, 77–78; law's mythologies and, 72; limitations of, 80, 82, 228n17; meanings of, 92–95; memory and, 91; multiplicity of, 89; outlawing in, 88–89; as politics, 78, 89–92, 95; as power, 95; religion and, 93–94; representation and, 78, 89–92; retributive, 82; ritual suicide for, 75–77; security and, 78, 86–89; TRCs and, 78; vigilante, 199
Justice and Judgment among the Tiv (Bohannan), 15–16

Kant, Immanuel, 94
Karachi, 109
Kazakhstan, 171–73, 235nn10–11
Kennedy, David, 80, 182
Kent, 60–61
Kesselring, Rita, 221
Khmer Rouge Tribunal, 80
knowledge, law and, 35, 206–11
Kohn, Eduardo, 221
kungax (Wet'suwet'en song about trails), 59–60, 228n11
Kyetuu, 61–62
Kymlicka, Will, 133–34

laïcité (philosophy about religion's place in politics and society), 128–30, 232n2
Lakota tribe, 132
language: dispute settlement and, 40–41, 48; education in, 46–47; Gluckman-Bohannan debate and, 15–17, 33–34; hegemony and, 36, 38, 52; heteroglossia of law and, 51–52; ideologies, 43–47; law, discourse and, 35–43, 47, 51–52; poetics of, 22, 39, 47–51; power through, 34, 36–39, 41–47; rights, 43–44; social construction through, 37; speech-acts, 34–35, 38; translation of, 237n9; universalized, 34
laterality, 124, 126
Latour, Bruno, 115

law: *adat*, 15, 56–57, 227nn7–8; as agency, 22, 118; colonial legacies and, 58; of concentric circles, 215–19; conservatism of, 71–72; education in, 46–47; equality and, 132, 206, 211–15, 239n4; exclusion shaped through, 117–22, 133–34, 138; global hegemony of, 4, 20–21; heteroglossia of, 51–52; history imagined through, 68–70; identity and, 24–26, 28, 92, 150–56, 203, 206, 215–16, 219; inclusion shaped through, 117–22, 131, 133–34, 138; Islamic, 49, 89, 106, 194–95; knowledge and, 35, 206–11; language, discourse and, 35–43, 47, 51–52; mythologies of, 70–72, 229n18; poetics of, 22, 39, 47–51; in post-utopian world, 206–7, 220; power through, 20, 29, 34–39, 41–47; transnational, 4, 22, 104, 209; universal norms of, 184–85, 192, 194. *See also* anthropology of law; indigeneity, law and; international law; justice; moral economy of gender; regulation
Law and Society Association, 7
lawfare, 58, 227n9
*Law in Culture and Society* (Nader), 26–27
Lazarus-Black, Mindie, 35, 38, 166, 170–71
Lebanon, 194–95
Leeman, Esther, 157–59
"Legal Anthropology: An Historical and Theoretical Analysis" (Goodale), 1–3
Lentz, Carola, 61–62
lesbian, gay, bisexual, or transgender. *See* LGBT
Lessing, Gotthold, 210, 238n2
Lévi-Strauss, Claude, 54
LGBT (lesbian, gay, bisexual, or transgender): moral economy of gender and, 175–78, 182–83; movement, 25, 130–31, 232n3
liberalist logics, of justice, 81
life, capitalization of, 121

Lipovec Čebron, Uršula, 187, 191
Lipset, David, 47–48, 226n11
Llewellyn, Karl, 2, 15
local dispute resolution mechanism (*gacaca*), 78, 83–84
Lombroso, Cesare, 11–12
Lorway, Robert, 182–83
lynching, 87–88

Macedonia, 190
Macfarlane, Alan, 9
Mahmood, Saba, 183
Maine, Henry, 27; *Ancient Law*, 9–10, 163, 165, 224n13; cosmopolitanism and, 219–20
Mainsant, Gwénaëlle, 135, 232n4
Makaremi, Chowra, 134–35
Makú people, 151
Malagón Barceló, Javier, 134
Malawi, 109–10
Malinowski, Bronislaw: anthropology of law and, 12–14, 16, 21, 53, 75–77, 164, 223n3, 226n1; *Argonauts of the Western Pacific*, 12–13, 226n1; *Crime and Custom in Savage Society*, 13–14, 75–77, 164
Mamdani, Mahmood, 55, 227n4
Marbury-Lewis, David, 100–101
Marbury-Lewis, Pia, 100–101
marriage, 10–11, 131, 163–64
*Marriage and the Family among the Plateau Tonga of Northern Rhodesia* (Colson), 164
Marx, Karl, 223n1, 224n13
*Mashabane v. Molosankwe*, 227n6
mass atrocity investigation, 104–5
"Masterpieces of the Ganges Delta" exhibition, 65–68
Matsuura, Kōichirō, 237n12
Maurer, Bill, 124–26
Maya people, 113
McEachern, Allan, 60, 228n12
McFate, Montgomery, 87

McGovern, Mike, 81

McKeon, Richard, 230n5

McLennan, John, 10–11, 163–64, 234n2

meaning, production of, 21–22

Medina, Laurie, 113, 145

Melhuus, Marit, 119, 122–24

Memo, Sara, 238n15

memory, justice and, 91

Merat, Zarir, 84

Merry, Sally Engle, 3, 7, 25, 208, 225n6; gender violence and, 104, 166, 168–69, 173–74; on justice, 92–94

Mertz, Elizabeth, 36–37, 39, 46–47

Meskell, Lynn, 63–65

Messick, Brinkley, 49

Mexico, 107, 120–21, 152–53

Mitchell, Jon P., 102–3

Moore, Sally Falk: anthropology of law and, 7, 14–15, 33–34, 165, 224n11; on Gluckman, 15, 33–34

moral creativity, in human rights, 105–7

moral economy of gender: contested body and, 179–82; ethnography and, 166–75, 178–83; FGC in, 181–82, 236nn17–18; gender violence and, 166–74; introduction to, 163–68; "invisible visible" and, 167, 175–78; LGBT and, 175–78, 182–83; transgression and, 182–83

Morgan, Lewis Henry, 11, 223n1

Morsink, Johannes, 192, 237n10

Mother Right (Das Mutterrecht) (Bachofen), 9–10, 163

Moyn, Samuel, 100, 220

Muehlmann, Shaylih, 49–51, 152–53, 226nn12–13

Musée Guimet, 65–68

museums, universal and national, 65–66

Das Mutterrecht (Mother Right) (Bachofen), 9–10, 163

Mythologies (Barthes), 70

mythologies, of law, 70–72, 229n18

The Mythology of Modern Law (Fitzpatrick), 71, 229n18

Nader, Laura, 6, 33, 165, 224n12, 225n3, 231n8; The Disputing Process, 17; Law in Culture and Society, 26–27

Nalin, David, 66–67

Namibia, 154–56, 182–83

nationalism: constitutional, 185, 189, 200; defined, 188; heated debates over, 237n6; legalization of, 25. See also ethnonationalism

national museums, 65–66

Native Title Act, Australian, 153–54, 234n11

nature, regulation of, 118–24, 136

negative peace, 82

Neier, Aryeh, 199–200

Nesper, Larry, 41–43, 225n7

The Network Inside Out (Riles), 103–4

New Order dictatorship, 85–86

New Zealand, 112

Niezen, Ronald, 78, 91–92, 141–42, 233n6

1965 Park, 86

Nisga'a First Nation, 148–49, 233n8

Northern Ireland, 107

Norway, 122–24

Nuer, 55, 227n3

Nuremberg Tribunal, 79–80, 82, 89–90

O'Barr, William, 39–40, 225n6

Obergefell v. Hodges, 131

Ojibwe, 41–43

oral history, 59–60, 228n11

Order and Dispute (Roberts), 17–18

The Origin of the Family, Private Property, and the State (Engels), 223n1

Osanloo, Arzoo, 106

Otavalo, Ecuador, 160–61, 234n14

Other, 142, 229n18

outlawing, 88–89

Palestine, 65, 109, 228n16

Papua New Guinea, 47–48

Parker, Ely S., 11

Pasqualino, Caterina, 195–96, 238n15

peace, 70, 82

Peebles, Gustav, 125–26

Permanent Peoples' Tribunal (PPT), 108

Peru, 161–62

Philippines, 114, 157–58

Philips, Susan U., 36–38, 41

philosophy about religion's place in politics and society (*laïcité*), 128–30, 232n2

Piketty, Thomas, 239n5

Pirie, Fernanda, 5

pluralism, 196; colonialism and, 57; de facto, 218–19; outlawing and, 88–89; value, 130

poetics of law, 22, 39, 47–51

Pogge, Thomas, 216, 239n6

Poland, 175–76

political economy, of international law, 110–14

politics: of aspiration, 102–3, 108–10, 147; cultural, 147–50; of immediation, 109; judicialization of, 81; justice as, 78, 89–92, 95; *laïcité* and, 128–30, 232n2; of recognition, 28, 159, 161; of representation, 78, 89–92

positive peace, 70, 82

post-utopian world, law in, 206–7, 220

Pottage, Alain, 71–72, 203

Powdermaker, Hortense, 234n3

power: of human rights, 93; justice as, 95; knowledge and, 35; through language, 34, 36–39, 41–47; through law, 20, 29, 34–39, 41–47; male, 10; state, 84, 132, 135, 160, 197, 199

PPT. *See* Permanent Peoples' Tribunal

Praed Street Project, 179–80

*Primitive Marriage* (McLennan), 10–11, 163–64

production of meaning, 21–22

property, regulation of, 118, 121–22

prostitution, 135, 179–80, 232n4

proto-anthropologists of law, 9–12, 26–27, 53, 163

public representation. *See* representation

race: colonialism and, 229n18; exclusion and, 188, 190; subject regulation and, 131–32

rape, 174

recognition, politics of, 28, 159, 161

*The Red Lily* (France), 211

regulation: capitalism and, 118; of collective identity, 119–20, 133–36; of debt, 125–26; ethnography and, 120–31, 134–35, 138; exclusion and, 117–22, 133–34, 138; human rights and, 123, 127, 133–34; inclusion and, 117–22, 131, 133–34, 138; introduction to, 22–24, 117–20; of nature, 118–24, 136; of property, 118, 121–22; by state, 22–23, 132–35; of subject, 119, 128–32, 136; Thompson on, 117–18, 120, 136–38; of value, 119, 124–27, 136, 232n1

religion: justice and, 93–94; *laïcité* and, 128–30, 232n2. *See also* Islam

Renteln, Alison Dundes, 237n8

repatriation movement, 66

representation, justice and, 78, 89–92

retributive justice, 82

Rey, Charles Fernand, 55–56

Richland, Justin, 44–46

rights. *See* human rights

Riles, Annelise, 103–6, 231n9

ritual suicide, 75–77

Rivkin-Fish, Michele, 180–81

Roberts, Simon, 17–20, 225n3, 227n5

Rocard, Michel, 134

Rome Statute, 80, 228n17, 229n4

Roosevelt, Eleanor, 98, 115, 186, 236n3, 238n1

Rosebud Reservation, 132

Rosen, Lawrence, 77, 89

Rosenblatt, Adam, 104–5

Roth, Kenneth, 228n17

*Rules and Processes* (Comaroff, John, and Roberts), 18–20

rules-relationship continuum, 40

Russia: fertility in, 180–81; revolution in, 142–43; TRC and, 85
Rwanda: *gacaca* in, 78, 83–84; genocide in, 25, 83–84, 229n5; ICTR and, 68–69, 80, 193–94

San people, 154–56
Santos, Boaventura de Sousa, 88
Sapignoli, Maria, 111
Sarfaty, Galit, 126–27
Schapera, Isaac, 14, 55–56, 227nn5–6, 227n8
Scott, James, 234n13
security: anthropology, 87, 229n8; citizen, 23, 78, 86–89
Security Council, UN, 80, 228n17, 229n4
Selim, Lala Rukh, 65–68
September 11, 2001, 135–36, 192
sexual rights, 130–31
sex workers, 135, 179–80, 232n4
shariʻa courts, 194–95
Shaw, Rosalind, 91
Shell-Duncan, Bettina, 181–82, 236n17
Sichuan, 106
Sieder, Rachel, 211–12
Sierra Leone Civil War, 91
Simpson, Gerry, 133
Singapore, 130, 185, 199–200, 236n2
Slotte, Pamela, 114–15
Slovenia, 190–91
Snajdr, Edward, 171–73, 235n11
Society of Legal Anthropology (*Sociedad de Antropología Jurídica*), 12
socio-legal studies, 7–8
Soeharto, 85–86
sorting society, 119, 123–24
South Africa, 82–83, 229n6
Southeast Asia, indigenous rights in, 112, 114
Spain, 195–96
Special Court for Sierra Leone, 80
Special Rapporteur on the Rights of Indigenous Peoples, 112–13, 145

speech-act, 34–35, 38
Speed, Shannon, 107
Spencer, Herbert, 234n2
*The Spirit of the Laws* (Macfarlane), 9
Standing, Guy, 143, 232n2
Starr, June, 20, 35, 165–66, 225n5, 235n6
state: calligraphic, 49; collective identity of, 135–36; ethnonationalism and, 196–99; power, 84, 132, 135, 160, 197, 199; regulation by, 22–23, 132–35; violence sanctioned by, 78
status, principal of, 10, 26
Stavenhagen, Rodolfo, 145
Strathern, Marilyn, 208
subject, regulation of, 119, 128–32, 136
Sudan, 227n3
suicide, ritual, 75–77
Supreme Court: of British Columbia, 59–60, 228n10; U.S., 6, 131
sustainable development, 114
swearwords, 49–51, 226n13
Sylvain, Renée, 154–56

Tanzania, 147–48
Thompson, E. P., 52, 117–18, 120, 136–38
Thoreson, Ryan, 130–31, 232n3
Timmer, Jaap, 196–97
title litigation, Aboriginal, 58–60
Todd, Harry, 17
Tokyo war crimes trials, 79, 80, 82
Tonga, 41
transgressive sexuality, 182–83
transnational law, 4, 22, 104, 209
Travers, Max, 7
TRCs. *See* truth and reconciliation commissions
Trinidad and Tobago, 170–71
TRIPS. *See* Agreement on Trade-Related Aspects of Intellectual Property Rights
Trobriand Islands, 13, 164
trouble cases, 2, 15
truth and reconciliation commissions (TRCs), 78, 82–85, 91, 229n6

*Tsigane* (Gypsy) society, 195–96, 238nn14–15
Tswana, 55–56, 227n5
Tukanoans, 151
Tylor, E. B., 238n13

UDHR. *See* Universal Declaration of Human Rights
UN. *See* United Nations
UN-DRIP. *See* Declaration of the Rights of Indigenous Peoples
UNESCO: UDHR and, 98–100, 230n3; Universal Declaration on Cultural Diversity, 192–93, 237n12; World Heritage Convention, 63–65, 228nn13–14
United Nations (UN), 115, 159; Commission on Human Rights, 98, 145, 230n5; Security Council, 80, 228n17, 229n4; Special Rapporteur on the Rights of Indigenous Peoples, 112–13, 145; UN-DRIP of, 144–45, 233n7. *See also* Convention on the Elimination of All Forms of Discrimination Against Women; UNESCO; Universal Declaration of Human Rights
United States (U.S.): ANCSA in, 159–60; Iraq invaded by, 184–85; Ojibwe in, 41–43; perspective on anthropology of law in, 7–8, 15; Rosebud Reservation in, 132; Supreme Court, 6, 131
Universal Declaration of Human Rights (UDHR): culture in, 192, 237n10; human rights and, 90, 96, 98–100, 192, 230n3, 230n10, 237n10, 237n12, 238n1; UNESCO and, 98–100, 230n3
Universal Declaration on Cultural Diversity, 192–93, 237n12
universal legal norms, 184–85, 192, 194
universal museums, 65–66
Urquieta, Cecila, 215

Urton, Gary, 161–62
U.S. *See* United States

value: pluralism, 130; regulation of, 119, 124–27, 136, 232n1
vernacularization, 3, 104, 110
vertical reason, 209
vigilante justice, 199
violence: gender, 104, 166–74, 235nn7–9; state-sanctioned, 78
von Benda-Beckmann, F., 15, 56–57, 224n8
von Benda-Beckmann, K., 15, 56–57, 224n8

waiting zones (*zones d'attente*), 134–35
Walker, Jeffrey, 71
Wallisian paradox, 149–50, 233n9
war on terror, 135–36
Warumungu people, 153–54
Weiner, Mark S., 11
Wenk, Irina, 114
Wet'suwet'en song about trails (*kungax*), 59–60, 228n11
*Whigs and Hunters* (Thompson), 117
White, James Boyd, 33, 47
Williams, Raymond, 187–88, 234n4
Wilson, Richard A., 68–70, 82–83, 102–3
Wolf, Eric, 53
women's rights, 103, 106, 169, 181–82
World Bank, 126–27
World Heritage Convention, UNESCO, 63–65, 228nn13–14
World Heritage Sites, 63–65, 228n16
world-making, anthropology of, 114–16
Wyzanski, Charles E., 90

Yugoslavia, 68–69, 80, 185, 189–91

Zapatista activists, 107
Zapotec, 164
*zones d'attente* (waiting zones), 134–35

# ABOUT THE AUTHOR

At the Bachofen monument in Basel, Switzerland, where a figurative representation of the Mother Right sits atop the tomb of the nineteenth-century proto-anthropologist of law. Photo by Gregor Dobler.

Mark Goodale holds a chair at the University of Lausanne, where he is Professor of Cultural and Social Anthropology. Previously, he was Professor of Conflict Studies and Anthropology at George Mason University and the first Marjorie Shostak Distinguished Lecturer in Anthropology at Emory University. He is the author of *Dilemmas of Modernity: Bolivian Encounters with Law and Liberalism* (2008) and *Surrendering to Utopia: An Anthropology of Human Rights* (2009) and the editor or co-editor of numerous other volumes on anthropology, human rights, legal pluralism, justice, Latin American politics and society, and methodology. The founding Series Editor of Stanford Studies in Human Rights, he is currently working on two ethnographies of Bolivia based on several years of research funded by the U.S. National Science Foundation and the Wenner-Gren Foundation for Anthropological Research: the first, a study of logics of justice; the second, a study of ideology, change, and pluralism.